The Justice of the
Western Consular Courts
in Nineteenth-Century Japan

Recent titles in
Contributions in Intercultural
and Comparative Studies
Series Editor: Ann M. Pescatello

Power and Pawn: The Female in Iberian Families, Societies, and Cultures
Ann M. Pescatello

Tegotomono: Music for the Japanese Koto
Bonnie C. Wade

Historical Archaeology: A Structural Approach in an African Culture
Peter R. Schmidt

Sacred Words: A Study of Navajo Religion and Prayer
Sam D. Gill

Liberalism in an Illiberal Age: New Culture Liberals in Republican China,
1919–1937
Eugene Lubot

Revolution and Counterrevolution: Mozambique's War of Independence,
1964–1974
Thomas H. Henriksen

Flying Dragons, Flowing Streams
Ronald Riddle

Communicating with Quotes: The Igbo Case
Joyce Penfield

Ideology on a Frontier: The Theological Foundation of Afrikaner Nationalism,
1652–1910
J. Alton Templin

Language, Science, and Action: Korzybski's General Semantics—A Study in
Comparative Intellectual History
Ross Evans Paulson

The Justice of the Western Consular Courts in Nineteenth-Century Japan

RICHARD T. CHANG

Contributions in Intercultural and Comparative Studies, Number 10

Greenwood Press
Westport, Connecticut • London, England

Acknowledgments

Grateful acknowledgment is made for permission to reprint previously published material: Richard
T. Chang, "A British Trial in Japan: *Regina* v. *Archibald King* (1875)," *Journal of Asian History*
10 (1976), pp. 134–150; Richard T. Chang, "The *Chishima* Case," *Journal of Asian Studies*, 34,
No. 3, May 1975, pp. 593–612.

Library of Congress Cataloging in Publication Data

Chang, Richard T.
   The justice of the Western consular courts in
nineteenth-century Japan.

   (Contributions in intercultural and comparative studies, ISSN 0147-1031 ; no. 10)
   Bibliography: p.
   Includes index.
   1. Consular jurisdiction—Cases.   2. Extraterritoriality
—Cases.   3. Justice, Administration of—Japan—History.
I. Title.   II. Series.
JX1698.J82C47   1984   341.4'88   83-12573
ISBN 0-313-24103-1 (lib. bdg.)

Library of Congress Catalog Card Number: 83-12573
ISBN: 0-313-24103-1
ISSN: 0147-1031

First published in 1984

Greenwood Press
A division of Congressional Information Service, Inc.
88 Post Road West, Westport, Connecticut 06881

Printed in the United States of America

10 9 8 7 6 5 4 3 2 1

To My Children
Perry and Penny

Contents

Tables

Preface

In 1876 Baba Tatsui, then a twenty-six-year-old man who had just completed two years' study of English law in London, published a booklet there called *The Treaty Between Japan and England*. It was a remarkable work in that it was destined to become the source most frequently cited by many Meiji publicists and later historians who attacked the inequity of the extraterritorial regime in Japan. In this work, Baba wrote that it was evidently in the interest of the British consuls in Japan "to protect their countrymen rather than to prosecute or convict them," and that the majority of the English residents in Japan had "strong prejudices against the natives of the country . . . and . . . against the native government." These facts alone, Baba went on to say, "show that the judges of the consular courts are not impartial, and therefore it is difficult to see how justice can be done in a court of justice where the judges have so much interest for the one and prejudice against the other."[1] In a similar vein in 1893 the *Kaishintō Tōhō*, a bimonthly periodical published by the Kaishintō, commented: "Injustice is the general rule in these [British and American consular] tribunals: justice is rare. Nevertheless, when they render just judgments we applaud their justice, hoping thereby to encourage them in the exercise of that quality."[2] Thus arose in the late nineteenth century the far-reaching generalization that the Western consular tribunals in Japan were so partial—toward Westerners and against Japanese—that they seldom rendered evenhanded justice.

This sweeping condemnation has been uncritically accepted and amplified by numerous historians who have written on the subject of revision of the unequal treaties in Meijii Japan. Moriya Hidesuke, for example, writes: "Consular jurisdiction was entirely abused. It is not surprising, therefore, that in the open ports the illegal application of it was frequent and the appearance of unruly foreigners was rampant." Yamamoto Shigeru observes: "Trials by foreign consuls were often biased in favor of protecting the interests of their own countries and therefore unfair, and this in turn created resentment on the part of the Japanese." Finally, Inoue Kiyoshi states: "In both civil and criminal cases the consular courts were likely to render decisions that were advantageous to foreigners and disadvantageous to the Japanese. In civil cases it was actually impossible for the Japanese to be tried fairly there."[3] Thus the pervasive generalization that for the Japanese defendant in a consular court injustice was the rule and justice the exception remains to this day an unquestioned major historical interpretation.

I once subscribed to this interpretation. Only after several years of research on the history of treaty revision in Japan did I begin to question whether the Western consular courts commonly treated Japanese litigants unfairly. Such a question led me to undertake a full-scale investigative study of the subject of justice in Western consular courts in nineteenth-century Japan. This book is the fruit of that research.

Conceptually, determining whether the Western consular courts in Japan did indeed seldom deal impartially with Japanese litigants requires two steps: (1) ascertaining how many *mixed* cases were adjudicated—cases with Western defendants and accused and Japanese plaintiffs and complainants; and (2) determining how many of the cases thus adjudicated were decided prejudicially against the Japanese litigants. The previously generally accepted interpretation would be valid only if at least one out of every two mixed cases were found to have been decided unfairly against the Japanese plaintiff or complainant.

Procedurally, these two criteria are applied here to two groups of mixed cases, publicized and unpublicized. The term "publicized" conveys the notion that a particular case was "widely discussed by both press and public"; "unpublicized" means that such widespread press coverage and public discussion did not occur in connection with the case under scrutiny. In examining the groups of publicized and unpublicized cases, therefore, four questions arise: How many publicized cases were there? How many of these cases were decided unfairly against the Japanese litigants? How many unpublicized cases were there? How many of these were decided unfairly against the Japanese litigants?

The focus of this inquiry is not on whether consular jurisdiction in Japan was unjust to the Japanese in the second half of the nineteenth century, since the overall inequity of the system is not likely to be denied. What is being questioned is the hundred-year-old Japanese interpretation that, as a rule, no Japanese could expect justice in the Western consular courts. An examination of this interpretation takes unequal consular jurisdiction as a given, with no evaluation of prevalent arguments for its abolition.

Of the two groups of publicized and unpublicized cases, the first includes a handful of cases on which hinges the Japanese interpretation of the prevalence of inequity in judicial decisions. Some of these cases have been cited and recited in many historical studies, both scholarly and popular, of pre- and post-World War II Japan. They have been adduced as conclusive pieces of evidence that inequity existed in the extraterritorial regime in Japan. These oft-cited cases number only five, all decided by British consular courts: the *King* case of 1875, the two *Hartley* cases of 1878, the *Drake* case of 1886 (more commonly known as the *Normanton* incident), and the *Chishima* case of 1892–1895. Full of legal issues, courtroom battles, and many elements of human drama, these cases may enthrall a researcher. They may also at times exasperate the scholar, for they have been subject to a host of simplistic, downright inaccurate accounts and misinterpretations. In an attempt to reconstruct and evaluate each of these cases by means of multiarchival research and legal analysis, the following three questions are addressed: Do the accounts of the case present both the Japanese plaintiff's and the British defendant's side of the story? Did the consular courts involved render their decisions in accordance with the law applicable? Had the plaintiff been English rather than Japanese, would the sentence or the decision have been harsher to the defendant than it actually was?

The second, unpublicized group is composed of all other mixed cases adjudicated by the Western consular courts in nineteenth-century Japan. There were numerous such cases. Listing and counting them, though largely a mechanical task, turned out to be a major research undertaking. Archivists around the world kindly responded to my queries concerning the possible existence of documents from which to ascertain the number of mixed cases. On the basis of the number of mixed cases recorded in the returns of British and U.S. cases that I was able to discover, I have estimated, first, the total number of cases adjudicated by the British and U.S. consular courts and, second, the total number adjudicated by the consular courts of the other treaty powers.

Of the book's seven chapters, Chapter 1 presents the first attempt ever made to provide an overview of the extraterritorial arrangements of all the Western powers that maintained commercial relations with nineteenth-century Japan. Chapters 2 through 5 deal with the second of the four questions mentioned— namely, how many of the publicized cases were decided unfairly against the Japanese litigants? These four chapters therefore concentrate on reconstructing and evaluating the five cases to ascertain whether they support the opinion in question: that, for the Japanese, injustice was the rule and justice, the exception. Chapter 6, on the other hand, is concerned with the twin questions of how many unpublicized cases there were and of how many of these were decided unfairly against the Japanese litigants. Consequently, the chapter details how the aggregate number of cases adjudicated by the Western consular courts in Japan has been estimated, and how many of the cases thus enumerated may have been decided unjustly. Chapter 7 presents the conclusions of my investigation.

In variant versions, Chapters 2 and 5 were published in the *Journal of Asian History* and the *Journal of Asian Studies*, respectively. The conclusion presented in Chapter 2 of this work, however, differs from that of the article published in the *Journal of Asian History*. I wish to thank the editors of these two journals for their permission to reprint the articles.

In writing this book, I have incurred greater debts of friendship and goodwill than one could imagine from the relative slimness of the book. But for the conceptual understanding and knowledge of law I gained at Harvard Law School and the Tokyo University Faculty of Law, I could not have written the book. For this legal training, I received support from the National Endowment for the Humanities and the Japan Foundation. Jerome Alan Cohen of Harvard Law School encouraged and facilitated my affiliation with Harvard; and Ishii Shirō of Tokyo University (Tōdai) paved the way for my connection with Tōdai. Martha Jean Chang of the Florida State Department of Education read and criticized Chapters 2 and 3; Malcolm Smith of the Monash University Faculty of Law, Chapter 3; Robert M. Spaulding, Jr., of Oklahoma State University, Chapter 4; and Alfred B. Clubok of the University of Florida, Chapter 6. I have profited from the advice and knowledge of Tanaka Hideo of Tōdai, Tanigawa Hisashi of Seikei University, Yamamoto Sōji of Tōhoku University, and, above all, W. R. Cornish of the London School of Economics and Political Science. Of all archivists around the world who responded to my inquiries as to the possible existence of returns of cases adjudicated by the Western consular courts in Japan, several deserve special mention here for either the valuable information they offered me on their own or the exceptional courtesy with which they entertained my persistent queries: Miss Eve Johansson and Miss M. E. Golfrick, both of the British Library in London; Ronald E. Swerczek of the National Archives and Record Service; P. H. Desneux of the Belgium Ministry of Foreign Affairs and Foreign Trade; and E. van Laar of the General State Archives at The Hague. For a variety of help and services rendered, I am grateful to Ray Jones and the interlibrary loan staff of the University of Florida Libraries; J. K. Dixon of the Privy Council Office in London; Key K. Kobayashi of the Asian Division and Sung Yoon Cho of the Far Eastern Law Division, both of the Library of Congress; the staff of the Public Record Office in Kew; the staff of the Harvard Law School Library; the staff of the National Diet Library in Tokyo; and the staff of the Tokyo University Faculty of Law Library. Finally, I thank Mrs. Rita Barlow for her editorial service and Mrs. Adrienne C. Turner for typing the manuscript.

Of course, I am solely responsible for any errors that may have crept into the book, and I welcome queries from any readers.

The Justice of the
Western Consular Courts
in Nineteenth-Century Japan

1

The Western Consular Courts in Nineteenth-Century Japan: An Overview

This chapter, the first attempt to provide an overview of the Western extraterritorial system in Japan, presents the organization, jurisdiction, and distribution of the consular courts set up in Japan by each of the sixteen Western treaty powers during the third quarter of the nineteenth century.

Today extraterritoriality means an alien's privilege of exemption from local law and law enforcement agencies while he or she is in a foreign country. In legal theory the alien's activities take place outside the territorial jurisdiction of the country where they actually occur. Extraterritoriality, including immunity from arrest and prosecution, extends to the visiting head of a foreign state and to diplomats and their families. Officials of the United Nations enjoy extraterritorial privileges when performing their duties.

Extraterritoriality was once granted to resident foreigners with no diplomatic or official position. This practice developed when law was personal rather than territorial, that is, regardless of where a person was, he or she came under the law of his or her nation.

In the nineteenth century Western powers, often by means of coercion, secured unilateral extraterritorial status for their citizens resident in Morocco, Turkey, Persia, Egypt, Siam, China, and Japan. The Western consul was usually granted jurisdiction to try all civil and criminal cases involving his countrymen. Extraterritoriality of this type meant "the extension of jurisdiction by a state beyond its borders," as well as immunity from the law and jurisdiction of a state in which an alien resided. Nondiplomatic extraterritoriality was strongly resented not only as an infringement of sovereignty but also as an opportunity for abuse. Whereas such extraterritoriality did not come to an end in China until 1946, it was abolished in Japan in 1899.[1]

In nineteenth-century Japan extraterritoriality of both types, diplomatic and nondiplomatic, was in operation. Only nondiplomatic extraterritoriality is of concern in this study, which focuses on Western consular jurisdiction in Japan.

With the exception of F. C. Jones' work which provides an overall view of the British and the U.S. consular courts in Japan,[2] there is virtually no literature on the subject of the Western extraterritorial regime there. This dearth of literature prompted my search for records of the sixteen powers' consular courts. Here, too, I encountered a scarcity of documentation. With the exception of Great Britain and the United States, none of the treaty powers has preserved an appreciable number, if any, of the records of its consular courts in Japan. Therefore, no full and satisfactory analysis of the extraterritorial arrangements of the other fourteen powers is possible, such as for Great Britain and the United States. In fact, the analysis of the fourteen powers' arrangements is of necessity incomparably shorter and far less comprehensive than that of the British and the U.S. arrangements. Nevertheless, both groups are presented in order to throw light, however meager, on the overall understanding of the Western extraterritorial regime in nineteenth-century Japan. The analysis of the fourteen powers' arrangements is based largely on information culled from extensive and prolonged correspondence with numerous archivists around the world.

The sixteen Western treaty powers were Great Britain, the United States, France, Germany, Austria-Hungary, Belgium, Denmark, Hawaii, Italy, the Netherlands, Peru, Portugal, Russia, Spain, Sweden and Norway, and Switzerland. Of these, the first four—Britain, the United States, France, and Germany—can be said to have had substantial commercial interests in Japan, while the interests of the other twelve powers were far less extensive. This may be evident in Table 1, which indicates the breakdown by nationality of Western shipping entered at the open ports of Japan in 1869.

Great Britain

Of the four trading nations, Great Britain was the foremost. Table 2 shows that Britain supplied an incomparably larger share of Japan's imports than did any other treaty power. In 1883, for example, its share of Japan's total imports, 44 percent, represented four times the value of the United States' 11 percent; in 1888, the two figures stood at the ratio of five to one.

Britain's preponderant commercial interests in Japan were dramatized in the report of British Minister Sir Francis L. Plunkett to the British foreign secretary, the Earl of Granville, dated July 22, 1884. Although the volume of American trade with Japan came next to that of England, observed Plunkett, the number of Americans resident in Japan was less than half that of the British, and the crews of American ships entering Japanese ports in 1883 numbered few more than one-sixth the number of those of Great Britain for the same year.[3] The American minister to Japan, Richard B. Hubbard, too, attested to the preponderance of British commercial interests in Japan in 1885, followed by those of the United States. According to Hubbard, the number of British subjects resident in Japan that year was 1,124, and of American citizens, 475. In sharp

Table 1
Western Shipping Entered at the Open Ports
of Japan in 1869

Flag	Ships	Tonnage
British	897	410,115(a)
American	352	509,008(b)
North German	179	74,150
French	48	29,042(c)
Dutch	47	12,969
Russian	50	19,128
Danish	26	6,707
Swedish and Norwegian	9	2,315
Hawaiian	4	1,610
Austrian	2	1,457
Portuguese	2	1,070
Other	4	1,096(d)
	1,620	1,068,667

SOURCE: DeB. Randoph Keim, A Report to the Hon.
George S. Boutwell, Secretary of the Treasury,
Upon the Condition of Consular Service of the
United States of America (Washington, D.C.,
1872), p. 60.
(a)Including mail steamers, 26 ships, 21,200
tonnage.
(b)Including mail steamers, 97+? ships,
355,615 tonnage.
(c)Including mail steamers, 12 ships, 12,668
tonnage.
(d)Under American, North German, and Dutch
colors; flags not distinguished.

contrast, the year's total resident population of European nationality, other than English, amounted to only 789. Moreover, during the year 1885, 28,896 British and 5,206 American merchant seamen visited Japan, while the total number of merchant seamen of other European nationalities who visited was only 8,466.[4] Stated another way, of the aggregate number of Western merchant seamen who visited Japan in 1885, 67.9 percent were British, 12.2 percent were American, and the remaining 19.9 percent European.

The British consular establishment in nineteenth-century Japan reflected the domination of the British commercial interests there. (The years in which both British and U.S. consulates were established in Japan are indicated in Appen-

Table 2
Japan's Imports from the Four Powers as a Percentage of Its Total Imports by Value, 1883, 1888, and 1893

Power	1883	1888	1893
Great Britain	44.0%	43.8%	31.3%
United States	11.0	8.6	6.8
France	6.4	6.3	3.7
Germany	4.1	8.0	8.2

SOURCE: Computed from The Statesman's Year-Book, vols. for 1890, 1895, 1896, passim. Nihon teikoku...tōkei nenkan, vols. for 1885, p. 2; 1891, pp. 167ff.; and 1894, p. 502.

dix Table 1.) "Great Britain is really the only Power which has made entirely adequate provision for the discharge of the duties imposed upon foreign nations by the necessity of exercising Consular jurisdiction," wrote Plunkett to Granville. "She is as much ahead of the other Powers in this respect as her interests are in excess of theirs."[5] So it was. Quite apart from and in addition to its legation in Tokyo, Britain maintained a professional consul at each of the three principal ports—Kanagawa, Hyōgo, and Nagasaki—and a professional consul or vice-consul each at Hakodate and Niigata. Table 3 shows the distribution of Britain's Japan service as of October 1, 1879.

The consular officers listed in Table 3 were professional consuls, commissioned by the queen and invested with ample judicial powers for the trial of all civil and most criminal cases; these were not merchants sitting as trading, or honorary, consuls. Clive Perry, an authority on international law, observes: "It is impossible for anyone who has read widely in the [British] Foreign Office papers to fail to be impressed by the very considerable expertise in international law . . . the rank and file of the Diplomatic Service has in the past possessed." Three factors may explain the British diplomats' expertise. First, "care was taken to select men of experience and probity for the British Consular Service and complaints of their unfitness were usually shown to be unjustified." (Unlike the United States, Great Britain made no distinction between the diplomatic and consular services. Instead, the distinction lay in the diplomat versus the clerk of the Foreign Office.) Second, a person serving in a diplomatic mission or ministry of foreign affairs is bound in time to acquire a reasonable working

Table 3
Distribution of Britain's Japan Service,
October 1, 1879

City	Rank	Name	Salary
Tokyo	Envoy and consul general	Sir H. Parkes	£4,000
	Secretary of legation	J. G. Kennedy	800
	Second secretay	Hon. J. Saumarer	400
	Japanese secretary	E. Satow	880
	Assistant Japanese secretary	E. Aston	600
	Vice-consul	J. Gibbins	300
	Medical officer	W. Anderson	250
	Student interpreter	L. Kucher	250
Kanagawa	Consul	M. Dohmen	600
	First assistant	J. Enslie	500
	First assistant	G. H. Hodges	400
	First assistant	R.R.H. McClatchie(a)	300
Hyōgo and Ōsaka(b)	Consul	M. Flowers	1,000
	First assistant	J. J. Quinn	400
	Student interpreter	J. McCarthy	250
Nagasaki	Consul	J. Troup	850
	Second assistant	W. A. Wooley	300
Hakodate	Consul	R. Eusden	850
Niigata	Vice-consul	H. W. Wilkinson(a)	600
On Leave	Assistant Japanese secretary	W. G. Aston	
	Consul	R. B. Robertson	
	First assistant	J. C. Hall	
	Second assistant	J. H. Longford(c)	
	Second assistant	E. B. Paul	

SOURCE: FO 46/250/341.
    (a)Drew extra allowances for their acting appointments.
McClatchie was acting as assistant interpreter to Her Majesty's Court
for Japan, and Wilkinson was acting as assistant judge of the same
court.
    (b)As of October 1879, there were two seals--one for a consulate
at "Hiogo" and the other for a vice-consulate at Ōsaka. FO
46/251/253.
    (c)Drew an allowance of £100 as interpreter in addition to a
salary as assistant.

knowledge of at least parts of international law. Third and finally, it was the
practice of the foreign secretary to encourage members of the Diplomatic Service to supplement this practical experience by appropriate reading and to proceed to an examination in international law, success in which brought additional financial compensation.[6] English diplomats serving in Japan customarily
sought leave to study for and take such an examination.[7]

The legal qualifications of the British consular officials, together with the speed with which they decided cases, were so extensive that even those Japanese who condemned all Western consuls for their alleged lack of legal qualifications excepted the British consuls from their condemnation, admitting that the British consuls had requisite experience in law.

The organization and jurisdiction of the British consular courts in Japan were provided for under the Foreign Jurisdiction Acts and a series of Orders in Council. Of these, two Orders together formed the immediate basis of British extraterritorial jurisdiction in Japan: the China and Japan Order in Council of 1865, amended by the China and Japan Order in Council of 1878.[8] All of Japan was divided into consular districts, each of which centered on one of the treaty ports. In his consular district, the consul was competent to convene a consular court which the Orders termed either Her Britannic Majesty's Court or a provincial court. In a summary way, that is, by a judge alone, the court could decide all civil cases in which the property or goods at stake were under $1,500 in value. Furthermore, the court could decide all criminal cases in which the maximum punishment did not exceed three months' imprisonment with or without hard labor, or a fine of $200. In all other cases, the court was required to adjudicate the case on indictment and with not fewer than two and not more than four assessors.[9] The court was empowered to impose (1) the punishment of imprisonment for any term not exceeding twelve months with or without hard labor and with or without a fine not exceeding $1,000, or (2) the punishment of a fine not exceeding $1,000.[10]

If there were not enough local British subjects "of good repute" who were fit to be assigned as assessors, the court was allowed to sit with one assessor or even without any at all. The assessors, unlike the jurors, had no voice in the decision of the court in any case, civil or criminal; they were simply representatives of the local British community called to insure that the law was equitably administered.[11] But, quite apart from the recommendation of the court itself, the dissent of an assessor from the conviction or from the amount of punishment awarded constituted the only channel whereby the judge of the Supreme Court at Shanghai, a court of appeal, reviewed the assigned punishment with a view to recommending a mitigation or a remission of the punishment by the foreign secretary or the British minister to Japan.[12]

The Supreme Court was composed of a judge, an assistant judge, a law secretary, and however many officers and clerks one of Her Majesty's Principal Secretaries of State thought necessary. The judge was required to be a member of the bar of England, Scotland, or Ireland, with seven years' standing at the time of his appointment or with service as assistant judge, legal vice-consul, or law secretary in the consular service.[13]

The 1865 Order in Council required unanimous verdicts from the five-person juries of a consular court.[14] Undoubtedly, the inability of many consular court districts to locate enough fit persons to serve as jurors accounts for the small jury size, five rather than twelve. The Supreme Court at Shanghai had the power to decide, with a jury, civil cases in which the property or goods at issue were worth $1,500 or more, but this provision was extended only by order of the foreign secretary to any consular court where it appeared to him there was a sufficient jury list.[15]

In a civil case involving $250 or more, any party aggrieved by the judgment of a consular court could apply to the court for leave to appeal to the Supreme Court, and was entitled to leave. In any other civil case, the consular court had the power to grant leave to appeal as did the Supreme Court in any case.[16] As regards criminal cases, anyone convicted summarily of an offense could have the consular court which had convicted him send his case to the Supreme Court for its opinion on any point of law. The consular court was authorized to re-serve for the consideration of the Supreme Court any question of law arising from the trial of anyone tried otherwise than in a summary way.[17]

Appeal from the Supreme Court to the Judicial Committee of the Privy Council at London was allowed in civil cases only and not in criminal cases. Any party aggrieved by the decision of the Supreme Court, could, within fif-teen days after it was made, apply to the Supreme Court for leave to appeal to the Privy Council.[18] Once leave was obtained, the party was required to trans-mit to the Privy Council the papers in the case concerned. Only upon receipt and registration of the papers at the Privy Council did the proceedings become a Privy Council Appeal. This procedure is still followed today. According to an Order in Council dated June 26, 1873, after papers had been dispatched to the Privy Council and an appeal registered, the appellant was directed to take, within twelve months, effectual steps to have the appeal scheduled for a hearing.[19]

By the China and Japan Order in Council of 1878, a Court for Japan was established at Kanagawa, replacing the old consular court there. The Supreme Court at Shanghai lost its extraordinary original jurisdiction, concurrent with the consular courts in Japan, and this concurrent jurisdiction was transferred to the Court for Japan. A judge and an assistant judge were appointed to the court. The consul at Kanagawa was to serve as assistant judge.[20] The judge was to draw an annual salary of £1,500 and an annual housing allowance of £250.[21] Like the chief justice—formerly referred to as the judge in the 1865 Order in Council—of the Supreme Court at Shanghai, the judge of the Court for Japan at the time of appointment was required to be a member of the bar of England, Scotland, or Ireland, of not less than seven years' standing.[22] In Japan, British subjects accused of crimes which in England were capital were subject to trial by jury before the judge of the Court for Japan. This court was *not*, however, an appellate court. Appellate jurisdiction remained with the Supreme Court at Shanghai. Chapter 3 discusses the circumstances under which the Court for Japan was established.

From the aspect of its appeal procedures alone, the British consular courts system in Japan surpassed those of all other treaty powers. The quality of the Court for Japan and of the Supreme Court for China and Japan unquestionably was outstanding. The Court for Japan, though not a court of appeal, could assume, as in the *Drake* case (see Chapter 4), original jurisdiction over extraordinarily serious or legally complex cases arising in the district of any consular court in Japan. The nearness of the location of the Supreme Court at Shanghai eliminated the likelihood that an appeal to the Supreme Court by the dissatisfied party, Japanese or foreign, would be precluded because of distance or expense.[23]

Undoubtedly, other treaty powers also made provision for appeals against the decisions of their consular courts. But in that case, states F. C. Jones, "such appellate jurisdiction was vested in the first instance in the resident minister for Japan, who normally had no legal training, and ultimately in the higher courts of their home territories, thousands of miles distant."[24] This statement is, however, either a half-truth or a hypothesis to be tested. In the case of the United States, for example, the statement is only partly true. It will be noted that in civil cases appellate jurisdiction was vested concurrently in the U.S. minister to Japan and in the U.S. Circuit Court in California. Today no one knows to what extent the statement in question held true for each of the treaty powers exclusive of Great Britain and the United States. It would require extensive study to learn how the appellate jurisdiction of each of the other fourteen treaty powers was exercised in Japan, if it ever was.

It should be clear, then, that British consular officials, who were subordinate to the British Foreign Office, were answerable to it for consular functions but not for judicial functions. The decisions they rendered as ex-officio judges could be reviewed, affirmed, or reversed only by the higher courts and not by the Foreign Office. Indeed, by today's standards, what is peculiar was the granting of judicial power to a consul. One way to interpret this former practice may lie in viewing this court as the lowest rung of the British judicial ladder. The court was not a *consular* court; it was a consular *court*.

The same accountability was required of U.S. consular officials in Japan. It will be shown that the route of appeal lay from their decision to that of either the U.S. minister to Japan or the U.S. Circuit Court in California, but never to the U.S. Department of State.

The United States

The United States maintained professional consuls at Kanagawa, Hyōgo and Ōsaka, and Nagasaki, but quite frequently was entirely unrepresented at Hakodate or Niigata.[25] For the United States, as for many other treaty powers, its Kanagawa consulate exceeded the aggregate importance of all its other consulates in Japan. The preponderant importance of the Kanagawa consulate was recognized in 1874 when it was elevated to a consulate general. The following is the list of persons employed at the consulate general as of December 31, 1886.[26]

C. R. Greenhouse	Consul general
G. H. Scidmore	Vice and deputy consul general
John McLean	Interpreter

W. R. Herbert	Marshall
R. McCane	Deputy marshall
R. Miura (Japanese)	Official clerk
Tomishima Rinzō (Japanese)	Messenger
Ishikawa Takejirō (Japanese)	Messenger

Congress authorized the establishment of consular courts in the Orient by an act of May 16, 1848. This statute was amended by several subsequent enactments, all consolidated in the Revised Statutes of the United States, Sections 4083–4130, an act of June 14, 1878.[27]

Under the terms of these statutes, the consul sitting alone was empowered to hear and determine all cases where the maximum fine did not exceed $500, or the maximum term of imprisonment did not exceed ninety days. But in all cases, if the fine exceeded $100, or the term of imprisonment for misdemeanors exceeded sixty days, the defendant might take the case, by appeal, before the minister of the United States to Japan. In other words, the consul's summary decision was unreservedly final only when the fine imposed did not exceed $100 or the term of imprisonment did not exceed sixty days.[28] Whenever the consul considered that assistance would be useful for reasons of legal perplexity or more severe punishment than usually prescribed, he was required to summon from one to four, and in capital cases not fewer than four, U.S. citizens "of good repute" to sit as associates in the trial. If any of the associates differed in opinion from the consul, the case would be referred to the minister for his adjudication.[29] Both the minister and the consul had original jurisdiction over capital cases for murder or insurrection against Japan by U.S. citizens, or for offenses against the public peace amounting to felony under the laws of the United States. If tried by the consul, however, there could be no conviction unless the consul and his associates all concurred and the minister approved.[30]

In civil cases, the consul sitting alone had the power to render judgment where the damages demanded did not exceed $500. If the damages exceeded that amount or the case involved legal perplexities, he was required to summon two or three U.S. citizens resident in the port to sit with him as associates in the trial.[31]

The two circumstances under which the avenue of appeal lay from the consul to the minister in *criminal* cases have already been discussed: where the consul sat with associates and one of them differed from him; and where the consul sitting alone imposed a fine of more than $100 or imprisonment of more than sixty days and the defendant decided to appeal. Furthermore, from any final judgment of the minister given in the exercise of original or appellate criminal jurisdiction, the accused might appeal to the U.S. Circuit Court in California when he considered the judgment erroneous in point of law.[32]

In *civil* cases where any of the associates differed from the consul, either party was allowed to appeal to the minister.[33] In addition, an appeal from the consul to the minister was granted when the matter in dispute exceeded $500 but not

$2,500. Where the amount exceeded $2,500, an appeal proceeded from any consular court to the U.S. Circuit Court in California.[34] Likewise, where the matter in dispute exceeded $2,500, an appeal could be conveyed from any final decision of the minister, given the exercise of original civil jurisdiction, to the same circuit court.[35]

The law to be applied was to be the relevant law of the United States supplemented by the common law and the law of equity and admiralty, to which might be added "regulations, decrees, and orders" having the force of law, which the minister was empowered to promulgate with the advice of such consuls as were accessible. The minister was required to transmit all these rules to the secretary of state to be laid before Congress for revision.[36] In practice, however, Congress revised none.

Apparently, only three cases were appealed from the consular courts in Japan to the U.S. Circuit Court in California during the second half of the nineteenth century.[37] By an act of Congress of March 3, 1891, the appellate jurisdiction was taken away from the U.S. circuit courts, and no appeal from the judgment of the consular courts was provided for.[38]

As to the quality of the American consular officials as ex-officio judges in the consular courts, there have been two opinions among American writers. The first is complimentary. In 1881 Secretary of State James G. Blaine, who favored legislative action to remedy the lack of "clearness, precision, and comprehensiveness of the statutes," made the following assessment of the U.S. consular court system abroad:

If, on the whole, the administration of consular justice abroad, in favor of American citizens, has worked with considerable regularity, utility and success, this result has been due rather to the right of extraterritoriality itself, and to the average common sense of business officers to whom the exercise of that right has been so broadly committed, than to the constitutionality or precision of the statutes.[39]

In his *American Consular Jurisdiction in the Orient*, Frank E. Hinckley noted: "In regarding the correspondence contained in these public documents [*Papers Relating to the Foreign Relations of the United States* and its antecedent, *Diplomatic Correspondence*] one cannot fail to appreciate the importance and excellence of the services of our diplomatic and consular representatives."[40]

The second opinion has decried the performance of the American consular officials, not without considerable justification. Upon inspecting the American consulates in Asia and South America in 1872, Special Inspector DeB. Randolph Keim stated: "Almost every consulate had some defects in its history, owing to the incompetency, low habits, and vulgarity of some of its officers during the endless round of evils incident to official rotation. Abuses had been committed in the collection of fees; in the exercise of judicial powers; in the adjustment of the business affairs of American citizens."[41] In 1904, after a consular inspection tour, Third Assistant Secretary of State Herbert H.D. Pierce reported:

Unfortunately, beset by the temptations which are rife in the East, it has sometimes happened that some of our consular officers, finding their salaries inadequate to meet the constant drain upon their resources, have yielded to this temptation and, under the cover of such protection as our unfortunate system of partial compensation by fees affords, have taken advantage of it to extort unwarranted charges for services of an unofficial character, and in other instances have employed their official positions to increase their incomes improperly, thus bringing the office into contempt.[42]

These disparaging contemporary observations have been incorporated into a historical interpretation accepted widely by American students of East Asian history, an interpretation attributable largely to the late historian Tyler Dennett who wrote:[43]

The American consular service throughout the [nineteenth] century presents a picture over which one would wish to draw the veil. The system of merchant consuls continued in China without change until 1854 when they were replaced at the five ports by others whose only legitimate emoluments were $1,000 a year for judicial services under extraterritoriality, and part of all of the fees of their office. . . . The men who displaced them [the merchant consuls] were often appointed from the lower ranks of political "hangers-on" in the United States and were placed where the cost of respectable living ranged upwards from three or four thousand dollars a year. . . . To the personal temptations which accompany residence in a foreign land where public sentiment is of slight support to personal character there was the constant temptation for peculation. The theory of government was to make the consular system support itself by the fees it collected, and the prevailing theory of the occupant of office was to gather in as much as the probably brief tenure of office would permit. . . . He [the consul] was never selected for his legal training.[44]

It is not germane to this study to evaluate these two diametrically opposed points of view. What is germane to the study, however, is to deal with a question that one might raise on account of both "the constant temptation for peculation" and the lack of legal training to which Dennett referred: how could the American consular officials have adjudicated mixed cases responsibly and impartially? The answer is that these and other shortcomings of the officials had little to do with most mixed cases adjudged by the officials. Close scrutiny of both the Keim and Pierce reports, on which Dennett's excoriation of the American consular service rests, reveals that, as far as the Japan service was concerned, the inspectors' criticism, censure, and indignation were all related to civil suits or disputes involving U.S. citizens and some Europeans. For example, when Keim visited Yokohama in 1871, a number of complaints were brought at once to his attention against American Consul General Lemuel Lyon for irregularities in discharge of his duties and for his overbearing manner. None of the individuals who complained were Japanese or speaking on behalf of any Japanese: they were all Americans.[45]

Dennett argued that the extraterritorial powers of the American consul were responsible in part for "the creation of ill feeling and hatred among the Orientals who were so miserable as to fall in his path."[46] Undoubtedly, this was true of certain American consular officials at certain places under certain circumstances, but it cannot be taken as proof that as a rule the American consular courts in Japan circumvented justice in regard to all Japanese litigants.

On the contrary, there is convincing proof that the multitude of faults condemned by Dennett had little, if anything, to do with the questioning of justice in the American consular courts in Japan. In fact, not one of the celebrated five cases on which has hinged the century-long Japanese condemnation of that justice was an American case. Rather, all of the five were adjudicated by the consular courts of Great Britain, the treaty power that it was conceded consistently maintained the best of all consular court systems in Japan.

The Other Western Treaty Powers

The returns of cases adjudicated by the consular courts of the Western treaty powers other than Great Britain and the United States are either nonexistent or too few in number to produce meaningful conclusions for the purposes of this study. There is, furthermore, a sharp difference in the amount of information available about the consular courts themselves from the two powers and that available from all the other governments. The remainder of this chapter presents two reasons for this glaring contrast. First, the number of cases tried by the consular courts of the fourteen powers was so small that their home governments probably regarded as unimportant the records of the courts, especially the returns of cases, with resultant neglect of their archival preservation. The relatively small number of cases, of course, reflected the fact that these powers had little commercial stake in Japan compared with Great Britain and that only a small number of their nationals resided in Japan. It is possible that the Netherlands was not the only European treaty power whose consular representatives in Japan did not even transmit their returns to their home government, presumably so few and insignificant were the records. Second, the archives of many of these countries suffered the ravages of war and natural calamities which those of Great Britain and the United States were fortunate enough on the whole to escape. For example, archives of the French consular courts at Tokyo, Yokohama, and Kōbe were destroyed, as were those of the Austrian consulate at Kōbe, apparently irreplaceably.

Austria-Hungary

In 1884, Austria-Hungary for the first time established a consulate general at Yokohama. Although the Hapsburg Monarchy had concluded a commercial treaty with Japan in 1869, for fifteen years it had not considered it necessary to maintain its own consulate there because so few Austrians were resident in Japan. Even as late as 1884, according to the *Jiji shimpō*, they numbered only thirty-two.[47] Until that year British consuls in Japan had had charge of Austro-Hungarian interests there. It would seem that some time after 1884 a consulate was opened at Kōbe, for it is known that the records of this consulate were destroyed by the Great Earthquake of 1923. During World War I, the building of the Austrian consulate general at Yokohama was damaged, and its records were removed to the Spanish legation at Tokyo which had protected Austro-Hungarian subjects during the war. It would seem, however, that these records, too, were destroyed. The extant records of the Ministry of Foreign Affairs at Vienna contain no accounts of mixed cases.[48]

Belgium

During the second half of the nineteenth century, the Belgian government maintained a host of honorary consuls in five Japanese ports as follows:[49]

City	Years	Number of Honorary Consuls
Tokyo	1868–1873	1
Tokyo	1895–1907	1
Yokohama	1866–1879	4
Ōsaka	1876–1900	3
Kōbe	1871–1901	5
Nagasaki	1866–1907	1
Nagasaki	1882–1907	1

Of these sixteen honorary consuls, the third consul at Yokohama filled his post for less than a year, whereas the second consul at Nagasaki held his office for twenty-five years from 1882 to 1907. The median length of service among the sixteen was five years. There are, however, no records of the Belgian consular courts in Japan because they were either destroyed during World War I or burnt during World War II by order of the German occupation authorities.[50]

Denmark

Although the Danish National Archives has preserved the records of the Danish consulates in Japan, they are exceedingly incomplete. An archivist who at my request examined cases adjudicated by the Danish consular courts at Yokohama and Nagasaki for the years 1873 to 1895 found about ten cases. Of these, only one case was a mixed one, an action for assault adjudicated on August 18, 1879, in favor of the Japanese complainant who recovered damages. All the other cases were between Danes and other Europeans. Although the sample was obviously small and unrepresentative of the incomplete returns of cases, it suggests that the total number of cases handled by the Danish consular courts was very small indeed, as was the proportion of mixed cases to all cases.

In 1868, a Danish consulate general was established at Kanagawa, and honorary consulates were established at Hakodate, Ōsaka, Hyōgo, and Nagasaki. Beginning in about 1890, however, both the consulate general and the hon-

orary consulates were abolished, and, instead, consulates were created at Yokohama, Hyōgo, and Nagasaki.[51]

France

In 1859 France established its first consulate in Japan at Edo and in 1877
redesignated it the French consulate at Tokyo. France founded a second consulate at Yokohama in 1870 and another one at Kōbe in 1879. Besides these
consulates, France maintained a vice-consulate at Nagasaki between 1865 and
1901. According to the Archives of the French Ministry of Foreign Affairs, these
consulates, once established, were in operation without interruption through
1899. Unfortunately for historians, however, the archives of both the Tokyo
and Yokohama consular courts were destroyed in 1945 as were those of the
Kōbe consular court in 1918.[52]

In his 1884 report on the Western consular establishment in Japan to Foreign Secretary Granville, British Minister Plunkett asserted that, although France
was second only to the United States in volume of trade, it had but one consul
in Japan, a professional one resident in Yokohama. At all the other open ports,
French interests were more or less vested in the British consuls there.[53] Plunkett's assertion does not accord with the records of the Archives of the French
Ministry of Foreign Affairs. Perhaps the French consulates, once founded,
continued to be maintained through the latter half of the nineteenth century,
even though the posts of consul and vice-consul did not remain filled contin-
uously.

Germany

Germany maintained a professional consul at Yokohama and another at
Hyōgo-Ōsaka and a merchant consul at Nagasaki. But there was no German
consular official at Hakodate or Niigata. From 1881 to 1890, the Swiss in the
Hyōgo-Ōsaka area were under the protection of the German consul there.[54]

The German consul was empowered to adjudicate bankruptcy cases and cases
in which the claims did not exceed 300 marks. He was also competent to adjudicate certain other types of cases, regardless of the value of claims involved.
These included cases between landlords and renters, employers and employees,
masters and servants, and cases involving loss of cattle, damage to wild game,
extramarital sexual intercourse, and the like. He had no power, however, to try
treason and other serious crimes which were supposed to be referred to the German Supreme Court (*Reichsgericht*) at Berlin. Also to the Supreme Court lay
appeal from any consular court in Japan.[55]

A few records from the German consulate at Yokohama have been preserved
at the Central State Archives at Potsdam, East Germany. These records pertain
to the years 1897–1899 and provide no basis for distinguishing mixed cases from
nonmixed. Most of the recorded cases seem to have been nonmixed ones involving Germans and other Europeans. Of a total of 193 cases, 105 are labeled
"cases involving temporary sequestration of property," and the other cases do

not involve such petty offenses as were frequently committed by Western seamen in open ports—assault and battery or drunken and disorderly conduct.[56]

Hawaii

With the appointment of American businessman Eugene M. Van Reed as consul general for Japan, the Kingdom of Hawaii established a consulate general at Kanagawa in April 1865.[57] The Hawaiian-Japanese Treaty of 1871 provided for no extraterritoriality, but, presumably by virtue of the most favored nation clause, Hawaii did exercise extraterritorial jurisdiction in Japan. Between January 1893 and April 1894, Japan exchanged with the Hawaiian government notes by which the Hawaiian government abandoned its extraterritorial jurisdiction.[58] My efforts to ascertain the possible existence of the records of the Hawaiian consular courts were fruitless.[59]

Italy

The first Italian consulate was established at Yokohama in 1864; and the second consulate, at Hakodate in 1870. In 1869, a year after the Meiji Restoration, Italian consular agencies were opened in Hyōgo, Nagasaki, Niigata, Ōsaka, and Tokyo, and for the next eight years Italy maintained a rather large consular network[60] as a result of its import trade in the eggs of silkworms from Japan. During the 1870s these constituted the bulk of Japan's exports to Italy—for example, in 1873, 87 percent of total exports involved the eggs of silkworms. In that year an agreement designed to facilitate and increase the export of the eggs was drafted between Japan and Italy. Under the terms of the agreement, Italy was to relinquish its extraterritoriality in Japan in exchange for the unrestricted right of Italians to travel in the interior of Japan. But the agreement was never signed owing to Great Britain's opposition.[61]

Failure to sign the agreement dashed Italy's hopes to obtain freedom of travel in the Japanese interior for its merchants and seems to have led to progressive reduction in the size of the Italian consular establishment in Japan. In 1876 the consular agencies at Tokyo and Niigata were closed. The year 1879 witnessed the closing of the agencies at Hakodate and Ōsaka. Consequently, from 1879 to 1895 the Italian consular establishment consisted of the consulate at Yokohama and the consular agencies at Hyōgo and Nagasaki. In 1895 a consulate general was opened at Tokyo and the consulate at Yokohama was closed.

There are no extant records of any Italian consular courts.[62]

The Netherlands

Throughout the second half of the nineteenth century, the Netherlands maintained a consulate at each of the three following port areas: Kanagawa, Nagasaki, and Kōbe-Ōsaka. The Kōbe-Ōsaka consulate was opened in 1868. In the following year the Yokohama consulate was established, as was the Nagasaki consulate.

According to the General State Archives at The Hague, no returns of cases adjudicated by the Dutch consular courts in Japan were transmitted to the home government at The Hague. Only the correspondence of Dutch ministers and consuls in Japan has been preserved at the Archives. It is known, however, that from 1870 onward Dutch consuls represented in Japan the interests of the United Kingdom of Sweden and Norway.[63]

Peru

With the signing of its Treaty of Friendship and Commerce of August 21, 1873, Peru became the last of the sixteen Western treaty powers to maintain commercial relations with Japan on an unequal basis. As of 1884, Peru was represented by a consul general at Yokohama.[64] It is uncertain when the consulate general was opened and where other Peruvian consulates may have been located. Inquiries made to both the Peruvian Ministry of Foreign Affairs and the General Archives of the National Institute of Culture uncovered no records of Peruvian consular courts in Japan.

Portugal

Concerning the Portuguese consular establishment in Japan, an inquiry was made to the Portuguese Ministry of Foreign Affairs, which responded that it possessed no records of mixed cases adjudicated by the Portugese consular courts in Japan. On the advice of the Foreign Ministry, another inquiry was made to the Portuguese Embassy in Tokyo, which made no response.

Nevertheless, at times the Portuguese consular court at Yokohama may have handled more mixed cases than did those of the other treaty powers with infinitesimal commercial interests. The *Japan Weekly Mail*, an English newspaper published in Yokohama, printed the judgments and sometimes even the minutes of proceedings of cases, both mixed and nonmixed, adjudicated by Western consular courts in Yokohama and Tokyo. The total number of sixty-five mixed cases were adjudicated by these courts and reported by the *Japan Weekly Mail* for the two cities in 1875, 1876, 1883, 1886, and 1893. Of these, thirty-three were British cases, nineteen were American, five German, four Portuguese, two French, one case Swedish-Norwegian, and one Dutch.[65] No one knows why the Portuguese consular authorities in the Yokohama-Tokyo area appear to have adjudicated more mixed cases for those selected years than did those of France, a major treaty power, and those of minor treaty powers like Sweden and Norway and the Netherlands.

Russia

Tsarist Russia established a consulate at Hakodate (1858), at Nagasaki (1873), and at Tokyo, Yokohama, and Hyōgo (1874).[66] Unique to Russo-Japanese relations throughout the period from 1855 to 1899 was the fact that the Russo-Japanese Treaty of 1855 provided for mutual extraterritoriality. As a result, the Japanese consuls exercised extraterritorial jurisdiction in Tsarist Russia as did their Russian counterparts in Japan.[67]

Spain

Strenuous efforts were made to locate possible extant records of the Spanish consulates in Japan, but none were found.[68] According to Plunkett, the British minister to Japan, as of 1884 Spanish interests at Hyōgo and Nagasaki were vested in the respective British consuls in those cities.[69]

Sweden and Norway

The United Kingdom of Sweden and Norway, which concluded a commercial treaty with Japan in 1868, seems to have maintained no consulates during the first few years immediately after the conclusion of the treaty. Dutch consuls, and at times German consuls, had charge of the interests of the United Kingdom between 1871 and 1901. Neither a thin file on consular jurisdiction that has been preserved at the Swedish National Archives nor the letters concerning Swedish and Norwegian subjects resident in Japan that have been kept at the General State Archives at The Hague contain any quantitative information about mixed cases involving Swedish and Norwegian subjects and Japanese.[70]

Switzerland

Today the consular affairs of Switzerland are managed by its embassy in Tokyo. In the second half of the nineteenth century, however, the Swiss government maintained four consulates as follows:

Yokohama	1864–1905
Ōsaka	1870–1890
Nagasaki	1864–1869
Hakodate	1864–1868

Moreover, Swiss residents in the Hyōgo-Ōsaka area were under the protection of the German consulate there from 1881 to 1890.[71] It is perhaps safe to assume, then, that, although the Swiss consulate at Ōsaka was not closed during the 1880s, no Swiss consul was there at that time.

The Three Principal Ports

The foregoing discussion has taken a country-by-country approach to the distribution of the Western consulates in Japan. In addition, something of a port-by-port review of the distribution of Western consulates is indicated in order to complete the discussion. One may have noticed in the foregoing that all the Western consulates were situated in seven ports: Yokohama (Kanagawa), Kōbe (Hyōgo), Nagasaki, Niigata, Hakodate, Ōsaka, and Tokyo (Edo). Of these, the first three, regarded as Japan's principal ports, will be discussed.

Of the three, Yokohama, primarily an exporting harbor, was unquestionably the largest and most important. Raw silk was the largest of the Japanese exports during the 1870s.[72] For example, on an *ad valorem* basis, raw silk accounted for 85 percent of Japan's total exports in 1875, 80 percent in 1876, 95 percent in 1877, and 90 percent in 1878.[73] The bulk of raw silk exported was shipped out of Yokohama. Hence, it is not surprising that most of the treaty powers had their consular officials of varying ranks reside in Yokohama even when they were unrepresented elsewhere in Japan. As of 1875, for example, the following twelve treaty powers maintained consulates at Yokohama: Belgium, Denmark, France, Germany, Great Britain, Hawaii, Italy, the Netherlands, Russia, Spain, Switzerland, and the United States.[74] The population of Yokohama was 193,000 in 1901. The foreign population in 1878 numbered 3,085, of whom about 1,500 were Western.[75]

Kōbe, unlike Yokohama, was largely an importing seaport. The population of Kōbe, Japan's fifth largest city, was 161,000 in 1895 and 215,000 in 1901. In 1899 it had over 2,000 foreign residents, more than half of whom were Chinese. The British numbered 534, the Americans 155, and the Germans 136.[76] Many treaty powers treated Ōsaka, the second largest city in Japan, as part of a two-ports consular district called Hyōgo-Ōsaka, although the consulate was actually located in Kōbe. The United States and Great Britain each maintained this two-ports district designation, as did other powers. On the other hand, some nations like Belgium and Switzerland had only merchant, or trading, consuls in Ōsaka and, unlike their British and American counterparts, evidently formed no two-ports districts. Kōbe was opened in 1869—ten years after the opening of Yokohama. In October 1892, Hyōgo, Kōbe's sister city, was also opened by the Japanese government to form part of the open port of Kōbe.

Nagasaki, a city of great antiquity and site of Christian martyrdom, was Japan's only open port between 1636 and 1859, and in the early days of European intercourse with East Asia was the most important seat of foreign trade with Japan. Although during the second half of the nineteenth century Nagasaki ceased to be a match for Yokohama or Kōbe from the viewpoint of Japan's foreign trade, it surpassed in importance Ōsaka, Niigata, and Hakodate. Even some of the treaty powers that maintained no consuls of their own in the other three ports were often represented in Nagasaki by their own professional consuls or by those of other powers there. The population of Nagasaki, the eighth largest city of Japan, was 107,000 in 1901. In 1898 the number of foreign residents was 606 (exclusive of the Chinese), of whom 40 were British and 566 other Europeans and Americans.[77]

British Minister Plunkett's 1884 report on the Western consular establishment in Japan provides a bird's-eye view of the minor treaty powers' distribution in Japan of their trading consuls. According to the report, at Yokohama there were trading consuls general for Switzerland, Denmark, and Peru. At Kōbe there were trading consuls for Belgium, Denmark, Hawaii, the Netherlands, Portugal, and Sweden and Norway; at Nagasaki, for Belgium, Denmark, Sweden and Norway, the Netherlands, and Portugal; and at Hakodate, for Denmark. At Kōbe, the British consul had charge of Spanish interests, and the German consul oversaw Italian, Swiss, and Russian interests. At Nagasaki the British and Russian consuls had charge of Spanish and Italian interests, respectively.[78]

The Double-Name Game

In nineteenth-century Western diplomatic correspondence and in the present-day literature on modern Japanese history, consular courts at Yokohama have often been referred to fictitiously as the consular courts at Kanagawa; those at Kōbe as the courts at Hyōgo; and those at Tokyo as those at Edo. The present work refers to these courts by their actual location—for example, "the Yokohama court" rather than "the Kanagawa court" when referring to judicial proceedings that actually occurred in Yokohama. However, when quoting directly from official records, it will be necessary to report the fictitious designation verbatim with a parenthetical notation as to the actual geographical site being referred to.

This double-name game may be rather confusing, if not annoying, but the custom derives from historical origins. The practice of recording fictitious designations, like "consular courts at Kanagawa," when in fact the courts being referred to were located at Yokohama, developed and prevailed because both the Japanese and the Western authorities, for their respective reasons, favored and utilized the custom of using fictitious designations.

Historical study shows why the Japanese authorities originated, and the Western authorites maintained, the custom with respect to Yokohama, why the Japanese authorities chose to open Kōbe in lieu of Hyōgo, and why the Western authorities referred to Kōbe as Hyōgo and to Tokyo as Edo.

The custom of using a factitious designation with respect to Yokohama arose because the Tokugawa Bakufu chose to open Yokohama instead of Kanagawa, the place stipulated in the 1858 treaties, and claimed that Yokohama was part of Kanagawa to avoid being accused of violating the treaties. In retrospect, the Bakufu's choice was indeed remarkable, since the drafter of the 1858 American Treaty, Consul General Townsend Harris, did not even include Kanagawa or Yokohama in the list of ten ports that he proposed be opened to foreign trade. Among the ten he proposed were Kyōto, Edo (the heart of present-day Tokyo), Shinagawa (now the southeastern part of Tokyo facing the Tokyo Bay to the east), and Ōsaka.[79] The Bakufu quickly talked Harris out of proposing the opening of Kyōto, the capital, on the grounds that domestic opposition to opening Kyōto was so strong that the opening, if forced, would surely precipitate a rebellion. Learning that Shinagawa has a shallow harbor, Harris withdrew his request to open Shinagawa and insisted on opening both Edo and Ōsaka. He believed that foreign trade could not grow in Japan if the two largest cities were excluded from access to it.

The Bakufu, on the other hand, firmly opposed opening Edo and Ōsaka, wishing to keep the Western "barbarian" representatives out of Edo proper, but at the same time wishing to locate the barbarians' residence not too far distant from Edo so that their activities could easily be observed and evaluated. Therefore, the Bakufu considered it best to require Westerners' residence to be somewhere between Kanagawa and Yokohama—away from Edo, yet accessible to official surveillance. Moreover, Harris' proposal to open Ōsaka ran counter to the perennial Bakufu concern with the potential threat to its authority from the *tozama* daimyō of Western Japan. Should Ōsaka be opened to foreign trade, the Bakufu feared, the daimyō maintaining financial officers (*kura yashiki*) at Ōsaka to sell their rice for cash might establish foreign trade with the Western treaty powers and subsequently circumvent the Bakufu's control.[80]

Still another source of the Bakufu's opposition to the opening of Edo and Ōsaka was the notion that opening Yokohama would transform Edo, the largest city and the center of consumption in Japan, into its commercial center; and that this economic supremacy would in turn enable the Bakufu at Edo to regain its hegemony over the numerous feudal domains in Japan.

The story is familiar of how the Bakufu's political supremacy began to erode following the Bakufu's receipt from Commodore Matthew C. Perry of President Millard Fillmore's letter demanding the opening of Japan to foreign commerce. To establish a broader base for Bakufu decisions than had been customary, Senior Councilor Abe Masahiro sought the advice of officials and daimyō. Abe's unprecedented action was generally regarded as a confession of the Bakufu's weakness, however. In consequence, the balance of the political scale began to tip in favor of the Imperial Court at Kyōto. To regain its hegemony, the Bakufu embraced the idea of opening Yokohama to foreign trade. The proponent of the idea was Iwase Tadanori, the Bakufu inspector (*metsuke*) reputed to excel in knowledge of military, naval defense, and foreign affairs who with Harris negotiated the 1858 American Treaty. Iwase's idea was to alter fundamentally the long-standing economic reality of Edo Japan: the concentration of its economic power in Ōsaka. He advocated that Edo supersede Ōsaka as Japan's economic center. In his view, opening Yokohama would enhance Edo's economic status, eventually transforming Edo into Japan's paramount economic center. With the opening of Yokohama, envisioned Iwase, all exported or imported commodities would arrive first at Edo before exportation or redistribution to all parts of Japan. With Edo having once become the nucleus of national commercial operations, the Bakufu would then be able to reassert itself as the repository and source of political power. This politicoeconomic consideration was one of the key factors that led to the Bakufu offer to Harris to open Kanagawa and Yokohama instead of Edo and Ōsaka.[81]

Harris's proposal thus conflicted with the Bakufu's, and out of this conflict came a compromise involving a distinction between open ports and open cities. The result was that in the 1858 American Treaty Edo and Ōsaka were designated open cities and Kanagawa was labeled an open port.

The phrase "open port" meant place of trade and permanent residence for Americans; the phrase "open city" meant place of trade only and therefore of only temporary residence. Article 3 of the American Treaty stipulated that in the open ports "American citizens may permanently reside; they shall have the right to lease ground, and purchase the buildings thereon, and may erect dwellings and warehouses. . . . The place which the Americans shall occupy for their buildings, and the harbor regulations, shall be arranged by the American Consul and the authorities of each place." In the cities of Edo and Ōsaka, on the other hand—the same article went on to stipulate—"Americans shall be allowed to reside . . . for the purposes of trade only. In each of these two cities a suitable place within which they may hire houses, and the distance they may go, shall be arranged by the American Diplomatic Agent and the Government of Japan."[82] Thus, the city and harbor of each open *port* were open to Americans for purposes of trade, whereas in each open *city* only the city, not the harbor, was open. No Western vessels were allowed to load or unload any cargo in the harbor of an open city. Like stipulations were made in the 1858 Dutch-Japanese Treaty, the 1858 Russo-Japanese Treaty, the 1858 Anglo-Japanese Treaty, and the 1858 Franco-Japanese Treaty.

In all of these treaties, Kanagawa, Hyōgo, Nagasaki, and Niigata were designated open ports (*kaikō*); Edo and Ōsaka, open cities (*kaishi*). In the end, however, only Tokyo (Edo) remained an open city after September 1868 when at the request of the treaty powers the newly created Meiji government reclassified Ōsaka as an open port. In so doing, the government was merely giving formal recognition to Ōsaka's de facto status as an open port. In drawing up regulations the previous year to govern the Western settlements in Hyōgo and Ōsaka, the Bakufu had already established an area where Westerners were allowed to lease ground and to erect dwellings as in the Western settlement in an open port. In Tokyo, now the only open city, Westerners were allowed to reside and engage in commerce in only a particular part (Tsukiji) of the city. But since the harbor of Tokyo, Shinagawa, was not open to foreign trade, foreign merchant vessels were not allowed to anchor there. Neither were foreigners permitted direct import and export of goods. Consequently, goods imported into Yokohama were consigned to Tokyo by shuttle barge; Japanese commodities purchased in Tokyo were transshipped to Yokohama, where they were loaded on foreign merchant vessels for export.[83]

In short, for these reasons—the Bakufu's desire to keep the Western "barbarian" away from Edo yet accessible to official surveillance, the Bakufu's determination not to open Ōsaka to foreign trade, and the Bakufu's wish eventually to regain political supremacy from Kyōto as a result of commercial development that would follow opening Yokohama—the Bakufu offered to open Kanagawa and Yokohama.

Ultimately, however, the 1858 American Treaty stipulated that Kanagawa alone, not both Kanagawa and Yokohama, be open as of July 4, 1859. What, then, accounts for the absence of any mention of Yokohama in the treaty? A possible explanation in a recent study by Ishii Takashi suggests that the area the Bakufu offered, the Kanagawa Bay area, comprised both Kanagawa and Yokohama; that Kanagawa, being the largest of the hamlets and towns in the area, was a representative place designation for the entire area; and that the Bakufu's desire to avoid the use of such a complicated expression as "Kanagawa and Yokohama" led the Bakufu to strike out the word "Yokohama," retaining only the word "Kanagawa."[84] If this suggestion is correct, the Bakufu's claim advanced at the time of opening Yokohama, that Yokohama was part of Kanagawa, was of less sophistry than historians previously thought.

After the conclusion of the American and other treaties of 1858, the Bakufu decided to open Yokohama only and not Kanagawa on the grounds that, should Westerners reside in Kanagawa, confrontations between them and Japanese samurai would be frequent. For centuries, Kanagawa had been a thriving post town and a flourishing port. But, being on the Tōkaidō—the main highway between Edo and Kyōto, a route followed today by the famous Japanese bullet train—Kanagawa was a place through which daimyō processions passed on their journeys to and from Edo. In those days the daimyō and their retainers were inimical to the Westerners. In contrast, Yokohama, a little fishing village then located across from the Kanagawa Bay and seven miles south of Kanagawa, was remote from the traffic of the Tōkaidō. Although the bay has largely been reclaimed since those days and what was once the town of Kanagawa now constitutes only a ward (ku) of the sprawling city of Yokohama, at the time Kanagawa was a key site on a major travel route. Hence, the Bakufu reasoned that bloody encounters between assertive Westerners and swashbuckling samurai might occur frequently if the Westerners were to be settled at Kanagawa; that there would be less likelihood of such encounters if they were domiciled at Yokohama.

The Bakufu opened Yokohama in July 1859. Claiming that Yokohama was part of Kanagawa, the place stipulated in the 1858 treaties, the Bakufu dubbed the Yokohama Magistrate the Kanagawa Magistrate and the tariff post at Yokohama the Kanagawa Customshouse. The Bakufu continued this practice until its own demise in 1867. In addition, the Bakufu created every inducement for Edo merchants and workmen, as well as newcomers from abroad, to move into Yokohama in order to build it up as a port suitable for Western residence. The British and U.S. ministers' objections to the Bakufu maneuvers fell on deaf ears. As it happened, though built on swampy ground, Yokohama had a far better harbor than Kanagawa. The net outcome was that Western merchants flocked to Yokohama. By 1860 over thirty Western firms had been firmly established in Yokohama.

The settlement of Western merchants in Yokohama forced all Western consuls to move one by one from Kanagawa to Yokohama and to recognize Yokohama as an open port. Since Kanagawa was the place mentioned in the treaties, the British, the United States, and other consulates and consular courts which were actually situated at Yokohama were by legal fiction described as situated at Kanagawa.[85]

Similarly, because Hyōgo, not Kōbe, was named in the treaties, all the consulates and courts actually located at Kōbe were by legal fiction described as situated at Hyōgo. Today, what was once the bustling town of Hyōgo constitutes only a ward of the city of Kōbe. But in the 1860s Kōbe was "just a sandy waste with a few fishermen's huts nestling under the pine trees that lined the shore."[86] Across the bay was the old town of Hyōgo on a busy highway between Ōsaka and western Japan. Once again, in keeping with its policy of isolating Westerners from Japanese, the Bakufu did not open Hyōgo to foreign trade as the treaties stipulated. Instead it opened Kōbe on January 1, 1868—a week before the Restoration of Imperial Rule (ōsei fukko) was proclaimed by the Imperial Court—but referred to it in official records as Hyōgo.[87]

Turning to Edo, one finds that even long after the Meiji government had renamed Edo Tokyo, the governments of Western treaty powers continued to refer to their consulates at Tokyo as being the ones at Edo (spelled "Yedo" in Western diplomatic documents). Through 1881, for example, the British Foreign Office referred to the British consulate general at Tokyo as "Yedo" rather than Tokyo.[88] The same legalistic grounds by which the fictitious designations of Kanagawa and Hyōgo consulates were maintained seems to account for the Western practice of calling Tokyo Edo. In other words, since Edo was the name mentioned in the treaties, Western consulates and consular courts at Tokyo continued to be referred to as being at Edo.

The foregoing has made it clear that there is an abundance of information about the organization, jurisdiction, and distribution of the British and U.S. consular courts in Japan and that there is a dearth of such information concerning those of the other fourteen treaty powers. Although this imbalance makes it difficult to generalize about the consular courts of all the powers, one may assert that there was a correlation between the magnitude of the powers' stake in Japan and the size and quality of their consular courts there. On the whole, the greater their commercial interest, the better and more numerous the consular courts.

As the Preface to this work emphasizes, this study in no way questions the overall inequity of the presence of consular jurisdiction in nineteenth-century Japan; that what is being questioned is the view that, as a rule, no Japanese could expect justice in a Western consular court. It is beyond doubt that extraterritorial arrangements in Japan had a variety of defects, some of which are alluded to throughout this study. The question under consideration here is, how seriously did these defects hinder the impartial execution of justice by the courts? More specifically, how many mixed cases were there whose outcomes reveal a miscarriage of justice? It is, therefore, necessary to reconstruct and evaluate the five publicized cases, the earliest of which is the King case.

2

The Honor of a Japanese Girl: The *King* Case (1875)

Regina v. *Archibald King*, a rape case tried at Her Britannic Majesty's Court at Yedo (the British consular court at Tokyo, hereafter referred to as the Court), is the earliest and the least known of the five oft-cited cases on which rests the well-established historical interpretation that the Western consular courts in Japan during the second half of the nineteenth century were so biased in favor of Westerners that justice was consistently denied to Japanese litigants. The case involved a thirteen-year-old Japanese girl of a saloon (*chaya*) who was reportedly raped by Archibald King, an Englishman, in Shiba Park, Tokyo. In 1875 the Court convicted King of the crime and sentenced him to six months' imprisonment.

This decision has been condemned by Japanese contemporaries and historians alike, who have asserted that the sentence was too light for such an atrocious crime and as such reflected the overall injustice of the Western consular courts in nineteenth-century Japan. The first person to criticize the outcome of the case was Baba Tatsui, the author of *The Treaty Between Japan and England*, published in London in 1876. In that remarkably pungent and rather pugnacious pamphlet, young Baba wrote: "There have been some crimes committed by Englishmen the nature of which is disgraceful even to describe; only recently a violent outrage was committed on a Japanese girl of thirteen, and this most shameful criminal act was punished in the Consular court with an imprisonment of six months."[1] Thirteen years later, Taguchi Ukichi, the economist and historian, said:

This incident occurred outside of the foreign settlement [in Tokyo]. But the case was not tried by a Japanese judge and according to Japanese law; it was tried by a British consul and according to English law. If the case were to be tried according to the law of Japan now in force the criminal would be sentenced to light penal servitude (*kei chōeki*) ranging from six to eight years. Nevertheless, the convict was sentenced only to six months' imprisonment.[2]

The Baba-Taguchi thesis, that the sentence was exceedingly light and therefore reflected the unfairness of the Western consular courts, has been reiterated by a number of historians who have written on the subject of treaty revision. For example, Yamamoto Shigeru has stated: "Trials by foreign consuls were often biased in favor of protecting the interests of their own countries and therefore unfair, and this in turn created resentment on the part of the Japanese. For example . . . only six months' imprisonment was meted out to an Englishman who had violated a girl under the age of thirteen."[3] Inoue Kiyoshi also has written:

As an unfair instance of the criminal proceedings adjudicated in the consular courts, Baba Tatsui's *Jōyaku kaiseiron* (On Treaty Revision), published quite early in 1876, cites a case in which the British consular court handed down a sentence only of six-month imprisonment to the criminal who had raped a Japanese girl under the age of thirteen in Shiba Park, Tokyo. This incident made a lasting impression on the Japanese. It was again cited in Taguchi Ukichi's *Jōyaku kaiseiron* (On Treaty Revision), published in 1889.[4]

Given the hue and cry heard for the past hundred years, it is rather astonishing to learn how little has been known about the facts and the decision of the case. A measure of the paucity of information about the incident is that Japanese sources fail to state when the alleged crime was committed. These sources never cite even the year, let alone the month and day. From Baba's work one learns that the crime was committed "only recently." The work's publication date, November 1876, is thus one clue which can be used to identify the case. A second clue is the well-known fact that King drew only six months' imprisonment. A diligent, time-consuming search notwithstanding, all that could be ascertained was, not a precise date, but the fact that the alleged crime was committed sometime between March and June of 1875.

In an earlier study to ascertain whether the adjudication of the *King* case did indeed buttress prevailing opinion in regard to it,[5] I suggested that, since there are no facts established through open court testimony with cross-examinations, the case is not relevant in evaluating prevalent opinion concerning the supposed lack of an evenhanded application of justice in cases involving Westerners versus Japanese. Since the publication of that study, however, I have discovered the minutes of the proceedings of the case that constituted part of the full report forwarded by the Court to the Supreme Court for China and Japan at Shanghai.[6] This discovery has led me to restudy the case and to reevaluate my own suggestion in order to determine whether the case lends support to the interpretation that the Western consular courts in Japan as a rule did not render evenhanded justice. The reassessment ultimately produced this chapter.

The chapter first presents the essential facts of the case and, second, analyzes them to determine whether or not the case supports the interpretation at issue.

Regina v. *Archibald King*

Probably early in June 1875, Ōkubo Ichiō, the governer of Tokyo Municipality (Tokyo *fu*), preferred the charge of rape against Archibald King, an Englishman, alleging that on the night of April 14, 1875, he had raped Kō, a
Japanese girl aged thirteen years and seven months old, in a room of a Japanese
tea house. At the trial she and her thirty-three-year-old mother, Yone, testified
tha Kō had never known a man, that King had knocked her down twice on the
floor mat of the room and had committed the outrage on her against her will
and by force, and that there had been blood on her undergarment. Anyone
who reads their testimony cannot help being impressed by its vividness. On the
other hand, the accused and his companion, Gray, rejected the testimony as
"absolutely incredible." They then testified that no rape had taken place; that
Kō was a prostitute; that she had sat on King's knee of her own free accord in
the room where the crime was alleged to have been perpetrated. Witness Gray
further elaborated, saying: "On entering the house I asked the old woman [Yone]
for beer which she gave. She handed the bottle to the girl Kō. She [Kō] attempted to draw the cork but she could not do so. She gave it to the accused.
She then seated herself on his left-knee. She did so of her free will."[7]

Whom are we to believe? For most of us, the answer must be obvious, for
the Court convicted King of the crime preferred against him. Since, however,
the trial judge was a mere vice-consul and since so much doubt as to King's
guilt was expressed by the British community immediately after the trial, a few
facts should be pointed out to dispel any doubts that might arise in the mind
of a skeptic. In the first place, King and Gray attempted unsuccessfully to settle
the matter privately by paying 20 *ryō* each. (The *ryō* was equivalent to the dollar in early Meiji Japan.) Would they have made this attempt had they not
feared the likelihood of prosecution and conviction? Of course not. In addition,
two of the three assessors who recorded their dissent from the Court's verdict
in the judgment of the Court had once, in the words of the trial judge, "most
unhesitatingly expressed their opinion that Gray's evidence could not be accepted as true." It was only at the time of sentencing that they accepted his
testimony as true.[8] Beyond this, the internal evidence in Gray's testimony makes
that testimony suspect. The allegation that in 1875—or for that matter, in 1975—
a thirteen-year-old Japanese girl seated herself on a Western male's knee in the
manner described by Gray—unhesitatingly, unabashedly, and unashamedly—
is just about as convincing as asserting that in 1875 the Japanese husband was,
like his American counterpart, in the habit of assuring his wife of his love and
fidelity by saying, "I love you, Darling!"

Apparently, Gray was an accomplice to the defendant. Yone testified that,
after King had commenced the act of rape, when she tried to go out to sum-
mon the police, Gray held her back and prevented her from doing so promptly.
Incredibly, Gray was not prosecuted as an accessory during the fact, owing to
some mistake on the part of the governor of Tokyo Municipality who omitted
Gray's name when he preferred the charge.[9]

On June 16, 1875, the Court found King guilty of the crime of rape as charged and sentenced him to six months' imprisonment. To enhance our understanding of the case, the judgment will be quoted at length:

The Vice-Consul addressing the prisoner said:

Archibald King,—a great responsibility is thrown upon me in having to deliver a verdict in this difficult and deplorable case. I feel this responsibility all the more as there is no appeal from my decision, and as the assessors have arrived at conclusions different from my own. The assessors desire your acquittal. Were I merely to consult my private feelings, I should not hesitate to meet their wishes; but, as a magistrate, I have a duty to perform, which does not admit of an appeal to my natural inclinations; and it is my profound conviction that you are guilty of the charge brought against you.

This is the second offense of this nature that has come before me since March. It is high time that such acts of violence be put a stop to; therefore, an example must be made.

Looking, however, to all the circumstances of the case, and taking into consideration your good antecedents, which have been testified to at the trial; and bearing in mind also that the object of the law is not so much vengeance on yourself as to deter others from the commission of a similar crime, I shall be lenient with you, and exercise my discretionary power in your favour to the utmost extent consistent with the object which the law has in view.

While in one sense my responsibility is materially increased by the dissent of the assessors, it affords me on the other hand some relief to know that if I err in my judgment, Section 77 of the Order in Council enables you, in consequence of this dissent, to apply for a mitigation or remission of the sentence.

Archibald King, I convict you of the charge of rape on the girl Kō, and sentence you to six month's imprisonment,

MARTIN DOHMEN,
Vice Consul, *Ex Officio* Judge.

The reason why we dissent from the verdict is, that we are not thoroughly convinced the accused committed the crime, and therefore, we wish to give him the benefit of the doubt.

Fred W. Sutton, ⎫
Herbert St. George, ⎬   Assessors

Note—The other assessor, Mr. Dallas, had left the Court before the conclusion of the proceedings; he, likewise, desired acquittal, but gave no reason for his opinion.[10]

The last sentence of the foregoing indicates that Dallas, the assessor, wished King's acquittal but failed to give his reason for his wish. It is probably safe to assume, however, that he had the same reason as the other assessors—they were not convinced that the prisoner at the bar, or the person on trial, had committed the crime of rape. Nevertheless, Vice-Consul Dohmen pronounced the prisoner guilty of the crime, for he was not only convinced of that guilt but also aimed at achieving a greater good within the British community, that is, deterrence. In other words, to the rhetorical question "Did King commit the crime?," Dohmen's answer was yes; the assessors' was no.

King was convicted "otherwise than in a summary way" of the crime of rape. In such a case, under the 1865 China and Japan Order in Council, there was no appeal from the decision of a consular court to the Supreme Court at Shanghai except where the court might, if it seemed fit, reserve for the consideration of the Supreme Court any question of law arising in the trial. In that event, the court should then state a special case, setting out the question reserved, with the facts and the circumstances on which it arose, and should send the case to the Supreme Court.[11] But, in practice, two provisions of the 1865 Order in Council made it possible for the Supreme Court to review the sentence passed by a consular court in China or Japan. The first was Article 77, which provided that the judge of the Supreme Court had the power to recommend to a higher authority a mitigation or remission of any punishment awarded by a consular court only if the court made such a recommendation or if an assessor dissented "from the conviction or from the amount of punishment awarded." The second provision, Article 80, read in part as follows: "Every Provincial [consular] Court shall forthwith send to the Judge of the Supreme Court a report of the sentence passed by it in every case not heard and determined in a summary way, with a copy of the minutes of proceedings and notes of evidence, and with any observations the Court thinks fit." As already noted, the three assessors, including the two who had previously believed Gray's testimony to be untrue, dissented from the conviction. Moreover, King wished to appeal it. Therefore, the Court sent to the Supreme Court a full report of the case and its observations. After review, the Supreme Court affirmed the sentence awarded.

Japanese and British Denunciations of the Court

Did King commit the crime? The Court's answer was yes; the assessors' was no. Ironically, however, the Court found itself denounced by both the Japanese and the local British community. The Japanese denounced the Court because they considered the sentence meted out to King to be too lenient. The British likewise denounced the Court because they agreed with the assessors' "verdict" of not guilty. It is appropriate to evaluate each of these diametrically opposed stances.

With the single exception of Taguchi, no Japanese writers seem to have expressed any opinion on what they thought King's sentence should have been. All that they have asserted is that the punishment was too light and, therefore, by implication, should have been heavier. There are two possible explanations for this seemingly inarticulate and inconclusive assertion. One explanation is that, since the Japanese have long accepted the generalization that the Western consular courts in Japan were unjust and unfair, these writers felt no need to prove the validity of their assertion of the absence of just punishment. No one is likely to amplify any statement which he or she believes will go unchallenged. The other possible explanation is that they simply have long since accepted the assertion because it was once made by such highly respected contemporary writers as Baba and Taguchi. The one explanation is no less plausible than the other, nor are they mutually exclusive. But since the first explanation offers no basis to evaluate the assertion, namely, six months' imprisonment was too light a sentence, the second explanation must be accepted, that is, all writers who have criticized the decision of the *King* case since Taguchi made known his criticism have implicitly shared his reasoning behind the criticism.

As already indicated, Taguchi wrote in 1889 that had King been tried under the law of Japan in force at the time, he would have had to serve a sentence of penal servitude ranging from six to eight years. The law referred to by Taguchi was the Penal Code of 1880, the law applicable as of 1889. Under the Code the crime of rape was punishable by minor penal servitude (*kei chōeki*), which by definition called for terms ranging from six to eight years.[12] Therefore, Taguchi's criticism contains a premise that King should have been punished in accordance with the applicable Japanese law. Taguchi's premise arose from his belief that, since King committed the crime outside of the foreign settlement in Tokyo, he should have been tried at a Japanese court and according to Japanese law. The fact is, however, that the privilege of consular jurisdiction, which all the subjects and citizens of the treaty powers enjoyed, had nothing to do with where they committed offenses. Regardless of the place of commission, the privilege exempted Westerners from being tried in any territorial court of Japan.

In spite of this mistaken belief, one inference which can be made from Taguchi's criticism is that he and other critics may have denounced the six-month imprisonment in question because they evaluated the sentence in the light of the laws of Japan which were applicable to the crime in their own times. This tentative explanation is supported by the fact that none of the penal codes which have been in force for the past hundred years has provided for the crime of rape any prison term shorter than two years.[13] During the century there have been three penal codes. The oldest of these, *Kaitei ritsurei* (The Revised Penal Regulations) of 1873, was in operation when King was convicted. This law provided for the crime of rape a single, fixed, ten-year term of penal servitude.[14] The Penal Code of 1880, which superseded *Kaitei ritsurei*, was in force when Taguchi criticized the sentence at issue. Under the Penal Code, any person convicted of rape was subject to minor penal servitude, terms of which, as already noted, ranged between six and eight years.[15] The Penal Code of 1907, which repealed the earlier 1880 Code, with a few revisions has been in effect until now. The 1907 Code stipulates that the punishment for rape is limited penal servitude (*yūki chōeki*) for any term not less than two years. Since limited penal servitude is defined as referring to prison terms between one month and fifteen years,[16] conviction of this crime leads to a prison term ranging between two and fifteen years.

Like the Japanese, the British community denounced the decision on the *King* case, but for different reasons. Apparently the British denunciation stemmed from the likelihood that English critics did not know two facts: (1) the legal function of a group of assessors was not the same as the legal function of a jury; and (2) there were no criminal offenses which a consular court was ordinarily competent to decide. Each fact requires amplification.

To Englishmen and other people who have adopted the common law system, trial by jury is a cherished protection against the possibility of judicial and administrative tyranny. Normally, in a jury trial the jury determines issues of fact and the judge passes on questions of law. A judge is not, however, bound "to receive at once the first verdict which the jury brings in. He may direct them to reconsider it. If their verdict is meaningless or inconsistent, he may refuse to accept it. If, however, they insist on a general verdict of guilty or not guilty [as distinguished from a special verdict], the judge must accept it." This was already the law of England in the 1870s.[17] Like the jury, the assessors expressed their opinion; unlike the jury, the assessors had no voice in the decision of the court in any case, civil or criminal. A court sitting with assessors was supposed to hear and determine a case with not less than two and not more than four assessors, but even this provision was not mandatory. If local circumstances did not permit the court to obtain enough local British subjects of "good repute" as assessors, it was allowed to sit with one assessor or even without any at all.[18] The assessors were simply representatives of the local British community called to insure that the law was equitably administered.[19] This law explains why Vice-Counsul Dohmen was able to set aside the three assessors' unanimous "verdict" of not guilty.

Not all criminal cases before the British consular courts in China and Japan were triable by jury. From the standpoint of the mode of trial, under the 1865 China and Japan Order in Council, which was in force in 1875, all criminal cases fell within four categories of offenses: (1) serious offenses, including those which in England were capital, tried, as a matter of course, with a jury; (2) offenses which might be tried with a jury when the court so directed; (3) those tried with assessors; and (4) those tried in a summary way, that is, by a judge alone. The Order in Council also provided for a Supreme Court for China and Japan at Shanghai, and for a consular court for each consular district in China and Japan. Each of the British consuls general, consuls, and vice-consuls held a consular court from which appeal lay to the Supreme Court. Whereas only the Supreme Court was competent to adjudicate the first two of the four categories of offenses, unless otherwise directed by the Supreme Court a consular court was competent to decide the remaining two categories only. It is evident, then, that in 1875 there were no criminal cases which a consular court was empowered to try, on its own authority, with a jury.[20]

Evidently, British residents in the Tokyo-Yokohama area did not know that normally they were not entitled to a jury trial in criminal cases prosecuted by the British consular courts there. As evidence of this, for example, in his letter to *The Japan Gazette*, a native Englishman based his attack on the fact that King's conviction by Dohmen was made in spite of the assessors' unanimous wish for acquittal. The writer questioned the judicial capacity of the judge, saying that the judge was a foreigner by birth, and he ended his indignant letter by calling upon Sir Harry S. Parkes, the British minister in Japan, to exercise the royal prerogative of pardon. This writer's indignation, denunciation, and demand—all stemmed from his ignorance expressed in the following words:

Is it not one of our most cherished safeguards that no man shall be criminally tried—to say nothing about being convicted—except by a legally constituted jury of his countrymen; and yet there is a man who has been condemned to imprisonment, and whose character for life is blasted—why? Not because he had committed the offense, but because he was denied his rights as an Englishman, and was tried on a criminal charge.[21]

Clearly, the writer knew nothing about the distinction between assessor and juror, nor did he know that the British consular court at Tokyo had no power to try King with a jury.

Conclusion

I now turn to the critical question of whether or not the outcome of the *King* case supports the interpretation in question, that the Western consular courts in Japan as a rule were so biased in favor of Westerners that justice was consistently denied to Japanese.

In answering this question, the three smaller questions mentioned in the Preface will be raised: (1) Do the existing accounts of the case present both the Japanese complainant's and the British defendant's side of the story? (2) Did the British courts involved render their decisions in accordance with the applicable law? (3) If the complainant had been English rather than Japanese, might the sentence upon the English defendant have been more severe? Should the answers to the first and the third questions be in the negative and the answer to the second in the affirmative, then it can be concluded that the *King* case fails to support the interpretation at issue, that as far as the Japanese were concerned, the Western consular courts in Japan seldom handed down just and fair decisions. On the other hand, the converse conclusion would be in order if the three answers should be otherwise.

The answer to the first question is a resounding no, for there have been no full accounts. As already indicated, this lacuna is attributable to paucity of information about the case.

With regard to the second question, each of the two British courts involved rendered its decision in accordance with the applicable law. It has already been shown that, under the 1865 China and Japan Order in Council, the Supreme Court had power to review King's conviction and sentence, which the Supreme Court subsequently affirmed. In passing sentence, the trial court was also governed by the applicable law. That law was the Offences Against the Person Act, 1861, Section 48 of which read: "Whosoever shall be convicted of the crime of rape shall be guilty of felony, and being convicted thereof shall be liable, *at the discretion of the Court* [italics mine], to be kept in penal servitude for life or for any term not less than three years, to be imprisoned for any term not exceeding two years, with or without hard labour."[22] It is beyond doubt, then, that the punishment imposed upon King, however light it may seem, conformed to this statutory provision.

To answer the third question, it is necessary to ascertain how the sentence in question compared with sentences in similar rape cases—in which the victims were English females, not Japanese—adjudicated in England in the third quarter of the nineteenth century. The necessity arises from the fact that the English court had by statute such great discretion that the punishment for the crime of rape could lawfully range all the way from "any term not exceeding two years" of imprisonment to penal servitude for life. A careful examination of *British Judicial Statistics* for the seven-year period from 1869 through 1875 reveals that during that period 1,011 persons were committed or bailed for trial at the courts of assizes and quarter sessions in England and Wales.[23] Of these 1,011,[24] 588 were acquitted, 3 were committed to confinement on account of insanity, and 420 were convicted. Table 4 shows the outcome of the trials of the 420 convicted.

In examining the above table, one may wonder at once what the difference was between penal servitude and imprisonment. Since the nineteenth-century British reference, *Judicial Statistics*, which makes this obsolete distinction, is referred to again in Chapter 4, it is essential to explain the distinction in some detail. To understand the distinction clearly, it is necessary to review briefly the progression from punishment by death to punishment by imprisonment in nineteenth-century England. Until 1800, the allotted punishment for treason and felony under English law had been death. By then, however, capital punishment was in practice being replaced by lesser substitutes, notably the secondary punishments of transportation (banishment to a penal colony) or imprisonment. Often the death penalty was commuted, or a secondary penalty was substituted for it. The usual form of commutation or substitution in the first half of the nineteenth century was transportation for life or imprisonment for a long term.[25]

In the midnineteenth century, the growing nonconvict inhabitants in British dominions such as Australia resisted further influx of convict population. As a result, in 1853 a Penal Servitude Act was enacted to designate imprisonment with hard labor at any penal establishment in Great Britain or its dominions. Thus, the term "penal servitude" was introduced into British criminal law in 1853.[26] The central authorities of the state bore responsibility for carrying out this punishment at national penitentiaries.

In addition to these national prisons, there were the local jails (or "gaols," which is the preferred British spelling) of county and borough. Although the jails were maintained in the name of the king, responsibility for their administration had early fallen on the sheriff of the county and had been extended by charter or custom to borough officials and other franchise-holders. By 1800, the local prisons were receiving, in addition to those awaiting trial, convicts

Table 4
Sentences Imposed on Persons Convicted of the Crime of Rape After Trials at the Courts of·Assizes and Quarter Sessions in England and Wales, 1869–1875

Disposition	Number	
Penal Servitude		
Life	4	
Over 15 years	20	
15 years and over 10 years	67	
10 years and over 7 years	139	(The median sentence falls into this category.)
7 years	73	
6 years and 3 years	64	
"Imprisonment with, in some Cases, Whipping, Fine &c. [etc.]"(a)		
Over 2 years	0	
2 years and over 1 year	26	
1 year and over 6 months	17	
6 months and over 3 months	5	
3 months and over 1 month	3	
1 month and under	0	
Detained in reformatories or industrial schools	1	
Fined or discharged on sureties	1	
Total convicted	420	

SOURCES: Computed from Great Britain, Parliament
(Commons), Parliamentary Papers, 1870, 63.621,
Cmnd. 195;1 1871, 64.102, Cmnd. 442;1 1872,
65.95, Cmnd. 600;1 1873, 70.99, Cmnd. 871;1
1874, 71.99, Cmnd. 1055;1 1875, 81.103;1 Cmnd.
1315;1 1876, 79.107, Cmnd. 1595.
(a) The Criminal Justice Act of 1948 abolished
whipping as a penalty that could be ordered by a
court.

awaiting transportation, civil debtors, and those who had been sentenced by the higher courts and petty sessions to terms of imprisonment. In 1877 the central Prison Commissioners were appointed to take over the administration of the local prisons. Since the commissioners were also the directors of the Convict Prisons, the two prison systems were brought under a single administration, even though the legal basis of the two remained distinct.[27]

Persons serving the sentence of penal servitude were convicts; persons serving the sentence of imprisonment were prisoners. The minimum period for penal servitude was three years, and the maximum was life. For imprisonment the minimum sentence was five days, and the usual statutory maximum was two years. There were some other distinctions in the treatment of convicts and pris-

oners. For example, although for good conduct either could earn remission of
a portion of a sentence, convicts were released on license only, whereas prisoners were simply discharged. The 1948 Criminal Justice Act abolished all these
distinctions between penal servitude and imprisonment. Before the act came
into force, however, there had been no differences in the treatment of convicts
and prisoners except those attributable to the difference in the length of sentence.[28]

As seen in Table 4, the median sentence, the sentence designating the middle point of the series of 420 sentences (the $210^1/_2$th sentence), ranged between
ten years and over seven years. Granted that in the third quarter of the nineteenth century there was neither any body able to lay down sentencing policies
to be pursued nor detailed comparative information about differences in sentencing between courts,[29] one cannot help observing that King's six months' imprisonment was at the low end of the penalty range and therefore lenient. On
the other hand, this lenience alone does not constitute proof that the adjudication of the *King* case bears out the partiality of the Western consular courts
in Japan. Such an inference would be quite fallacious, for the process of sentencing, as distinguished from the process of trial, was within the discretion of
the trial judges (assizes) and justices (quarter sessions), with the result that there
were marked disparities of sentence for comparable offenses and circumstances.
This fact remains largely unchanged today.[30]

Nevertheless, quite apart from the lenience of King's sentence, there is another reason why the answer to the third question may be yes. The Court evidently prejudged the outcome of the *King* case by assuming that King's crime,
if proved, would not call for a punishment harsher than one year's imprisonment. Under the 1865 China and Japan Order in Council, the maximum punishment a consular court was empowered to impose was twelve months' imprisonment with or without hard labor and with or without a fine not exceeding
$1,000. Moreover,

Where the crime or offence with which any person charged before a Provincial [con-
sular] Court appears to the Court to be such that, if proved, it would not be adequately
punished by such punishment as the Court has power to impose, and the accused is not
to be sent for trial to Her Majesty's dominions, the Court shall reserve the case to be
heard and determined by or under the special authority of the Supreme Court [at
Shanghai].[31]

In adjudicating the *King* case, the Court did not seek this special authority.
Evidently, therefore, it was the opinion of the Court prior to the trial that King's
crime, if proved, could be adequately punished by such punishment as the Court
had power to impose. In other words, by assuming that the crime, if proved,
would not call for a punishment harsher than one year's imprisonment, the
Court evidently prejudged the outcome of the case. Once again, making allowance for the fact that information presented in this study about the sentences
meted out to the convicted 420 rapists may have been unknown to the Court,

the Court's pretrial assessment of the gravity of King's crime seems to have been rather biased in favor of the accused, since it was known to the Court that the maximum statutory punishment for the crime was penal servitude for life.

For these reasons—the relative lenience of King's sentence and the Court's biased pretrial assessment of the gravity of King's alleged crime—one may conclude that had the complainant been English rather than Japanese, the sentence imposed on King might have been more severe than the one actually imposed on him.

The *King* case, therefore, lends support to the interpretation that the Western consular courts in Japan as a rule did not render evenhanded justice.

3

Extraterritoriality on Trial: The *Hartley* Cases (1878)

The extent to which the decisions in *Regina* v. *John Hartley* (1878) and *Regina* v. *Hartley & Co.* (1878) have rankled in Japanese minds for the past hundred years may be shown by the comments of several Japanese historians. Hanabusa Nagamichi writes that the *Hartley* cases were "ones in which the English merchant John Hartley, while trying to smuggle opium into Japan in contravention of a trade regulation appended to the Anglo-Japanese Treaty of 1858, was caught twice by the Japanese authorities. . . . In each case he was found not guilty [!]."[1]

Inoue Kiyoshi states: "The *Hartley* cases represent a classical example of the unfair and improper adjudication of treaty-violating cases." Kawashima Shintarō attributes the failure of Foreign Minister Terashima Munenari's attempt at treaty revision to the *Hartley* decisions:

The moral of the *Hartley* cases was the fact that, so long as such clear wording of the Treaty was the prohibition of opium importation could be made void by a distorted interpretation by an English consular court, the recovery of Japan's sovereign right to enact all customs regulations would be of no effect unless Japan recovered simultaneously her sovereign right to interpret such regulations.[2]

Speaking of the alleged unfairness of consular court decisions which created resentment among the Japanese, Yamamoto Shigeru cites the *Hartley* cases as prime examples, saying: "An English consular court held that an Englishman who imported opium, prohibited by the Treaty [of 1858], was not guilty once import duties on it were paid." (It will be shown that this statement is entirely inaccurate.) Finally, Roy Hidemichi Akagi refers to the first *Hartley* case both as "a typical instance" of the Western treaty powers' shameful "interference with the enforcement of the Japanese laws necessary for the protection of Japanese life and general welfare," and as evidence of "the unreasonableness of extraterritoriality."[3]

During the 1870s Japan attempted repeatedly to undermine the extraterritorial regime, but Great Britain and other treaty powers blocked these attempts. The opium question raised by the *Hartley* cases epitomizes this conflict between Japan and Great Britain from 1872 to 1881.

Jurisdiction and the Law

Japan's indignation over the *Hartley* decisions reflected profound disagreement with Great Britain on the extent to which the treaty powers were entitled to exercise extraterritoriality in Japan. It is, therefore, necessary to review what extraterritoriality meant and how its extent was defined by treaties that Japan entered into during the third quarter of the nineteenth century.

Historically, extraterritoriality meant an extensive exemption from both the local jurisdiction and the laws of the country in which foreigners dwelled. Three prenineteenth-century examples illustrate this. First, the laws of the Visigoths provided that "when foreign merchants have disputes with one another, none of our judges shall take cognizance, but they shall be decided by officers of their own nation and according to their laws." Second, the Turkish Firman of 1453, the first document which conferred extraterritorial rights on Christians in the Ottoman Empire, granted the Genoese the right to retain their own laws and customs and to choose from among themselves an *ancien* to decide their own disputes. Finally, under the terms of the 1664 treaty between the Dutch East India Company and Siam, the Company's chief had the power to take cognizance according to Dutch laws of cases of grave crime committed by Dutch citizens in Siam.[4] Although many authorities on international law have defined the word "extraterritoriality," perhaps none has given a better definition than Henry Wheaton. In the Dana edition of his *Elements of International Law*, he defines the word as foreigners' "exemption from the local laws and jurisdiction of the country where they reside."[5]

Today it is taken for granted that each state is entitled to exercise exclusive jurisdiction over all persons, native and foreign, within its territories. From this viewpoint of the territoriality of law, extraterritoriality means a derogation from the sovereignty of a nation which grants it, as it meant in the nineteenth century. But before the rise of modern nation-states, extraterritoriality was granted gratuitously. Then the underlying assumption was the personality of laws—namely, that the laws of the nation to which an individual belonged followed him wherever he went and that he was entitled to their protection and benefits without reference to the laws of the state in which he sojourned.

The underlying issue of the opium cases controversy was whether nationals of the Western treaty powers were exempt from both local jurisdiction and the national laws of Japan. The issue involved the two main concerns of private international law, or the conflict of laws. The first was, before the courts of what nation should a case be brought? The answer was the principle *actor sequitor forum rei*, that is, the plaintiff followed the defendant into the court of the defendant's state.[6] Under the terms of the Japanese treaties with the Western powers, in each criminal case the accused was to be tried by a court of his nationality. For example, Article 5 of the Anglo-Japanese Treaty of 1858 stipulated:

Japanese subjects, who may be guilty of any criminal act towards British subjects, shall be arrested and punished by the Japanese authorities according to the laws of Japan. British subjects, who may commit any crime against Japanese subjects, or the subjects or citizens of any other country, shall be tried and punished by the Consul, or other public functionary, authorized thereto, according to the laws of Great Britain.

The same principle also applied to civil cases, but the application was sanctioned either by treaty or by practice and not by treaty alone.[7] In any event, the net outcome was that in either a civil or a criminal case no Westerner could be sued in any court of Japan, being wholly exempt from the territorial jurisdiction of Japan. Among the treaty powers, therefore, there was no question as to this exemption.

There was, however, no such unanimity among the treaty powers regarding the second concern of private international law, on which the opium controversy impinged. Here the question was, by the laws of what nation should the rights of the litigants be determined? More specifically, by the laws of what country should a Western consul in Japan be governed in adjudicating mixed cases arising under existing treaties? The extraterritorial provisions of the various Western treaties with Japan were virtually identical in form and in substance. The treaties' most-favored-nation clauses enlarged the jurisdiction to the fullest extent granted to any treaty power, and thereby made the privileges uniform for all treaty powers.

Nevertheless, between 1872 and 1874 there surfaced three conflicting constructions—American, British, and Japanese—of the extraterritorial provisions in the existing treaties.

From 1874 on, the United States, which hitherto had adhered to the British construction (to be explained shortly), maintained a clear, consistent construction of its own, a construction greatly appreciated by the Japanese government. This was that under the American-Japanese treaties Americans resident in Japan were exempt from the territorial jurisdiction of the Japanese courts, but were in no way exempt from the territorial laws and regulations of Japan as long as these were not in conflict with existing treaty rights. This construction was enunciated authoritatively by Secretary of State Hamilton Fish in his instructions of January 7, 1874, to John A. Bingham, the U.S. minister to Japan:

The rights of the authorities of Japan to enact and promulgate laws for the government, security, and order of its own people cannot, of course, be questioned; and of the character and sufficiency of these laws, that government must be the sole judge. Citizens of the United States resident in Japan are expected and required to observe and obey such laws in the same manner and to the same extent that the like obligations rest upon the subjects of that Empire.

In short, the municipal laws and regulations of Japan were binding upon the citizens of the United States.

Fish went on to say:

> In regard to the enforcement of these laws, and the imposition of penalties for their infraction, citizens of the United States have secured to them, by the provisions of the existing treaties, the right of being tried in the consular courts of their own nation, established in Japan, and according to the mode prescribed by the laws of the United States, and are protected from the infliction of any other penalties than those prescribed or warranted by the laws of their own country. So long as these privileges are recognized and respected by the government of Japan, there can be no cause of complaint on the part of this government in relation to the promulgation of any municipal law or regulation which the legislative authority of that country may deem necessary to the public interest and welfare.[8]

Fish's statement calls for two observations. First, in essence he made a distinction between substantive law and procedural law—a fundamental, dichotomous category of law.[9] He declared that Japanese law defined what acts by Americans in Japan constituted offenses, and what constituted their substantive rights and obligations; that American law, as interpreted by an American consular court, prescribed how Americans who either committed offenses or incurred obligations should be punished or treated. Stated in another way, Japan had the right to enact laws and regulations binding upon all Americans in Japan. The United States was under obligation both to apply those laws and to make and enforce judgments. Second, the American construction as laid down by Fish imposed upon Americans the obligation to observe and obey the laws of Japan, whereas the British construction did not impose such an obligation upon British subjects in Japan.

The Fish doctrine received judicial notice in 1875, when in *United States v. Middleton* (1875) the U.S. consular court at Kanagawa held that Americans in Japan were exempt from obedience to Japanese laws only insofar as the treaties with Japan provided such exemption.[10] Moreover, Eli T. Sheppard, the American legal adviser to the Foreign Ministry, who did much to acquaint the Japanese government with the American construction laid down by Fish, expounded the limits of the extraterritorial provisions in the treaties. He wrote: "The treaty provisions relate exclusively to *the mode of trial and the measure of punishment*" (italics in original). At the same time, he stated that the exemption of American citizens from the jurisdiction of the Japanese courts was not an immunity from the general obligations and restraints of the territorial laws of Japan, for Japan had never surrendered its inherent sovereign power to impose those laws.[11]

From the perspective of the past hundred years, it would seem fair to observe that the American construction was the fairest and most judicious of the three. Sheppard, after making a careful study both of many authorities on international law of the midnineteenth century and of the extraterritorial provisions in the British and American treaties with Japan, reached the following conclusion: "Complete extraterritoriality [exemption from both substantive and procedural law] can be claimed . . . by virtue only of the express or implied consent of Japan; but the law of nations existing at the time the treaties were signed absolutely forbids and repels such an implication."[12] It will be shown that the law officers of the British Crown and certain officials of the British Foreign Office entertained essentially the same view.

Although there were other British constructions of the extraterritorial provisions in the British treaties with Japan, Parkes' construction ultimately prevailed and will be referred to here as the British construction. Parkes maintained that the extraterritorial provisions of the existing treaties with Japan exempted the nationals of the Western treaty powers not only from the jurisdiction of Japan but also from its laws and regulations. Western consular courts could enforce only Western laws, not Japanese laws. Hence, he argued, any municipal laws or police regulations of Japan, if they were to be binding upon British subjects, must first be converted into British equivalents. And this process of conversion required the British minister's assent. In his memorandum of May 25, 1881, he expressed this viewpoint with greater eloquence than anywhere else:

The same cardinal question arises in the case of these [Draft] regulations [of 1880] as in that of all others affecting British subjects which have been or may be proposed by the Japanese Government. Are they to be approved by Her Majesty's Government as they stand, and simply because they are represented to be Japanese law? and, if so approved, how are they to be enforced on British subjects?

I presume that these or any other Japanese regulations can only be enforced on British subjects in Japan by a British court, i.e., by being made British regulations under the China and Japan Order in Council, 1865, and I believe it to be a principle of private international law that no foreign court is obliged to enforce an unreasonable law of another nation.

It is for Her Majesty's Government to judge whether these regulations are reasonable, or whether they require modification, before Her Majesty's Minister in Japan can be instructed to clothe them with the authority of British Regulations. . . . [13]

Parkes' arguments implied that British subjects could, with impunity, defy and disobey any police or municipal regulations of Japan unless such regulations had previously received the approval of the British minister. They further implied that Japan had surrendered its inherent sovereign power to legislate over all foreigners within its territories.

In brief, the British construction claimed that nationals of the treaty powers were exempt from the substantive law, the procedural law, and the territorial jurisdiction of Japan. According to the American construction, however, the exemption extended only to the procedural law and the jurisdiction and not to the substantive law, as long as the substantive law did not conflict with treaty rights of Americans.

The Japanese construction was precisely the opposite of the British construction. The Japanese government argued that, except for rights expressly conferred by treaties upon Westerners resident in Japan, these Westerners were not exempt from Japanese laws governing the rights or from the jurisdiction of Japan. They were, therefore, subject to the substantive law, the procedural law, and the territorial jurisdiction of Japan. Between 1873 (when the first draft regulations concerning importation of opium were issued) and 1879 (when Foreign Minister Inoue Kaoru yielded to the British demand that Japan cooperate with Parkes in drafting its regulations), the Japanese government took the view that a privilege not expressly granted by treaty was a purely internal matter on which the government had no obligation to consult representatives of the treaty powers, and on which it alone had power to make decisions. Specifically, Japan argued that the treaties did not stipulate that subjects of the contracting parties in Japan had a right to import medicinal opium. Hence, it rested entirely with the Japanese government to give or withhold permission to import the drug, and to make foreign subjects amenable to whatever regulations it might see fit to enact. Permission, if granted, would be, as aptly put by Parkes, "an act of grace." In the case of British subjects, therefore, they were to obey such regulations, not in the form of British regulations, but rather as Japanese regulations.[14] Tokyo repeatedly told London during the opium controversy that the need of opium for medicinal purposes and the right of foreigners to import it were "in their nature totally different questions." In other words, the need did not confer the right; the Japanese government alone had power to grant or withhold that right.

Had Japan not insisted upon placing British chemists and druggists under its territorial jurisdiction and procedural law, the question of the importation of medicinal opium could have been resolved between 1873 and 1875, and there would have been no *Hartley* cases.

Opium, the Indispensable Medicine and the Contraband

Opium was and is the sovereign pain-killer. In 1680 Thomas Sydenham, a founder of modern clinical medicine who has been called "the English Hippocrates," observed: "Among the remedies which it has pleased Almighty God to give to man to relieve his sufferings, none is so universal and so efficacious as opium."[15] The alkaloid which gives opium its analgesic (pain-relieving) actions is morphine. Morphine was the first of the alkaloids the discovery of which enabled the pharmacy of nineteenth-century Europe to develop into modern rational therapeutics. This discovery was regarded as so important that in 1831 the Institute of France awarded the discoverer, German apothecary and chemist William Adam Sertürner, a prize of 2,000 francs.[16] Sir William Osler, a Canadian physician and medical historian who taught medicine at Johns Hopkins and Oxford until 1919, referred to morphine as "God's own medicine." Since his day, scores of synthetic and semisynthetic agents equal to morphine in their ability to relieve pain have been introduced, but it is doubtful that any is clinically superior. Morphine remains the standard against which new analgesics are measured. Along with its narcotic surrogates, it retains its "very special place in the never-ending combat against pain."[17]

It is not surprising, therefore, that in the 1870s, the decade with which this chapter is concerned, medicinal opium with its relatively high morphine content was viewed as indispensable. Various descriptions of medicinal opium found in documents pertaining to the *Hartley* cases bear witness to that indispensability: "the medicine of the first necessity," "the medicine of the most valuable and necessary," and the medicine "imperatively needed by British subjects."

British physicians in Yokohama, the largest of the ports open to Western residents in late nineteenth-century Japan, prescribed medicinal opium regularly. According to a certain Dr. Siddal, an English physician practicing in Yokohama, as of 1878 approximately 37 percent of all prescriptions that a practicing apothecary was called upon to make required medicinal opium. British apothecaries there also supplied medical stores to merchant vessels in the Yokohama harbor in compliance with the Board of Trade Regulations, and the medical stores enumerated "opium pills, Laudanum, Paregoric, Diarrhoea powder, Dover powder, and five articles containing opium." "I could not," testified John North, an English apothecary and expert-witness at the trial of the first *Hartley* case, "prepare those medicines without opium; opium forms the principal ingredient. It is a staple medicine. It is an indispensable one. If we made our opium preparations without opium, that is, the principal drug, we would be liable to prosecution, as we are bound to make our preparations according to the London Pharmacopoeia." Dr. Siddal estimated that 200 pounds of medicinal opium were required annually for the 1,500 Western residents and the crews of the more than 300 Western vessels that docked at the Yokohama port.[18] It is no wonder, then, that Sir Harry S. Parkes said that "no community of civilized persons could dispense with this essential medicine."[19]

In spite of its extensive pharmaceutical use in the Western (especially British) community in Japan, opium was contraband under the treaties between Japan and the Western treaty powers. Paragraph 8 of Regulation II appended to the Anglo-Japanese Treaty of 1858 read:

The importation of opium being prohibited, any British vessel coming to Japan for the purpose of trade, and having more than three catties' weight of opium on board, the surplus quantity may be seized and destroyed by the authorities; and any person or persons attempting to smuggle opium, shall be liable to pay a fine of fifteen dollars for each catty of opium so smuggled or attempted to be smuggled.

Similar clauses appeared in treaties Japan concluded with other Western treaty powers.

The first treaty embodying a prohibition of this sort was the Dutch-Japanese Additional Convention of 1857, Article 14 of which stipulated: "The importation of opium into Japan is forbidden." This stipulation was evidently intended to avert the spread of the evil of opium-smoking. Some Chinese at Nagasaki had induced two Japanese women to smoke opium. So injurious were the effects upon their systems that they died, shortly before the Convention of 1857 was made. The Bakufu, therefore, inserted the stipulation, which was then reaffirmed by the Tariff Convention of 1866 as follows: "Clause III.—Prohibited Goods. Opium."

These international compacts barred from importation all opium, not specifically smoking or medicinal opium. This absence of a qualifying word caused disagreement between Japan and Great Britain as to the applicability of the prohibition to medicinal opium. Out of this disagreement came the controversy over the *Hartley* cases. One obvious question here is, if medicinal opium was so indispensable, why was the term "opium" not qualified by the word "smoking," or why wasn't the prohibition worded so as to exclude medicinal opium? According to Parkes, Clause III of the Tariff Convention of 1866 was understood by the framers of the tariff, of whom he was one, to apply to smoking opium only, and they did not expressly mention medicinal opium because they thought it would have been contrary to common sense to suppose that the Japanese government could possibly object to the importation of an indispensable drug.

Whatever the intent of the framers, for fourteen years from 1858 to 1872, Western residents in Japan continued to import opium. It should be pointed out that usage was (and remains) one of the most important sources of international law. The Bakufu never objected to importation in the eight years before or in the six years after the Tariff Convention was instituted. The convention stipulated "Drugs and Medicines such as Ginseng &c. [etc.]" to be among "Class IV.—Goods subject to an Ad Valorem Duty of Five Per Cent on the Original Value." Under this stipulation, from 1866 to 1872 medicinal opium was imported as a drug.[20]

Apparently, no Japanese records reveal either the inner thoughts of the leaders who decided to prohibit the unrestricted importation of medicinal opium or the process whereby they reached their decision. Given their severely limited knowledge of international law and diplomacy, however, one may safely assume that not until 1872 or slightly earlier did they realize that the wording of the prohibition in the Anglo-Japanese Treaty of 1858 and the Tariff Convention of 1866 made no distinction between medicinal and smoking opium. Not until 1872 did they formulate the interpretation on which rested their objections to the importation of medicinal opium: that both the treaty and the convention prohibited the importation of all kinds of opium.

More positively, it would seem that the Japanese decision to place a strictly literal construction on the prohibition stemmed from the "independent foreign policy" (*jishuteki gaikō*) that Soejima Taneomi initiated when he became foreign minister in November 1871. Ignorant of diplomacy, aware of Japanese nonsophistication, and repeatedly bullied by arrogant Western diplomats, the government leaders of early Meiji Japan had been fearful of and often subservient to these diplomats, Soejima being one of the few leaders who could stand up to them. From missionary-teacher G. F. Verbeck, he had gained a knowledge of English and European institutions and economics and a smattering of international law which most of his fellow leaders lacked. Most significantly, he was by temperament self-assertive and independent-minded.

Soejima's foreign policy owed much not only to his self-confidence, but also to the influence of the first legal adviser to the Foreign Ministry from 1871 to 1876—Erasmus Peshine Smith, an American lawyer. Smith helped embolden Soejima to become assertive and firm with Western diplomats. Insouciant and impudent, Smith is said usually to have worn Japanese clothing and two curved swords while strutting on Tokyo streets. He advocated that Japan pursue a non-subservient, autonomous foreign policy, and he clashed with Western representatives accustomed to browbeating Japanese government leaders. British Minister Parkes intimated to Soejima a desire for Smith's dismissal—a suggestion Soejima repudiated with the tacit backing of American Minister Charles E. DeLong.

Soejima, encouraged and assisted by Smith, became involved in a number of diplomatic exploits. One was the *Maria Luz* incident of 1872 in which the Japanese government set free and sent home 224 Chinese coolies, bought in Macao, who were on board a Peruvian ship en route to Peru which had entered Yokohama for repair. Japan had not yet established commercial and diplomatic relations with Peru. All the Western consuls in Yokohama except the British, expressed disapproval of the Japanese action. Peru demanded damages; Japan refused to pay. The dispute was arbitrated by Alexander II of Russia in Japan's favor. In this first international proceeding to which Japan became a party, it was Smith who guided the Foreign Ministry in dealing with the incident and took charge of its legal disposition from start to finish. For this service, in September 1875 he was received in audience by Emperor Meiji, who awarded him an imperial rescript on his service and a long, curved sword.[21] The boldness and determination with which the Japanese government liberated the Chinese, despite the disapproval of the Western community, attested to the strength of the foreign policy Soejima had initiated. It is not without significance, then, that Japan's unilateral decision to put an end to the importation by Westerners of medicinal opium coincided with the *Maria Luz* incident. Japan began to pursue in earnest independent lines of action in foreign affairs.

Opium Controversy

Beginning in July 1872, Japanese customs at Yokohama confiscated and held small supplies of Turkish opium imported by Western drug importers. The Japanese government had not given Western representatives any notice that the government wished to change its previous fourteen-year practice. In response to these unannounced seizures of Turkish opium, the representatives met in mid-December and agreed to make the following representation to Foreign Minister Soejima the next month: The quantity of Turkish opium required by the Western community in Japan was small. But if the Japanese government should consider that the smallness of the quantity imported was no sufficient guarantee for its exclusive use for medicinal purposes, it would be easy to devise the means to prevent opium from being diverted from its legitimate use by requiring that Western apothecaries and chemists submit their accounts periodically to the inspection of *their* consuls.

Foreign Minister Soejima made no immediate response to this joint note. Four months later, the Western representatives informed Acting Foreign Minister Ueno Kageyasu that the subject of the January note demanded immediate attention in the interest of public health, and they requested the release of the small quantities of Turkish opium then detained by the Yokohama customs. Thereupon, Ueno simply announced as a decision of his government that Turkish opium might be imported for medicinal purposes, subject to Japanese regulations enclosed with his note. In the note he informed the representatives that these regulations should be regarded as provisional pending the establishment of fuller rules regulating the importation of drugs. By this decision, observed Parkes, Ueno left it to be inferred that the representatives need not be consulted. Parkes' observation was perceptive. Henceforth, Japan took the position that control of importation of drugs was purely an internal affair about which no foreign representative need be consulted, since Japan had never granted to the treaty powers the right to import Turkish opium. Parkes and other representatives, however, considered this position to be in violation of the existing treaty arrangements.[22]

Japanese regulations of May 12, 1873, provided that foreign apothecaries might be permitted to import, every two months, such quantity of medicinal opium as the Japanese government might allow to each apothecary on payment of a duty of 10 percent—twice the amount of the duty that could be levied on drugs and medicines under the Tariff Convention of 1866—and on condition that the foreign apothecaries should submit to such regulations as the Japanese government might see fit to establish. The apothecaries were to be bound to dispense opium under a physician's certificate, to report monthly to the Japanese authorities the amount they had dispensed, supported by every certificate or prescription under which it had been dispensed, and to keep their books open for examination at any time by an officer sent from the prefectoral government. Furthermore, they were to be subject to a fine not exceeding ¥500 if this examination disclosed any irregularity, such as the sale of a larger amount of the drug than they were authorized to dispense; to the seizure and forfeiture of all opium found on their premises at the time of the violation; and to future deprivation of the privilege of importing a further supply. In addition, they were forbidden to sell opium in any quantity to any Japanese.

The regulations then defined not only what constituted an infraction, but also what punishment should be meted out, and what the maximum should be—all to be determined unilaterally by Japanese authorities. Concerning the incompatibility of these provisions with the treaty rights of Westerners in Japan, Parkes in 1879 wrote to Foreign Secretary Salisbury as follows:

Your Lordship will perceive that these Regulations would have placed the foreign chemists and druggists under the control and jurisdiction of the Japanese authorities. As the condition of being furnished with a supply of medicinal opium, which was indispensable to their professional business, and to the want of their foreign customers and patients, they were to be subject to most inquisitorial interference and restraints, and also to heavy fines and penalties by Japanese officers to whom under Treaty they owe no submission, and who have no more right to fine a foreign chemist or to decree the forfeiture of his property than they have to impose similar penalties on a merchant or any other foreign subject.[23]

With the single exception of the American representative, the Western representatives agreed that the Japanese position on medicinal opium could not be accepted; it involved a serious encroachment on treaty rights. They proposed a substitute for the Japanese regulations. Under the proposed agreement, all medicinal opium imported into any open port in Japan was to be stored only in the bonded warehouses of the Japanese government, and no new permit to take opium out of bond was to be granted to a foreign apothecary until he had proved to the satisfaction of his consul and of the Japanese superintendent of customs that he had disposed of the quantity named in his last permit in the manner required by rules proposed by the representatives. In return, the representatives concurred in almost all of Ueno's demands—the importation of only medicinal and not of smoking opium, the 10 percent duty, and no sale of opium to any Japanese. The draft agreement also provided for as strict a scrutiny of the way in which the apothecaries disposed of each supply of opium as Ueno had specified. But it also specified that this scrutiny should be conducted by the apothecary's consul, or if desired, in the presence of the Japanese superintendent of customs. The representatives could not accede to the Japanese provision that Japanese officers be allowed to enter, whenever they pleased, and independently of consular concurrence, the premises of Western apothecaries in order to examine their papers and books and to inspect their stocks of medicine.[24]

The proposed agreement was just as unacceptable to Tokyo as the first regulations had been to Western diplomats. The heart of the matter was, who had the power to punish subjects and citizens of the treaty powers for infraction of Japanese regulations?

The Japanese government's attempt to make opium regulations binding on Westerners in Japan while simultaneously trying to meet objections raised by Western representatives continued from 1873 to 1875.[25] The outcome was that the government issued four sets of draft regulations, in addition to the one already discussed (see Table 5 below). Under the terms of these five regulations, all Western apothecaries were to be subject to the jurisdiction of Japan. Of the five, the first three were designed to regulate the West's importation of medic-

Table 5

Japan's Draft Regulations Regarding Opium and Parkes' Response, 1873–1875

	Regulations Proposed by Japan			Parkes' Response		
Set	Date of Issuance	Title	Number of Articles	Date	Response	Number of Articles
1	5/12/1873	Regulations for the Importation of Turkish Opium for Medicinal Use	12	5/31/1873	Agreement as to Importation of Medicinal Opium, proposed by Western representatives	7
2	6/23/1873	Rules for Regulating the Importation of Opium for Medicinal Purposes	25		No countermeasures or corrections offered by Parkes or by other Western representatives.	
3	4/22/1875	Third Set of Japanese Regulations for the Importation of Opium	13	?/?/1875	Regulations for the Import and Sale of Medicinal Opium	13
4	?/?/1875	Fourth Draft of Regulations for the Sale of Medicinal Opium	5	?/?/1875	Draft Regulations for the Supply of Medicinal Opium by the Japanese Government	4
5	?/?/1875	Fifth Set of Japanese Regulations for the Supply of Medicinal Opium	7	9/9/1875	Corrections Suggested (See the text of this chapter below.)	

SOURCE: FO 46/360/179–374; FO 46/361/32–48.

inal opium; the other two were intended to forbid such importation entirely and to regulate the sale to the Western dispensers of medicinal opium, which the Japanese government alone would import, to meet the needs of Westerners in Japan.

The table also shows Parkes' response to each of the five sets of regulations. By means of the three counterproposals that followed the first, third, and fourth sets, respectively, he tried to meet what he considered to be "every legitimate" demand of Japan, while at the same time reserving to British consuls the power to punish British apothecaries for any breaches of Japanese regulations. There was no meeting of the minds between Tokyo and Parkes. When the superintendent of customs at Yokohama instituted the first *Hartley* case in December 1877, Parkes told Foreign Minister Terashima face to face that the case was "a consequence of our not having agreed to regulations under which medicinal opium might be imported."

One may further observe in the table that the five sets of regulations were issued at highly irregular intervals. The reason was that they accompanied a series of negotiations that took place only consequent to Japanese seizures of opium and that Japanese customs authorities seized supplies of medicinal opium only intermittently. The total amount entered for importation by British subjects from July 1872 to October 1875—over three and a half years—and detained at the Customshouse at Yokohama, was only 148 pounds. Four British apothecaries, the only Western ones practicing in Yokohama in 1872, estimated the yearly amount of medicinal opium required by the Western community there at 400 pounds, half of which was sold to Japanese physicians and druggists. If one assumes conservatively that the Westerners imported 1,200 pounds from July 1872 to October 1875, the detained 148 pounds represented only 12.3 percent of the total. Surely, the enforcement of the Japanese ban on importation appears to have been lax and haphazard. There is no evidence that customs interfered with the Westerners' importation of medicinal opium between October 1875 and July 1877. Parkes later reported to London that during this two-year period Western apothecaries obtained all the medicinal opium they needed, although he did not know by what means.[26]

Before closing our discussion of the opium controversy of 1872–1875, it is necessary to understand Parkes' criticism of the draft regulations. From 1865 to 1883, he represented the foremost treaty power with the largest commercial interests in Japan. This, combined with his colorful and energetic personality, made him the prime mover among Western representatives on virtually all issues involving Japan and the treaty powers. Moreover, on most issues of the nineteenth century, the British Foreign Office followed the advice of Parkes, the man on the spot.[27] As a result, his views on the draft regulations, while initially not fully accepted by the Foreign Office, ultimately prevailed.

Parkes found the five Japanese sets of draft regulations to be defective in four ways. The first defect, the most fundamental and serious of all, has already been discussed: encroachment upon the British subject's immunity from the laws and jurisdiction of Japan. He was especially alarmed about the possibility that the subjection of British apothecaries resident in Japan to territorial juris- diction might serve as an entering wedge to the eventual subjection of all the British in Japan, that is, to the abolition of extraterritoriality. Parkes was willing to accede to an agreement that no Westerners be allowed to import medicinal opium and that they obtain their supplies of it entirely from the Japanese au- thorities if, and only if, any Western violators should be dealt with by their own Western authorities. Foreign Minister Terashima never accepted this point, even after the opium controversy was revived following adjudication of the two *Har- tley* cases in 1878. [28]

In Parkes' view, a second defect was that each set of regulations contained much that was "superfluous . . . incomplete, confused, and badly worded." In his judgment, the regulations were so poorly worded and so ill-constructed as to be at times ambiguous or even unintelligible; they were liable to occa- sional legal doubts and difficulties in their application. Parkes argued:

If I . . . have to act upon any regulations which they [the Japanese government] pro- pose and desire British subjects to conform to, I have carefully to consider the form and wording of those Regulations. I have to put the substance of the Japanese draft into intelligible English and into sense before I can issue a Regulation, under the Order in Council, which is to have the force of law, and to be executed in formally constituted Courts. But any alteration, even of the wording of their so-called regulations, gives the Japanese government dissatisfaction, and still more the conversion of them into British regulations. [29]

A third defect Parkes found in the draft regulations was that they were too restrictive. Concerning the first set of regulations, the contents of which have already been analyzed, in 1879 Parkes wrote to Lord Salisbury that as a con- dition of being supplied with medicinal opium, foreign chemists were to be subject to "most inquisitorial interference and restraints." He also referred to the Regulations of 1878, issued following the adjudication of the *Hartley* cases, as "arbitrary and wholly superfluous interference" by Japanese officials. Parkes stated that he agreed with the *Japan Herald*, which characterized the disposi- tion of the Japanese "to be extremely exacting in the minutest particulars when- ever they think they have the power." In his memorandum of April 28, 1880, to the Foreign Office, he went so far as to state that the Japanese regulations "not infrequently contain absurd and unreasonable conditions." [30]

Fourth, and finally, Parkes' view of the British as "civilized" and the Japa- nese as only "semi-civilized" made the Japanese regulations unacceptable to him. "I feel bound to state plainly to your Lordship [Lord Salisbury]," wrote Parkes in 1879, "my conviction that the object of the Japanese government in seeking to impose these wholly unnecessary restrictions upon foreigners, is not to pre- vent opium reaching their own people . . . but that they thereby aim at bring- ing foreigners under the vexatious grasp of their authority." He went on to say:

It would afford no small degree of pleasure to subordinate Japanese officials to oblige foreign chemists to dance attendance in their public offices once or twice a week to receive the absurd supply of five ounces of medicine; to demand the inspection of their books and papers. . . . I should deeply regret to see a respectable class of British subjects placed in such degrading position.[31]

Of the four defects he identified, Parkes spoke openly of only the first two to the Japanese authorities. It would seem that even he considered the other two defects to be less than legitimate grounds for objecting to the regulations, even though they concerned and caused him to oppose the regulations. His dissatisfaction is not hard to understand. Even today Japanese regulations and ordinances are, in many respects, too restrictive and too "inquisitorial" from the American, if not the Western, point of view. The British perception of the Japanese as being less than "civilized" in the latter half of the nineteenth century was something to which, unlike the American, the British seldom, if ever, gave open, public expression.[32] This leaves only the first two defects for evaluation.

As already noted, there is no denying that the first defect, the encroachment of the Japanese regulations upon extraterritoriality, represented an unreasonable, excessive feature of the regulations. Although American adviser Sheppard believed that the British claim to the right to import medicinal opium under the existing treaties was totally unwarranted, even he considered that the Japanese claim to apply the procedural law of Japan, as well as its substantive law, to the nationals of treaty powers was inconsistent with the extraterritorial provisions. In 1879 he wrote that, as to "penalties and punishments prescribed by Japanese law, the consular courts may justly hold that they are not applicable to their own nationals."[33]

As to the second defect, the English translations of the five sets of regulations were certainly far from perfect in both construction and wording. In January 1880, with regard to imperfections of this sort in the Draft Regulations of 1879, the Japanese minister to Britain, Mori Arinori, admonished Foreign Minister Inoue Kaoru to exercise great care in drafting Japanese regulations, especially those relating to foreigners. Mori pointed out, among other things, that it was not enough to translate a Japanese regulation into ordinary English, and that lawyers should be relied on to make proper use of legal terminology so as to insure both the accuracy and intelligibility of the translation.[34]

How defective were the English translations? Juxtaposed below are the first two of the fourth set of regulations, with Parkes' suggestions for improvement:

Japanese *Draft of Regulations for the Sale of Medicinal Opium*	Observations by Sir H. Parkes
WHEREAS the importation of opium is prohibited by the Treaty, and it is intended to maintain this prohibition; and	The allusions refer to the words or sentences printed in italics in the text.

Japanese Draft of Regulations for the Sale of Medicinal Opium	Observations by Sir H. Parkes

whereas the use of opium as a medicine being indispensable, *the following regulations for the sale of opium (for medicinal use)* are established:—

The omission of this sentence and the substitution of the following one appears necessary:—

"Its importation for medicinal use has hitherto been allowed. It being necessary, to regulate the manner in which opium shall henceforth be sold by foreigners for medicinal use, the following regulations are established:—"

1. The preparations of opium recognized by the European or American *Pharmacoporios*, with the exception of extract of opium *(solution in spirits and water or other dissolving material)*, may be imported and sold in Japan as other drugs and medicine.

Pharmacopoeias.

These words would exclude tincture of opium (laudanum) and many other preparations of the Pharmacopoeias.

2. The Japanese local authorities will *always* request every Consul within whose Consular district his countrymen are carry-on business as druggists and chemists to furnish the said local authorities, at the end of every year, with the estimate of such quantity of opium *as is required* for foreign use in the succeeding year.

"Always" is unnecessary.

Add "through the Consul."

"As each of them may require" is probably what is intended to be said.

It was rather unfortunate that Terashima was so intent upon asserting Japan's sovereign rights not delegated by treaty to the Western treaty powers that he refused even to recognize, when pointed out by Parkes, such obvious errors in the English translations. But in retrospect, while making allowance for this insecure, touchy attitude of the Japanese government, the semantic and constructional imperfections of the translations in themselves cannot be taken to have rendered the regulations utterly worthless, as Parkes claimed. Any law or regulation, however perfectly drafted, is always subject to judicial interpretation and may later be found to be wanting in some respects. A prime example is the inadvertent omission of the word "smoking"—should one accept Parkes' claim—before the word "opium," in the 1866 Tariff Convention clause prohibiting importation of opium. Certainly, the equity of a British consular court could have mitigated the imperfections of any Japanese regulations applied by the court. Moreover, there is plenty of evidence that the defect at issue was not serious enough to warrant Parkes' decrying of the regulations. The law officers

in London found no fault in point of law with either the Quarantine Regulations of 1878 or the 1878 Draft Regulations for the Sale of Opium.[35] While
the opium controversy was raging, the U.S. government ordered the Americans
in Japan to conform to the Japanese Hunting Regulations of 1874, the Press
Regulations of 1876, and the Quarantine Regulations of both 1878 and 1879.[36]

What the Japanese Foreign Ministry needed during much of the 1870s was
an English-speaking legal adviser as able as Henry W. Dennison, an American
lawyer who served the Foreign Ministry with devotion and distinction from 1880
until his death in 1914. Some of his English-language diplomatic notes were
so well written that they are reported to have been admired even by the British
Foreign Office.[37] To what extent his predecessors, Smith and Sheppard, exercised less care and diligence in their draftsmanship than did Dennison later, no
one knows. Perhaps one may say that the Japanese government, which was so
adept in selecting and retaining fine foreign advisers and teachers for a limited
period only, should have demanded of these two American and other advisers
to the Foreign Ministry more precision and exactness than they seem to have
contributed. F. V. Dickins, who served on the staff of the British legation under Parkes, observed: "The Japanese regulations . . . were sometimes mere es-
says in draftsmanship proceeding from irresponsible foreign advisers entirely
without experience in such matters."[38] Making allowance for Dickins' anti-
American bias, it would seem that the American advisers' draftsmanship and
the care with which they translated Japanese regulations were not of the highest
caliber.

So much for Parkes' objections to the draft regulations. It is now necessary
to consider why Japan insisted upon imposing these regulations on the nationals of the treaty powers. One reason has already been discussed: Japan's resolve
to exercise inherent sovereign powers not expressly delegated by treaty. Another
reason was that the Japanese government, fearful of the spread of opium-smoking, did not give full credence to the distinction between smoking and medicinal opium.[39] Instead, the government believed the two to be interchangeable,
both suitable for smoking. In November 1875, rejecting Parkes' contention that
the importation of medicinal opium was not prohibited by treaty, Foreign Minister Terashima asserted: "Opium being an article of such nature that it can be
used for both medicinal and also for smoking purposes, it was on account of
the exceedingly deleterious effects caused by smoking it that one general prohibition was laid down." In March 1879, rejecting Parkes' request to release
fifty pounds of medicinal opium detained at the Customshouse in Yokohama,
Terashima stated that the Japanese government had "no intention of ever granting to foreign subjects the right of importing opium whether medicinal or
smoking." Parkes was indignant over the Japanese suggestion that the British
make medicinal use of Japanese opium, the morphine content of which was
only 4 percent. Since the Japanese government had been importing Turkish
opium for use at its own army and navy hospitals, he reasoned that Japan was
trying to persuade the British to use opium which it considered unfit for its own

New Yokohama Customshouse, 1873

people. But, it would seem, the suggestion was not malevolent, as Parkes believed; rather, it reflected the Japanese incredulity. Furthermore, that incredulity was not an attitude deliberately assumed to enforce the treaty prohibition; it seems to have been genuine. In his 1876 order prohibiting the importation of opium in perpetuity (*eikin*)—issued nearly two years prior to the first *Hartley* case—Home Minister Ōkubo Toshimichi stated that the Japanese government would import Turkish opium from abroad to make up for an insufficiency of Japanese opium. The following year the government appropriated ¥18,000 to the Home Ministry to import Turkish opium for medicinal use by Westerners in Japan and to "remake" (*saisei*) Japanese opium, which Westerners did not "as yet" trust.[40]

Regina v. John Hartley

On December 14, 1877, John Hartley, an English importer of drugs and medicine, had certain goods entered for import at the Yokohama Customshouse, and he claimed that one of the cases contained scurvy grass and cochineal. When examined there, the case was found to contain two tins comprising fifteen catties of opium, as well as the two articles mentioned. When counsel for the Customshouse J. F. Lowder invited Hartley to explain the concealment of opium, he answered: "Well! I wish to pass that opium as cochineal."

On December 26, 1877, Motono Moriuchi, superintendent of Japanese customs (*zeikanchō*) at Yokohama, brought suit against John Hartley at Her Britannic Majesty's Court at Kanagawa (hereafter referred to as the Yokohama Court). Hartley was charged with having smuggled or attempted to smuggle twenty pounds (fifteen catties) of opium into Japan. Motono also applied for infliction of a penalty under a stipulation of the 1858 treaty between Great Britain and Japan. Regulation II of the six "Regulations under which British Trade is to be conducted," the regulations appended to the treaty, stipulated in Paragraph 8:

The importation of opium being prohibited, any British vessel coming to Japan for the purposes of trade, and having more than three catties' weight of opium on board, the surplus quantity may be seized and destroyed by the Japanese authorities; and any person or persons smuggling or attempting to smuggle opium, shall be liable to pay a fine of fifteen dollars for each catty of opium so smuggled or attempted to be smuggled.

This first *Hartley* case would have been obscure had it not been for the defense offered by the accused: that the opium in question was medicinal opium, not opium used for smoking, and that the prohibition in Regulation II contemplated only smoking opium. This defense made the case an extraordinary one. Thereupon, Lowder, the counsel for the Japanese customs, wished the Court to decide only whether the accused was guilty of violating that particular provision of the treaty, and all subsequent arguments for both the prosecution and the defense were directed to that issue alone.[41]

Japanese historians have alleged that the Court was unfair and unjust in dismissing the original charge. The facts of the case, however, do not support this allegation. The Court found that the opium in question was indeed medicinal opium; that it was necessary to import such opium, "an inestimable blessing to suffering humanity," into Japan to obtain it in sufficient quantity; that until 1872 medicinal opium had been imported without Japanese interference; that since 1866, under the Tariff Convention of that year, medicinal opium had occasionally been imported on the payment of an *ad valorem* duty of 5 percent on original value; and that there had been no agreement between Great Britain and Japan regulating the importation of the drug. In view of these findings, the Court reasoned that it would lead to absurdity to conclude that the prohibition applied to medicinal opium and that it was importable under the Tariff Convention. Consequently, on February 20, 1878, the Court declared the accused not guilty of violating the prohibition and dismissed the original charge of smuggling opium. Since the original charge had not been decided upon, the Court considered that the Japanese customs authorities should have an opportunity to deliberate what course they should take with respect to the accusation. The Court therefore ordered that the two tins containing the opium should remain in charge of the Customshouse under the seal of the Court until further application.[42] As late as 1889, they so remained.[43]

Japan objected most energetically to the judgment[44] of the Court, on three grounds. First, the holding that the prohibition did not apply to medicinal opium was contrary to the clear wording of the 1858 treaty. Tokyo reasoned that this holding, unless resisted, might lead Japan to be flooded with opium, which, though not primarily intended for smoking, might easily be used for that purpose and, once in the country, would be difficult for Japanese authorities to control. (It is possible that its high morphine content makes medicinal opium rather unpalatable to smoke, for it is known that "the opiums most prized by smokers are not those containing most morphine."[45]) Second, Japan argued that Hiram Shaw Wilkinson, consul-judge of the Court, had no power to adjudicate the case, either as "Vice-Consul of Niigata"—which he was not at that time, as Japan was misinformed in this regard—or as acting law secretary of the Supreme Court at Shanghai. Since the case did not arise in the consular district of Niigata, he had no power to try the case. Nor did he have such power in the capacity of acting law secretary. Under the 1865 China and Japan Order in Council, he was empowered to try such criminal charges as might originally have been brought before the Supreme Court, and which had been specifically referred to him by the judge "for the dispatch of urgent business." The *Hartley* case was not so brought before the Supreme Court, or so referred by the judge. Third, and finally, Japan claimed that the decision rendered by a servant of a high contracting party, relating to the interpretation of an important point in a bilateral treaty, particularly in direct opposition to the views of the other high contracting party, could not be taken as conclusive.[46]

Regina v. Hartley & Co.

While *Regina* v. *John Hartley* was still pending at the Yokohama Court, Motono preferred two new charges there against Hartley. The first was that on January 8, 1878, Hartley smuggled or attempted to smuggle eleven catties of opium into Yokohama. The second charge was that a case containing both this opium and 221 pounds of gum was discharged without having been duly entered at the Customshouse. Because of the second charge, the prosecution sought to have the case and its contents confiscated.

The Court found that the opium seized was not medicinal opium; the accused was guilty of smuggling the opium. On April 6, the Court fined him $165 for the eleven catties of opium seized as provided in Paragraph 8 of Regulation II, the fine being $15 a catty. An order was issued for the Japanese authorities to destroy all but three catties of the opium in accordance with the same paragraph and for the reexportation of the remainder. The Court ruled that the gum which formed part of the contents of the case in which the opium was smuggled was not liable to confiscation.[47]

Ueno Kageyasu, the Japanese minister in London, on July 27, notified Lord Salisbury that he had been instructed by his government to appeal both against the reexportation of any of the opium and against the ruling that the gum was not liable to confiscation. These Japanese objections derived from the tortuous arguments for appeal to the Privy Council by Lowder as counsel for the Yokohama Customs.

As to the three catties of opium allowed to be reexported, Japan maintained that the permission to a vessel coming to Japan to have a maximum of three catties of opium *on board*—a stipulation of Paragraph 8 of Regulation II—did not apply to smuggled goods landed ashore, and that it was the invariable rule in all countries that such goods are liable to confiscation. The Court should, therefore, have had these three catties also confiscated under Paragraph 3, which read: "Any goods that shall be discharged, or attempted to be discharged from any ship, without having been duly entered at the Japanese Custom-House . . . shall be liable to seizure and confiscation." This Japanese view was advanced in response to the ruling of the Court that this paragraph did not apply to prohibited goods. The Court was of the opinion that prohibited goods were incapable of being duly entered.

With respect to the 221 pounds of gum contained in the same package as the opium, Tokyo contended that the gum, as well as the three catties of opium, should have been confiscated. It took the view that the gum became "tainted" by being part of the package in which prohibited goods were contained; that the discovery of prohibited goods in any package rendered not only such goods, but also any other goods in the same package, liable to seizure and confiscation. The Court, however, had ruled that the gum had been duly entered and that Paragraph 3 was inapplicable to it.[48]

Quite apart from making its vigorous representations to London, Tokyo pursued two other courses of action in response to the judgments of the Court. The first, as already enumerated, was a decision to appeal from the judgments to the Judicial Committee of the Privy Council, the court of last resort for all British colonies and overseas settlements. It did not take Tokyo long to reach that decision. In reference to the first judgment, on March 7—only two weeks after the judgment had been rendered—Foreign Minister Terashima notified Parkes of Japan's intention to appeal. Then, on May 18 Terashima informed Ueno that Japan intended to appeal also that part of the second judgment which, as already discussed, Japan found objectionable. He instructed Ueno to ask Sir Henry James, Q.C., and presumably his junior counsel John Shortt, both of whom seemed to have advised Tokyo previously, to apply for leave to appeal. On these two barristers' recommendation, Ueno retained Wilson, Bristow, and Carpmael, a firm of solicitors that had successfully represented Japan in a case involving a Naval Ministry order of ammunitions, to ascertain whether an appeal against Wilkinson's judgments would lie, as a matter of right, to the Privy Council.

After careful research, the firm advised Ueno on June 17 that no such appeal lay as a matter of right. But if a petition were presented to the Queen in Council asking for leave to submit a special case for the opinion of the Judicial Committee on the proper construction to be placed upon terms of the 1858 treaty relating to prohibition of the importation of opium and referring, of course, to the second judgment, Her Majesty would be advised to direct the opinion of the Judicial Committee to be given. The firm further advised Ueno: "Should your Excellency approve the course we have suggested we will at once prepare such a Petition and have it presented in due course."[49] Such approval never came.

The second course of action that Tokyo undertook was an attempt to nullify the judgments by diplomatic negotiations rather than by appeal. In his communication to Lord Salisbury of June 4, 1878, Ueno registered Tokyo's objections to Wilkinson's second judgment and stated: "It would be satisfactory if Your Lordship were able to inform me that Her Majesty's Government is of opinion that the decision of Mr. Wilkinson is not binding. This action on the part of Your Lordship would probably prevent the necessity of an appeal to the Judicial Committee." That the British Foreign Office, by a stroke of declaration or statement, had power to reverse or rescind the judgment of a British consular court was an erroneous notion of the Japanese government. This notion caused Japan to keep pressing the British Foreign Office to issue a repudiation of Wilkinson's judgments. On August 8, for example, Ueno wrote to Salisbury:

I . . . understand that Her Majesty's government does not approve of the judgment rendered . . . which asserted that British subjects were entitled under the Treaty to import Medicinal Opium. . . . I am sure that a decided expression of opinion from Your

Lordship on this subject would be much valued by the Government of His Majesty the Emperor. [50]

As a purely executive department, the British Foreign Office neither had nor claimed any authority to determine questions of law. In retrospect, one may find it rather difficult to understand why Tokyo was unaware of this or had not been reminded of it by such foreign advisers as Lowder or Sheppard. On the other hand, the limits of consular jurisdiction were also quite unfamiliar to at least one member of the British Parliament. In December 1878, MP Mark Stewart inquired in the House of Commons whether the Foreign Office had "confirmed or reversed" the decisions in the *Hartley* cases. By the end of 1879, however, the Japanese Foreign Ministry realized that its British counterpart could do nothing to undo the decisions. [51]

Issue of Jurisdiction

One may recall that Tokyo raised three objections to Wilkinson's judgment in the first *Hartley* case and two more objections to his judgment in the second *Hartley* case. Of the five objections, the first two were of great concern to the British Foreign Office: (1) Japan regarded as absolutely erroneous the construction placed by Wilkinson on the general prohibition against the importation of opium stipulated in the Anglo-Japanese Treaty of 1858 and in the Tariff Convention of 1864; and (2) Japan protested the unlawful exercise of jurisdiction by Wilkinson. The other three issues did not concern the Foreign Office nearly as much because they could be settled readily once the central issues of jurisdiction and construction had been resolved. The issue of jurisdiction was the more pressing, since Tokyo might appeal the two judgments to the Judicial Committee of the Privy Council.

The seed of the issue of jurisdiction was sown in January 1871. At that time, under the direction of Foreign Secretary Granville, Acting Judge Charles W. Goodwin of the Supreme Court for China and Japan at Shanghai appointed Nicholas J. Hannen to the post of "Acting Assistant Judge of the Japanese Branch of the Supreme court at Kanagawa" and empowered him under Article 38 of the 1865 China and Japan Order in Council to try cases. Article 38 provided that from time to time the judge of the Supreme Court might visit any "provincial" (consular) court and try any case pending or arising within its district, or might appoint the assistant judge or the law secretary of the Supreme Court to visit any provincial court for that purpose. [52] Visitation by any one of these three judicial officials was clearly intended to be a short-term, temporary, and recurring arrangement. But presiding by the assistant judge or the law secretary over the Yokohama Court became a permanent arrangement from its inception through 1878. Subsequent correspondence among Hannen, Goodwin, and Sir Edmund Hornby, judge of the Supreme Court, suggests that "the Japan Branch of the Supreme Court at Kanagawa," an anomalous entity, was created to adjudicate cases that the consular court there had no power to adjudicate under the 1865 Order in Council. These cases included grave criminal cases calling for jury trial and admiralty cases.[53]

Hannen, the acting assistant judge at Yokohama, considered his court the Supreme Court for China and Japan "on circuit" and not "the Provisional Court at Kanagawa." Acting Judge Goodwin at Shanghai agreed, but when Hannen asked Goodwin to issue a duplicate seal of the Supreme Court to its branch at Kanagawa, Goodwin deferred issuing one "until further direction from home." No further steps were taken in the matter. The seal of the Provincial Court at Kanagawa was the only seal ever used until the establishment of a Court for Japan under the 1878 China and Japan Order in Council.[54]

The next question that emerged in connection with the anomalous nature of the Yokohama Court was that of appeal. This question arose in June 1872, a month following the return to Shanghai of Judge Hornby.[55] Hannen entertained the view that no appeal lay from the decisions of the assistant judge of the Supreme Court at Kanagawa to the Supreme Court at Shanghai, except by way of rehearing before the judge as provided for in the 1865 Order in Council. He reasoned that the assistant judge represented the Court; therefore, appeal lay only to the Privy Council. But the Foreign Office, when consulted by Hornby, did not consider it desirable that appeal from Yokohama be made directly to the Privy Council. In August 1872, Judge Hornby ruled that decisions of the assistant judge should be reviewed by the judge. He took the position that, until the Order in Council was amended, the Yokohama Court should remain a provincial court "under the presidency of Her Majesty's Assistant Judge" but that steps should be taken to enable him to exercise an admiralty jurisdiction over vessels coming within the jurisdiction of the Court. This meant that Judge Hornby provided a twofold jurisdiction for that Court: that of the Supreme Court in admiralty actions only and that of the Provincial Court at Kanagawa in all other actions. Hornby also directed Hannen to consider himself responsible for presiding over the Provincial Court in all but admiralty cases and directed him to invoke the power of the Supreme Court only in exercising admiralty jurisdiction. In admiralty cases only, therefore, appeal should lie directly to the Privy Council.[56] It was under this ruling that in adjudicating the *Hartley* cases, actions in admiralty, Wilkinson, the presiding judge of the Yokohama Court, represented the Supreme Court.

The two separate but simultaneous sittings of the Supreme Court, one at Shanghai and the other at Kanagawa, together with the arrangement whereby the acting law secretary was left in charge of the Kanagawa Court, caused the British Foreign Office to wonder whether these arrangements were lawful under the 1865 Order in Council. With the appointment of a new judge of the Supreme Court who was then on his way to China, the foreign secretary, the Earl of Derby, decided to seek an opinion of the law officers as to the legality of the arrangements. On behalf of Lord Derby, on March 13, 1878, Sir Julian Pauncefote put four questions to the law officers: (1) Was it competent for the judge, under the 1865 Order in Council, to delegate for hearing and determination by the assistant judge or the law secretary any class of cases in general terms, or was his power limited to the delegation of particular cases? (2) Could the Supreme Court sit at the same time in two places, the judge presiding over the Court at one place and deputing the assistant judge or the law secretary to preside over the Court at another place; or could the judge alone hold sittings of the Supreme Court all over China and Japan under the Order in Council? (3) Was the authority given by Goodwin, the late acting judge, to Wilkinson, as acting law secretary, to hear and determine all summary civil and criminal cases arising in the Supreme Court at Kanagawa, and such other cases as the acting judge might specially refer to him, warranted by the Order in Council? (4) Was the arrangement by which, on Goodwin's departure from Japan, Wilkinson was left as acting law secretary in charge of the Supreme Court, warranted by the Order in Council?

The law officers, on May 10, gave Lord Salisbury, Lord Derby's successor, the following opinion: (1) Under the Order in Council, the assistant judge or the law secretary could hear only the cases that were specially referred by the judge from time to time; the judge could not delegate for hearing and determination by the assistant judge or the law secretary any class of cases in general terms, but only particular cases. (2) The Order in Council did not require that the judge alone should hold sittings of the Supreme Court all over China and Japan. (3) The authority given by Goodwin to Wilkinson to hear and determine all summary cases arising at Kanagawa was not warranted by the Order in Council, but an authority to hear and determine cases specially referred to the law secretary by the acting judge would have been warranted by the Order in Council. (4) The arrangement under which Wilkinson was left as acting law secretary in charge of the Supreme Court at Kanagawa was not warranted by the Order in Council. [57]

Of the four arrangements under which Wilkinson took charge of the Court, in the opinion of the law officers, only one was warranted under the Order in Council. In brief, they considered that Wilkinson had unlawfully exercised the powers of the Supreme Court for China and Japan. The implication was clear that his two decisions on the *Hartley* cases had resulted from faulty exercise of the jurisdiction of the Court. Therefore, if Japan had appealed the decisions to the Judicial Committee of the Privy Council, as it once intended, the decisions could have been reviewed and set aside as nullities. To make this conclusion comprehensible requires an explanation of the distinctions in English law between appeal and review, and between void and voidable acts.

An appeal means that some superior court has power to reconsider the decision of a lower court on its merits. As a rule, rights of appeal are given by statute. Review, on the other hand, is based not on the merits but on the legality of the lower court's proceedings. "At the root of the matter is jurisdiction, or simply, power." If there is a right of appeal, and the appeal succeeds, the appellate court substitutes its own decision for that of the court below, and disposes of the case conclusively. But if an unlawful act or decision is quashed on judicial review, the result is merely to establish that it has no existence in law, that is to say, it is a nullity. Fresh proceedings then can be instituted. [58]

Unlawful acts or decisions that can be quashed on review fall into two categories—void and voidable. A voidable act or decision means that it is legally valid and remains valid unless the court reviews and annuls it. Voidable acts involve such trivial defects as the authorized person's errors in interpreting the relevant legal provisions and disregarding some judge-made rules pertaining to the mode of exercising his power. They can be invalidated only in proceedings especially formulated for the purpose of directly challenging such acts. They are said to be subject only to direct attack, as opposed to collateral attack.

By contrast, no proceeding is indicated for the express purpose of invalidating the *void* act, which can be attacked collaterally. Since the act is a nullity from the very beginning, there is nothing to be made voidable. Hence, it can be disregarded and impeached in any proceeding before any court, whenever it is relied upon. A decision which is in excess of jurisdiction is a void decision. A distinction between void and voidable acts is made in order to preclude legal anarchy which might result from annulments of numerous acts on trivial grounds.[59]

One of the defects as to jurisdiction is want of jurisdiction, which "denotes action taken beyond the sphere allotted to the tribunal by law. . . . Furthermore, want of jurisdiction is regarded as a usurpation of power unwarranted by law. It is considered so radical a defect that it cannot be cured by the acquiescence or consent of the parties concerned."[60] It was precisely want of jurisdiction which Wilkinson's two decisions represented. He adjudicated cases which neither the judge nor the acting judge of the Supreme Court for China and Japan specifically referred to him. In theory, as already stated, no proceedings are in order for the express purpose of invalidating the void act. In practice, however, English courts have decided jurisdictional questions on appeal.[61] Hence, had Japan, upon appeal, prevailed upon the Privy Council to review the decisions at issue as instances of the illegal exercise of jurisdiction by Wilkinson, there was sufficient precedent as of the 1870s to suggest that the Privy Council might very well have adjudged the decisions to be null and void.

Upon receipt of the law officers' opinion of May 10, 1878, the British Foreign Office decided to remedy the unlawful arrangements of the Yokohama Court. On August 10, 1878, Pauncefote informed Ueno that a new court for Japan would be established in a few months. Four days later, the Privy Council issued the short China and Japan Order in Council of 1878 creating the promised court, Her Britannic Majesty's Court for Japan. The Court was to come into force on January 1, 1879. Thus the establishment of the Court was caused in part by the *Hartley* cases. It is true that, even prior to adjudication of the first *Hartley* case, the Foreign Office had doubted the validity of "the Japan Branch of the Supreme Court" and had for some time contemplated remedying the unlawful jurisdiction of that branch.[62] On the other hand, it is also true that Pauncefote did not seek the law officers' opinion until March 13, 1878. By that time, the first *Hartley* case had already been adjudicated and the second was pending. Undoubtedly, therefore, these cases contributed to the making of the Court for Japan.

The new Court, composed of a judge and an assistant judge, supplanted the Provincial Court for the district of the consulate at Kanagawa, and the consul for that district ceased to have authority to hold a provincial court. The Court for Japan now held not only an original jurisdiction within the district of the consulate at Kanagawa but also an extraordinary jurisdiction throughout Japan which was concurrent with the jurisdiction of the several provincial courts in Japan. Above all, the Court, like the Supreme Court for China and Japan, was empowered to exercise admiralty jurisdiction. Article 11 of the Order in Council, 1878, read: "Any proceeding taken in China or Japan against one of Her Majesty's vessels, or the officer commanding the same, as such, in respect of any claim cognisable in a Court of Vice-Admiralty, shall be taken only in the Supreme Court or in the Court for Japan, under the Vice-Admiralty jurisdiction thereof respectively." As an aside, the Order in Council abolished the post which Wilkinson was holding when he adjudicated the *Hartley* cases—the law secretaryship of the Supreme Court.[63]

Issuance of the 1878 Order in Council eliminated the anomaly of the Yokohama Court. But it did not immediately relieve the Foreign Office of its anxiety and embarrassment about that anomaly, which any Japanese appeal to the Privy Council was bound to expose. This kept Pauncefote in a state of discomfort, uncertainty, and anxiety. In his internal memorandum to Lord Salisbury of November 30, 1878, for example, Pauncefote recommended that Parkes be instructed to find out whether the Japanese foreign minister intended to proceed with appeals from the Wilkinson decisions; and that in making this inquiry the minister be reminded that Parkes' failure to obtain a satisfactory set of regulations for importing medicinal opium for the past three years arose from Japan's insistence on direct enforcement of such regulations against British subjects without intervention of the British consular authorities. On December 21, when he was about to transmit the second *Hartley* case to the law officers for their opinion, Pauncefote wrote another memorandum to Lord Salisbury in which he confided his worst fear of the possible exposure: "In my opinion both the Judgments are wrong, and in any case we *must* [italics in original] fail before the Privy Council."[64] In the meantime, as already noted, the Japanese government, which wished to settle the opium controversy by diplomatic negotiation rather than by appeal, kept pressing the British Foreign Office to disavow Wilkinson's decisions, under the mistaken impression that such a disavowment would be tantamount to a reversal on appeal.

Fortunately for the British Foreign Office, however, Japan never appealed nor even applied for special leave to appeal.[65] By January 1880, Pauncefote was relieved to see little prospect for appeal. He was able to assert that no further explanation of Wilkinson's judgments was called for unless Japan made its threatened application to the Privy Council, which he thought improbable because of the lapse of time.[66]

Why did Japan ultimately elect not to proceed with an appeal? Out of ignorance, Japan preferred a declaration by the British Foreign Office to the effect that Wilkinson's decisions were not binding. But extant Japanese diplomatic records pertaining to the opium controversy suggest two more fundamental reasons why in the end Japan did not appeal. The first was the feeling of the Japanese leadership that it was sufficient for Japan to exact from Great Britain an admission that the decisions were wrong and that to take further action would be unkind, uncalled for, and even unwise.

On February 7, 1879, Salisbury officially communicated to Ueno the report of the law officers that the decisions on the *Hartley* cases could not be upheld.[67] But Ueno had learned the content of this report a week earlier and had written to Foreign Minister Terashima that there was now no point in pressing an appeal. Two months later, Ueno once again conveyed to Terashima the thought that, since Salisbury had conceded that the decisions were wrong, an appeal to the Privy Council would not only cause Salisbury to lose face (*memmoku nashi*), but would also strain Anglo-Japanese relations. Soon thereafter Ueno became assistant vice-minister for foreign affairs, and the threatened appeal was never carried out. In July 1881, his successor in London, Mori Arinori, explained to Foreign Secretary Granville that Japan had not proceeded with the appeal because of Salisbury's statement that the decisions could not be upheld.[68] It would seem, therefore, that Terashima and other leaders of Tokyo came to accept the characteristically Japanese point of view advanced by Ueno—namely, that the British admission of wrongful decisions was sufficient.

Salisbury undertook to disclose the law officers' opinion, which is confidential, probably because in his judgment the opinion was precisely what the Japanese had asked for. The disclosure also reflected the British Foreign Office's one-time resignation that the Japanese government was certain to carry out its threatened appeals, which in turn would divulge the unlawful arrangements of the Yokohama Court presided over by Wilkinson to the detriment of the Foreign Office.

The second reason why Japan chose not to appeal was national pride. Foreign Minister Inoue's instructions to Mori, dated November 9, 1879, contained the following statement: "From the outset, we had no intention of demanding an appeal against such a petty merchant as Hartley."[69] Brief as it was, this statement betrayed a reality that non-Western countries in the late nineteenth century had to face in dealing with powerful Western countries whose nationals enjoyed extraterritoriality.[70] From the standpoint of private international law, an individual wronged in a foreign state is normally expected to exhaust all legal remedies available locally in that state prior to seeking the diplomatic intervention of his government. The Japanese government would demean itself and act like a private subject if it submitted itself to the jurisdiction of a consular court. On the other hand, it had the option of representing itself as a government in relation to the British government, thereby avoiding a prolonged appearance before a foreign court of law—an appearance which the Japanese government undoubtedly would have found demeaning. As already noted, the Japanese government, after having announced that it would pursue the first option of appeal, resorted to the second option of representing itself vis-à-vis the

British government. It will be seen that the second, preferred option proved to be fruitless.

Issue of Interpretation

One may recall that the Yokohama Court held that the prohibition against importation of opium applied only to smoking opium and that medicinal opium was excluded from the prohibition. Confronting the second issue of interpretation of the treaty prohibition against importing opium, the British Foreign Office evidently reasoned that, if this distinction between two kinds of opium were valid, importation by Westerners of medicinal opium would be legal under the existing treaties and there would be no need for Japanese regulations governing the import of opium. In the face of Japan's insistence on enforcing such regulations against British residents in Japan, the Foreign Office wished the distinction to be valid beyond doubt so as to terminate the protracted and fruitless effort to persuade Japan to make its regulations suitable for enforcement by the British consular authorities against any British subject in violation of the prohibition. As a result, the Foreign Office repeatedly sought the opinion of the law officers as to the legality of the distinction, and altogether they obtained four such opinions.[71]

Since the issue of interpretation was inextricably intertwined with the advice of the law officers, a few words should be said about the status and nature of the opinions of both government legal advisers and law officers. Although these opinions are not law, in most cases they govern the actions of governments, and "the main source of [international] law, apart from multipartite treaties, is to be found in the practice of government." Lord McNair, an English jurist and former president of the International Court of Justice, observes: "It is a delusion affecting the minds of many laymen and not a few lawyers that governments in the conduct of foreign affairs act independently and capriciously and without reference to legal principle. . . . the ordinary, routine, nonpolitical business of the world is carried on by Ministers of Foreign Affairs and their diplomatic agents against a background of [international] law." To be sure, the high-level foreign policy decisions of the government are often matters of policy rather than of law. But the government strives to make decisions of this kind, let alone routine diplomatic business, in such a way as to conform to, or at least give appearance of conformity with, international law as much as possible.[72]

Confidentiality helps insure that the opinions of the law officers of the British Crown are highly objective. Although the law officers are accountable to Parliament for their multifarious duties, their opinions are not, as a rule, laid before Parliament or cited in debate. Moreover, the opinions given to the British government are not likely to be published for a considerable time, if ever. Therefore, the law officers can deal with matters quite objectively and without regard to any factor other than expressing their legal conclusions.[73]

The issue of interpretation devolved heavily upon Sir Julian Pauncefote, later a negotiator of the second Hay-Pauncefote Treaty of 1901, which secured to the United States a free hand in the construction and defense of the Panama Canal. In 1878 he was the first person appointed legal assistant under-secretary of state.[74] As an "in-house" lawyer to the Foreign Office, he was supposed to help the foreign secretary in dealing with cases of insufficient importance to go to the law officers and in preparing cases submitted to the law officers. Ueno, the Japanese minister in London, attributed Pauncefote's sympathy for Japan's protests against Wilkinson's decisions, in part, to his friendship with Pauncefote. But it would seem that this sympathy arose mainly from Pauncefote's genuine belief that the Yokohama Court had erred in making a distinction between smoking and medicinal opium. On June 5, he advised Salisbury to undertake certain measures in response to the protests from both Japan and the Anglo-Oriental Society for the Suppression of the Opium Trade.[75] One of these measures was to obtain an opinion from the law officers on whether, under the Tariff Convention of 1866, opium being the only prohibited article (Class III), it was lawful to import medicinal opium as distinguished from smoking opium under Class IV, which fixed an *ad valorem* duty of 5 percent on drugs and medicines. In Pauncefote's view, the judgment in the first *Hartley* case was wrong, and opium being "absolutely" prohibited, the description "drugs and medicines" had to be read subject to the exception of opium. Salisbury accepted the advice, and Pauncefote transmitted the question to the law officers on June 12.[76]

They gave their opinion on July 2, reporting: "Medicinal Opium unless expressly named in Class IV amongst 'Drugs and Medicines,' is a prohibited Article under Class III and cannot be distinguished from 'smoking opium.' "[77]

Again in December 1878, Pauncefote sought an opinion of the law officers, stating that the Japanese government was disposed "to proceed no further with the appeal if Her Majesty's Government should concur in their view that the conclusions at which Mr. Wilkinson arrived in both cases were erroneous in point of law." On January 17, 1879, the law officers reported that the second decision could not be upheld either and that nothing in Wilkinson's full report on the first decision induced them to modify the opinion expressed in their report of July 2, 1878.[78]

Although he had been deeply involved in such European affairs as the Berlin Congress of 1878, Foreign Secretary Salisbury reacted decisively to this opinion. On February 4, 1879, he sent a cypher telegram to Parkes informing him that they had been advised neither judgment could be upheld, and instructing him both to transmit to London Japan's proposed regulations for the importation of medicinal opium and to press "for immediate facilities." Three days later, Salisbury gave Ueno a long-awaited reply to the Japanese protests against the two decisions. Salisbury wrote:

I have the honour to state to you that I am advised that the judgments in the cases of opium smuggling in Japan, which formed the subject of your letter of the 12th of December as well as of previous Communications, cannot be upheld, and I have to observe that, under circumstances, it becomes all the more necessary that immediate steps should be taken for the regulation of the importation into Japan of medicinal opium.[79]

Salisbury's action brought to a new height the war of treaty construction that Japan had waged intermittently since 1872 and to little avail against Great Britain. The battle was no longer between Tokyo and Parkes, but between Tokyo and London. As early as August 1878, Salisbury had instructed Parkes to offer his cooperation to Terashima in framing such regulations as would be acceptable to Britain, but Terashima declined to enter into any conversation or agreement with Parkes in this matter. Instead, he insisted upon the full exercise of Japan's right to issue its own regulations to be enforced by Japanese authorities alone against all Western nationals. He now supplied Parkes with another set of regulations issued on October 14, 1878: the Regulations for the Sale of Opium (*Ahen uriwatashi kisoku*). These regulations formed part of a larger set of regulations called the Regulations for the Sale and Production of Opium (*Yakuyō ahen baibai narabi seizō kisoku*). The Regulations for the Sale of Opium were in the nature of a Japanese municipal law that would apply to all persons resident in Japan, whether Japanese or foreigners.[80]

Terashima's continued insistence that Japan exercise unilateral control over Western nationals, coupled with the law officers' opinion disapproving Parkes' interpretation of the prohibition against importing opium, led Parkes to ask the British Foreign Office to inform him on what grounds the law officers considered that neither of Wilkinson's judgments could be upheld. In making this request, Parkes pointed out that Western nationals could not observe the Japanese regulations without sacrificing their immunities from interference by local Japanese authorities. Salisbury, who fully appreciated Parkes' point, addressed the following question to the law officers on May 26, 1879: if the Japanese government was indisposed to enter into an agreement concerning the importation and sale of medicinal opium, should it not at least issue special regulations framed "strictly in harmony with their Treaty rights which, as regards British subjects, Her Majesty's Government cannot consent to waive in any degree?" This inquiry was certainly an instance of Lord McNair's observation that, even when government takes action contrary to the opinion of its legal advisers, it strives to minimize the gap between what it does and what it ought to do according to the legal advice given. On July 10, the law officers reported that the Japanese government was competent to make such regulations respecting the sale of opium as those referred to them by Salisbury and to enforce them on foreigners.[81] This was their third opinion associated with the *Hartley* cases.

After having received a copy of the 1878 regulations on July 2, Salisbury on July 12 notified Tomita Tetsunosuke, the Japanese chargé d'affaires, as follows:

These regulations are at the present time under the consideration of Her Majesty's Government in communication with the Law Advisers [officers] of the Crown, but they represent serious difficulties, and I think it is to be regretted that your Government did not agree to the Regulations proposed by the Foreign Representatives at Yedo in May 1873. Until the importation into Japan of this article is placed on a footing satisfactory to both Governments no rules can be issued by Her Majesty's Minister at Yedo for the guidance of British subjects or to remove doubts as to the interpretation of the Treaty. In the meanwhile let me assure that Her Majesty's Government have no wish to dissuade your Government from an appeal to the Privy Council should they be desirous of resorting to that course.[82]

Four days later, Pauncefote called Tomita to the Foreign Office to inform him of three objections to the 1878 regulations. First, the Foreign Office was of the opinion that the quantity of opium to be sold semiannually (about five ounces) was insufficient. Second, it desired to modify Article 6, which provided for examination of the Western apothecaries' accounts by local Japanese authorities. The modification proposed that either an inspection by a British consul or one in the presence of a British consul be substituted for examination by Japanese authorities alone. Third, and finally, London objected to Article 7, which in part stipulated that apothecaries "suspected of having disposed of opium for smoking purposes" should also be denied a further supply of it. If the Japanese government were prepared to meet these objections, Pauncefote assured Tomita, the British government would instruct Parkes to have all British subjects in Japan obey the 1878 regulations.[83]

While London was awaiting Tokyo's response to the objections, tension was rising between London and Tokyo over other matters—quarantine, pilotage, and hunting. All Japanese regulations relating to these subjects raised the same issue: unilateral enforcement by Japanese authorities against the nationals of treaty powers. Once again Salisbury sought the opinion of the law officers on the two decisions in question. On August 12, 1879, Pauncefote transmitted to them papers pertaining to the decisions, along with Wilkinson's report to Parkes of February 20, 1879, defending his competency. The law officers were requested to reconsider their previous opinion as to the decisions in the light of the extraneous considerations that had gone into rendering the decisions. They were also asked to explain how their previous concurrence with the American construction on the extraterritorial provisions as laid down by Secretary of State Fish in his instructions to Bingham of January 7, 1874, could be reconciled with the opinion expressed in their report of July 10, 1879, that Japan had power to enforce the latest draft of regulations for the sale of opium. These regulations, pointed out Pauncefote, imposed penalties to be recovered in Japanese courts and were, therefore, inconsistent with the American construction.[84]

The law officers rendered their fourth and last opinion on the *Hartley* cases on September 22, 1879, reporting that they were unable to see anything in Wilkinson's report which modified their previous opinion as to the two decisions. The law officers stated: "We still think both judgments are wrong." Concerning the more important issue of Japan imposing penalties on Westerners, however, the law officers wrote that they had not intended to express any opinion that "penalties to be recovered by Japanese courts were capable of being enforced against British subjects."[85] The law officers, therefore, reaffirmed their concurrence in the American construction. Undoubtedly, Salisbury and Pauncefote felt relieved to learn that the law officers did not mean to say that Japanese authorities had a unilateral right to enforce Japanese laws against British subjects.

On November 19, 1879, in response to London's three objections to the 1878 regulations, Inoue dispatched to Mori another set of ten regulations entitled The Revised Draft of Opium Regulations (*Ahen kisoku kaiseian*). First, this draft made no change in the proposed semiannual supply of approximately five ounces to each apothecary, for Inoue considered that amount quite generous (*kabun no taka*). Second, an examination by Japanese authorities of both the prescription of a physician and the application of a buyer for medicine containing opium was to be substituted for an examination of the accounts of each apothecary. Owing to this narrowed scope of the examination, Inoue notified Mori, the presence of a Western consul at the Japanese officals' examination would be unnecessary. Finally, the severe penalty of refusing a supply of opium to an apothecary on the grounds of mere suspicion of his having disposed of opium for smoking purposes was removed; the penalty would result only from conviction on such a charge.[86] It is clear, then, that under the 1879 draft regulations Japan would have met only the third and last of the three British objections and that it would have continued to claim authority to enforce its regulations directly against the nationals of treaty powers.

In spite of Japan's intransigence, Inoue departed from the hard-line policy, doggedly pursued by his predecessors from 1872 to 1879, of not consulting or listening to the British representative. By removing the punishment based on mere suspicion, Inoue incorporated a British view into the 1879 draft regulations. This departure meant that Japanese laws and regulations to be imposed on Westerners were to be drafted in consultation with the treaty powers, thus affording them an opportunity to safeguard their treaty rights, especially immunity from the territorial jurisdiction of Japan.

The British Foreign Office evidently objected to the 1879 draft regulations also. The Foreign Ministry issued another set of eleven regulations early in 1880. Whereas the 1879 regulations provided fines up to ¥500, the amount stipulated in the 1880 regulations ranged from ¥10 to ¥200. Such differences, however, provided no basis for acceptance. Both drafts contained the provision to which London had strongest objection: unilateral enforcement by Japanese authorities against Western violators. Like the 1879 regulations, the 1880 regulations would have infringed upon extraterritorial privileges.[87]

At this juncture, London saw no immediate way out of the impasse. On behalf of Foreign Secretary Lord Granville, on July 28, 1881, Lord Tenterden, the permanent under-secretary, communicated to Mori that parts of the 1880 regulations were "unnecessarily stringent and harassing." As opium imported by the British into Japan was imported only in the small quantities required for indispensable medicinal purposes, Lord Tenterden continued, "the inquisitorial regime" to which it was proposed to subject Western medical men, apothecaries, and hospitals had no precedent as far as he was aware in the legislation of any other country, and was all the more remarkable in Japan where the growing of opium by Japanese subjects was not prohibited. To arrive at a satisfactory solution of this long-pending question, the British Foreign Office proposed that it be discussed by representatives of the treaty powers with those of Japan in the course of the approaching negotiations for revision of the treaties.[88]

So ended Japan's undeclared and unsuccessful attempt in the 1870s to drive a wedge into the extraterritorial regime. Since the early negotiations for the revision of the unequal treaties failed, the question of opium remained unresolved until 1899, at which time these treaties were completely scrapped and replaced with new treaties.

This attempt throws new light on the universally accepted view that Foreign Minister Terashima's attempt to revise the treaties, beginning in 1876, never sought the abolition of extraterritoriality but aimed solely at regaining tariff autonomy.[89] This is a highly misleading half-truth, for in the 1870s the Japanese government actually pursued both goals.

The above account shows how erroneously the Japanese-language literature on the *Hartley* cases has described their ending. According to this literature, Japan was obliged to drop the cases because on February 7, 1879, despite its long, sustained efforts to solve the opium controversy by diplomatic negotiation instead of appeal, Great Britain announced unilaterally that Japan had to frame a set of regulations for the importation of medicinal opium.[90] This statement is untrue in two ways: first, Britain did not, all of a sudden, inform Japan of the necessity of framing such regulations early in 1879; and furthermore, no less adamantly than Britain, Japan, too, had insisted upon having regulations of that kind. It was as a result of their fundamental disagreement on the terms of the regulations that the two countries had been unable to agree upon a set of regulations. Second, the *Hartley* cases could have had a tidy, clear-cut ending as Japanese historians seem to have wished if the Japanese government had made the appeal it had once contemplated. Japan's reluctance to exhaust the legal remedies available to it was responsible for the cases ending in smoke as they did.

"Unreasonable" Law

Great Britain accepted as right and proper the Japanese view that all importation of opium was prohibited by treaty and that Japan had the sovereign right to issue any regulations governing the procurement by the Westerners of medicinal opium. At the same time, however, Great Britain rejected all the draft regulations which Japan framed as being not "suitable." How did Great Britain reconcile these two diametrically opposed positions? Although the second position has been shown at length, the first position has only been alluded to and requires amplification.

British acceptance of Japan's right to issue the regulations in question was shown when key officials of the British Foreign Office subscribed to the American construction of the extraterritorial provisions of Japan's treaties. One of these officials was Foreign Secretary Lord Salisbury himself. In transmitting to the law officers Salisbury's third inquiry concerning the *Hartley* cases, dated May 26, 1879, Pauncefote pointed out that Japan appeared indisposed to enter into any agreement with Great Britain relating to the sale of opium and that Japan insisted upon the right to issue its own regulations in the matter. He further pointed out that with respect to the Japanese position "Lord Salisbury apprehends . . . they [the Japanese government] are acting in their strict rights, as we cannot compel them to supplement the existing Treaty for a further agreement. . . ."[91]

Another official who adhered to the American construction was Pauncefote. To be sure, as already noted, he initially identified himself with the Japanese point of view, saying that Wilkinson had erred in distinguishing medicinal from smoking opium. By mid-1879, however, he came to believe, as Parkes had previously contended, that, medicinal opium being the drug "of the first necessity," the framers of the Tariff Convention of 1866 would undoubtedly have made provision for it had they appreciated the difficulty. This change in attitude, however, did not mean that Pauncefote embraced Parkes' point of view, or what has been called the British construction. Rather, he subscribed to the American construction. In notifying Tomita of three objections to the 1878 regulations, on July 16, 1879, Pauncefote said that it was wrong for Parkes to insist that Japan had no power to frame regulations binding upon foreigners. In fact, he told Tomita that he agreed with Fish and Bingham that Japan had the right to enact laws and regulations binding upon Western nationals in Japan provided they did not violate the treaty rights of those nationals. He also said that it was the consular courts which had the power to apply and enforce these laws against their nationals.[92]

Still another adherent to the American construction among key British officials was Sir Edward Hertslet, librarian of the Foreign Office from 1857 to 1896,[93] whose knowledge of international law was vast. On May 31, 1880, he submitted to Foreign Secretary Granville and Pauncefote a memorandum reviewing the state of Japanese regulations concerning quarantine, pilotage, and the sale of opium, to which the law officers raised no objections from the standpoint of law. In the memorandum he stated:

As regards the general question of the liability of British subjects to obey the Laws of Japan, I have no doubt whatever that the L[aw]. O[fficers]. are right. I cannot concur with Sir H. Parkes in the view that the Convention of 1854 is superseded by the Treaty of 1858, and even if it were practically obsolete, the Exposition of its art. IV agreed to between the two Governments . . . expressly declares that British subjects are admitted on condition *of their conforming to the Law of Japan* [italics in original]. But they can only be punished by their own Authorities, for the infraction of them.

In closing his memorandum, Hertslet cited recent volumes of the U.S. Foreign Relations series as being conclusive on the subject.[94]

It is evident, then, that the law officers were not the only officials of the British government who subscribed to the American construction. The officials of the Foreign Office also accepted that construction. Nevertheless, as already noted, the position of the Foreign Office was that Japanese regulations, if they were to be binding upon British subjects, must be framed in consultation with the British minister in Japan.

The key to the Foreign Office's ambivalent attitude seems to have been an implicit British view that no Japanese regulations framed unilaterally by the Japanese government met the quality standards of a "civilized" state. As with many historical explanations of human motivation, there is no proof of this explanation, but there is sufficient evidence to suggest it. The evidence consists mainly of the Foreign Office's actions relating to the opium question and the adamant, vociferous objections Parkes raised against the possible unilateral enforcement by Japan of Japanese regulations against British subjects. The actions of the Foreign Office have been amply discussed. It only remains to show Parkes' objections raised prior to London's 1881 notification to Tokyo that regulations for the sale of opium should be dealt with as part of the forthcoming negotiations for revision of the unequal treaties.

The reason it can be assumed that Parkes' view had a definite bearing on the Foreign Office's position is that he was the man on the scene and that such a man would usually have had the foreign secretary's ear. Until 1905 the clerks of the Foreign Office had had no part in policy-formulating processes. Even the permanent under-secretary "scarcely thought it decent to express a personal opinion on big questions." At a hearing before the Select Committee of 1872 on the Diplomatic and Consular Services, an official who later became chief clerk testified: "We clerks are ready to do anything and everything that is required of us by the Under-Secretary of State or the Secretary of State; but in point of fact the Secretary of State may be said himself to do the work of the Office." The primary sources of information and intelligence on which the foreign secretary based his decisions during the nineteenth century were letters, private ones in particular, from ambassadors and ministers abroad. Foreign secretaries, notably Salisbury, freely indulged in the private letter habit; they seldom consulted anyone in the Foreign Office on matters of importance. But the reform of 1905 produced a great change. Now the clerks began to write their own suggestions, "in the detailed way that was formerly so much deprecated, on each paper that came before them." Until then, for example, no one in the China Department had known China firsthand. The British minister in China was the only expert on that country on whom the foreign secretary heavily depended.[95]

In his memorandum of April 28, 1880, to the Foreign Office, Parkes objected to the Japanese authorities' proposed assumption of jurisdiction over British subjects for infractions of Japanese opium regulations, on account of probable infringement by the Japanese police on the rights of the accused. Parkes stated that the Japanese police might make domiciliary visits, arrests without warrants, and carry off movable property; that the police might imprison persons, examine them in private, torture them to elicit evidence, and make them incriminate themselves and others; or that the police might keep them in prison for an indefinite period without making any charge. "Are Regulations of this nature," asked Parkes, "to be accepted and enforced on British subjects through the instrumentality of the British authorities because they form a portion of Japanese municipal law—or should those Authorities be a party only to the enforcement of such Regulations on their countrymen as are reasonable and necessary, and accord with the principle of justice as administered among civilized States?"[96]

Parkes raised the same issue in his memorandum of May 25, 1881, in which he argued that the draft regulations of 1880 were harassing and unreasonable. As he contended:

I believe it to be a principle of international law that no foreign country is obliged to enforce an unreasonable law of another nation. . . . I am bound to say that I think these Regulations are, in some respects, unnecessarily vexatious and inquisitorial; that the proposed penalties cannot be adopted without modification . . . that special difficulty will arise in regards to the clause which makes selling opium for smoking or converting it for smoking punishable by 'transportation with hard labour for a term [unspecified].' "[97]

Parkes' contention seems to have helped shape the Foreign Office's attitude. In his communication of July 28, 1881, to Tomita, Lord Tenterden characterized the 1880 regulations as "unnecessarily stringent and harassing," closely echoing Parkes' words.[98]

Conclusion

Let us now consider the three questions posed in evaluating each of the five cases. If the answers to the first and third questions are negative and the answer to the second question is positive, it can be concluded that the *Hartley* cases fail to support the interpretation at issue, that the Western consular courts in Japan seldom handed down just and fair decisions. On the other hand, the converse conclusion will be in order if the three answers are the opposite of what has been indicated.

First, do the existing accounts of the *Hartley* cases present both the Japanese plaintiffs and the British defendant's side of the story? This chapter suggests that none of the accounts presents both sides, nor does any present either side adequately. One reason is that the writers did not know all relevant facts. Another reason is that they failed to take into account the context in which the seemingly outrageous judgments were rendered.

Second, did the Yokohama Court render the judgments in accordance with the law applicable to each case? This question is the most difficult of the three, and the answer to it needs to be examined in detail.

In the *Chishima* case of 1893–1895, the subject of Chapter 5, Japan, the complainant, appealed the judgment of the trial court and in the end obtained a satisfactory adjudication as far as the case proceeded. Since, however, Japan elected not to appeal the judgments in the *Hartley* cases, one finds it impossible to answer the question raised on the same basis as one would answer it with regard to, for example, the *Chishima* case. One cannot, of course, be certain of the outcome of appeals in the *Hartley* cases, had they been made. It is difficult even to speculate whether the Privy Council would have taken into account the extralegal considerations that went into the judgment in the first *Hartley* case. That judgment rested on the distinction between medicinal opium and smoking opium. On the other hand, it is far less difficult to speculate about what the Privy Council might have decided on the issue of want of jurisdiction. If Japan had appealed, the judgment might have been quashed on the grounds of procedural irregularity, namely, the faulty exercise by "the Supreme Court at Kanagawa" of its jurisdiction. Therefore, the question of whether the judgments were rendered in accordance with the law applicable can be considered solely on the basis of the judgments of the trial court. Here the law applicable was the prohibition against opium importation.

Undoubtedly, those judgments were contrary to the clear wording of the prohibition. The law officers upheld the Japanese protests when they expressed the opinion that the distinction between medicinal opium and smoking was unwarranted under the existing treaty terms. One might, therefore, argue that the judgments resting on unwarranted distinction were wrong and that the *Hartley* cases were adjudicated unfairly and unjustly. But such an argument would amount to an unfair, unreasonable assessment, for two reasons. First, although law strives to realize the ideal of justice, the realm of justice is wider than that of law. For the sake of justice, the judgments in question should be evaluated in the wider, historical context. Second, more appropriately, even in the domain of law the literal construction is a norm but not the only norm. Justice Stephen J. Field of the U.S. Supreme Court once wrote:

It is a canon of interpretation to so construe a law or a treaty as to give effect to the object designed, and for that purpose all of its provisions must be examined in the light of attendant and surrounding circumstances. To some terms and expressions a literal meaning will be given, and to others a larger and more extended one. The reports of adjudged cases and approved legal treaties are full of illustrations of the application of this rule. The inquiry in all such cases is as to what was intended in the law by the legislature, and in the treaty by the contracting parties.[99]

In the historical context, it is irrefutable that the two *Hartley* cases would not have arisen had the opium controversy been resolved between 1872 and 1875. The controversy was not resolved then because both Japan and Great Britain were adamant in maintaining their respective positions. It follows, therefore, that the party maintaining the less justifiable position should bear greater responsibility for the *Hartley* cases. The question becomes, then, which position, the British or the Japanese, was the less justifiable.

In my view, the Japanese position was less justifiable, namely, that Japan had power to enforce its laws and regulations against British subjects in its territories without the intervention of British consular authorities. This position had no basis in treaty. But the British position that Japan had no such power under treaty rested squarely upon treaty provisions. At this juncture, one might be tempted to argue that the unequal treaties that Japan entered into at gunpoint were invalid and that Japan should have set aside its treaty obligations and assumed jurisdiction over the Westerners in Japan. Such an argument would be untenable on two grounds. First, duress does not invalidate consent in the law of nations as it does in the private law of contract. "A dictated treaty is as valid legally as one freely entered into on both sides."[100] Second, in the 1850s the Tokugawa Bakufu freely and willingly—though out of ignorance—conceded extraterritoriality to the Western "barbarian," reasoning as it did that it would be better for them to deal with their own criminals and scoundrels and to settle disputes between them.[101]

Not only did the Japanese position lack treaty sanction; it also rested on an unrealistic, unattainable expectation. Japan expected Great Britain and the other treaty powers to entrust their nationals unreservedly to the territorial administration of justice. This expectation was unrealistic on several counts. First, at that time punishments for crimes in Japan were severe and cruel when compared with those in the treaty powers. For example, under the penal code in force from 1873 through 1881, the punishment for theft of public property worth between ¥250 and ¥299 was penal servitude for life, and the punishment for theft of property valued at ¥300 or more was death by strangulation.[102] In addition, not until 1876 was torture formally abolished as a legal means of extracting a confession from the accused. Moreover, a national judiciary, though organized in 1875, could not function at once as an effective national system of impartial courts of justice worthy of the name. Finally, although the primary objective of most Westerners in Japan was trade, no body of laws gave them a clearly defined regulation of commerce. The last point needs elaboration.

One function of law in any society is "that of enabling members of the society to calculate the consequence of their conduct, thereby securing and facilitating voluntary transaction and arrangements."[103] Suppose John Smith, a British merchant, can write a check on his account at a Mitsubishi bank in Tokyo with some confidence that the bank will honor his check. This confidence is based in part upon the legal obligation imposed upon the bank to honor all checks drawn upon sufficient funds. Likewise, he can with confidence put down earnest money on a ton of Shizuoka tea to be exported, knowing that Yamamoto Saburō, the seller, is required by law to perform his part of the bargain. Thus, law makes it possible to predict with assurance what others will do. To fill this vital social function, law must be published and made known to all before it can be applied and enforced. This simply was not yet the case with Japanese law in the 1870s.

Little of the Japanese law was known or even knowable by any foreigners. Until its demise in 1867, the Bakufu had maintained the policy of making its laws and rules known to only a small number of officials for their guidance in enforcing them against the "ignorant masses" (gumin). The first codes of law based on Western legal principles, the Penal Code (Keihō) and the Code of Criminal Instruction (Chizaihō), went into effect only in 1882, and nearly a decade was to elapse before two other Western-style codes were enacted. In fact, not all of the Commercial Code, so essential to commerce and trade, was in force until 1899. It is not surprising, therefore, that during the 1870s all the treaty powers except the United States opposed any attempt by Japan to drive an entering wedge into the extraterritorial regime. The British foreign secretary, Lord Granville, was in effect speaking for all the powers when on October 2, 1881, he wrote to Mori: "The system of ex-territorial jurisdiction is no doubt attended with inconvenience in certain cases, but it must remain a necessary condition of the relations between Western nations and those of the East so long as their judicial systems are widely dissimilar."[104]

Hence, although Sir Harry S. Parkes was irascible and contemptuous of the Japanese, he could not be faulted for attributing to the lack of procedural safeguards his opposition to Japan's attempted encroachment on extraterritoriality. Justice Felix Frankfurter once observed: "The history of liberty has largely been the history of the observance of procedural safeguards."[105] Robert J. Jackson, another associate justice of the U.S. Supreme Court, stated that it might be preferable to live under Russian law applied by common law procedures than under the common law enforced by Russian procedures.[106]

At the height of the opium controversy, even some Japanese, both in and out of the government, believed it was unrealistic for their government to hope to subject Westerners in Japan to Japanese law and to exercise direct control over them. In the summer of 1876, for example, Vice-Foreign Minister Sameshima Naonobu noted that the Japanese felt the extraterritorial and tariff clauses of the treaties put Japan under a foreign yoke. But at the same time he admitted to Parkes that it would be altogether premature for Japan to claim at that time the surrender by the treaty powers of the extraterritorial privileges. Sameshima also said that Japan was not as yet prepared to exercise jurisdiction over foreigners, since it had neither suitable laws nor suitable courts.[107] Moreover, some Japanese observed that the Westerners did not as yet wish to obey the laws of Japan in much the same way as the Japanese themselves did not wish to obey the laws of China or Korea. For example, the Chōya shimbun, a major newspaper, more than once questioned the wisdom of the Japanese government in trying to control the Westerners.[108]

Given Japan's greater responsibility for the opium controversy, coupled with the country's fourteen-year failure to object to the importing of medicinal opium, and the indispensability of such opium as the sovereign pain-killer, it would be difficult to assert that the Yokohama Court violated the intent of the prohibition against opium importation. In other words, it would be less than fair and just to state that the Court did not render the *Hartley* decisions in accordance with the "law" applicable.

Third, and finally, would the decisions of the Court have been more severe if the complainant had been English rather than Japanese? More specifically, had the complainant been English, would Hartley, the prisoner at the bar, have suffered harsher penalties than he actually did? In fact, Ueno raised this question in his communication to Salisbury of July 12, 1878: "I would request your Lordship to consider whether in all probability a very different sentence would not have been passed in this country [England] on a foreigner, detected twice attempting to smuggle goods, whether prohibited or not, into England." Concerning the penalties meted out to Hartley in the second *Hartley* case, Ueno went on to deplore them as "inadequate" and "trifling," not a "properly deterrent punishment."[109] Ueno's observations, however, missed the mark on two counts. First, Hartley was not a foreigner convicted twice of attempting to smuggle goods. The penalties were determined in part by the decision on the first *Hartley* case. In that case, the Yokohama Court did not determine whether he had attempted to smuggle or had smuggled opium. Instead, at the request of counsel for the Japanese complainant, the Court decided only the issue of whether the importation of opium of every description was prohibited by treaty. Second, despite Ueno's deprecation of the penalties, they were in perfect conformity with the treaty terms. More broadly, since no extraterritorial regime ever operated in Great Britain, no cases similar to the *Hartley* cases ever arose there. Therefore, one cannot properly entertain the question but must regard it as merely rhetorical.

Of the three questions examined, the first has been answered in the negative, the second more or less in the affirmative, and the third has proved to be unanswerable. One may, therefore, conclude that the adjudication of the *Hartley* cases fails to sustain the interpretation that the Western consular courts in Japan as a rule did not render evenhanded justice.

4

Captain Drake's Failure to Discharge His Trust: The *Drake* Case (1886)

Shortly after 7:00 P.M. on October 24, 1886, the British freighter *Normanton*, en route from Yokohama to Kōbe, was overtaken by a rainstorm off the coast of Ōshima Island at the southern tip of Kii Peninsula, Wakayama Prefecture. It struck a rock and sank in an hour. All but one of the thirty-nine officers and crew took to two lifeboats, while all of the twenty-five Japanese passengers went down. John William Drake, master of the *Normanton*, explained that, although he had directed the Japanese passengers to take to the boats, they had not responded because they could not understand English. The Japanese public did not believe his explanation. A naval court of inquiry held at Her Britannic Majesty's Consulate at Hyōgo found that "the Master, Officers, and others of the European Crew did all in their power to save the lives of the passengers." This finding, together with the fact that all but one of the Occidentals had been saved while all the Orientals except for one Chinese boy had been lost, brought utmost dismay to the Japanese government and people. To assuage the public wrath, the government preferred a charge of manslaughter by negligence against Captain Drake to Her Britannic Majesty's Court at Hyōgo. Ultimately tried at Her Britannic Majesty's Court for Japan at Kanagawa (hereafter referred to as the Yokohama Court), he was found guilty as charged on December 8, 1886, but was recommended for mercy by the jury and sentenced to three months' imprisonment. For the Japanese public, the sentence was a travesty of justice, too lenient for the loss of twenty-five lives. It simply reflected, they felt, the fundamental inequity of the Western consular court system in Japan. The *Normanton* incident generated intense anti-British feelings which in turn helped arouse public indignation against the treaty revision plan Foreign Minister Inoue Kaoru had been pursuing for eight years. The public indignation contributed to both the demise of the plan and his resignation in 1887.

The *Normanton* incident was unique in three ways. First, it devolved into a far more serious matter than could have been anticipated. This effect is evident when one considers the Japanese response to a similar maritime tragedy which reportedly caused the contemporary Japanese to forget the *Normanton* incident. In 1890, the sultan of Turkey dispatched a Turkish man-of-war to Japan in order to present the emperor of Japan a medal. On September 26, en route from Yokohama to Kōbe, the Turkish warship, manned by 650 men, struck a rock in virtually the same location where the *Normanton* had run into one four years earlier, and sank. With the warship went down 587 men, including the captain. This incident, which was far more tragic in number of fatalities than the *Normanton* incident, was reported as a matter of course by Japanese newspapers, and there were no reported outpourings of grief, sorrow, or even regret as had been witnessed after the *Normanton* tragedy.[1] In the earlier sinking, the Japanese lamented the innocent and senseless death of their twenty-five compatriots, they deplored Drake's failure to save their lives, and they wished to dispel their feelings of resentment and anger. But these feelings alone do not account for their hyperemotional response to the tragedy. The response was more complex. A feeling prevailed that they were despised as semibarbaric, held in contempt, and regarded as inferior to the Westerners. Therefore, they believed that the tragic incident could not have occurred without this superiority complex in the Westerners.[2]

Second, from the standpoint of the Japanese public, probably no other single incident associated with any of the five publicized cases provoked so swift and so total an indignation among the Japanese populace as did the *Normanton* incident. The central incident of the earliest of the five, the *King* case (1875), was the heinous crime of rape, but it involved a single person, not the large number of victims of the *Normanton* incident. Furthermore, there were fewer newspaper readers in 1875 than in 1886; hence, proportionately more Japanese had greater knowledge of the *Normanton* incident than of the rape. The two *Hartley* cases dealt with important issues of treaty interpretation, but since the legal issues concerned the Japanese government rather than the people, the general population did not become so excited about the issues as they did about those pertaining to the *Normanton* incident. Finally, in the 1893 collision of the *Chishima* with the *Ravenna* (Chapter 5), the Japanese understood only some of the issues and those in a piecemeal fashion. As a result, the sinking of the *Chishima* did not emotionally stir them up so wholly and quickly as did the *Normanton* incident.

Third, the *Normanton* incident was an event unmatched in the history of British merchant marine service. On November 18, 1886, the *Chōya shimbun* reported that, according to a noted Japanese jurist, there had not been any shipwreck in which, while all passengers on board a British ship were drowned, its master and crew saved themselves; that there had been but one American incident of this sort.[3] By all counts, this finding still stands. At this juncture, one might recall a maritime episode which might erroneously be cited as one disproving the finding—the *Jeddah* episode. (This episode inspired Joseph Conrad to write the first half of his masterpiece, *Lord Jim*.) The British steamship *Jeddah* was used to carry Muslim pilgrims from Singapore to Jeddah, an Arabian port on the Red Sea. It left Singapore on July 17, 1880, for Penang, where it took on board nearly 1,000 pilgrims and proceeded directly for Jeddah. After a stormy passage, the ship developed a leak off Cape Guardafui. On August 8, the master, Joseph Lucas Clark, and his European crew abandoned the ship with the 1,000 lives on board and took to lifeboats. Rescued by a British steamship, they were taken to Aden, where they reported that the *Jeddah* had foundered. The appearance of the *Jeddah* at Aden a day later, towed by a French steamship with its passengers still on board, sparked a scandal and subsequent inquiry. A British naval court of inquiry held at Aden into the cause of the abandonment of the *Jeddah* found that no immediate danger of foundering had existed and suspended Captain Clark's certificate of competence for three years. But he was never tried because of insufficiency of evidence for criminal prosecution.[4] Had he been tried, there would have been a British case, the sentence of which could serve as a precedent and a basis for evaluating Drake's sentence in the *Drake* case.

Did the Yokohama Court's handling of the *Drake* case bear out the Japanese claim that, *as a rule*, no Japanese could expect evenhanded justice from the Western consular courts? More specifically, do the existing accounts of the case present both sides, those of both the Japanese plaintiff and the English defendant? Did the Yokohama Court render its decision in accordance with the law applicable? If the Japanese plaintiff had been English, would the defendant have been given a more severe punishment than the one actually imposed upon him?

By distinguishing the *Drake* case from the incident that produced it, one may evaluate the case more effectively. Connected with the case were three pivotal incidents, each of which caused the Japanese to feel humiliated and outraged afresh: the drowning of the Japanese passengers and the survival of the Western crew members; the Japanese press's erroneous reporting of the finding of the naval court of inquiry as a decision of a court of law; and the sentencing of Drake to three months' imprisonment. The first incident, tragic as it was, had nothing to do with the justice of the Western consular courts in Japan. The second incident, like the first, was unrelated to the justice of the courts—the subject of inquiry—although both infuriated the Japanese. Only the third incident, being an integral part of the *Drake* case, was related to the subject of inquiry. Therefore, even though this chapter touches upon the first two incidents, it does so only so far as they impinge upon the case itself.

The Normanton Incident

Four years old at the time of its loss, the *Normanton* was a 1,533-ton freight steamer owned by Adamsonbell and Company in Yokohama. In early 1885, the steamer started from Antwerp on its voyage to China and Japan. Designed chiefly as a cargo carrier, it was not certified by the Japanese government to carry passengers. Nevertheless, for some time it had carried passengers, both on the way out from Antwerp and while plying off the coasts of China and Japan. There was no accommodation for passengers except the ship's alleyways.

The thirty-nine member crew—thirty-eight adults and one boy—included a master, three mates, four engineers, ten deck hands (a German carpenter, a boatswain, and eight able seamen), three stewards, two cooks, fourteen firemen, and a "donkey-man," a man in charge of a "donkey-engine" (a small steam engine, usually used for subsidiary operations on board ship). The crew was composed of four ethnic groups: (1) Chinese—a steward, a cook, and the boy; (2) Hindu—another cook and the fourteen firemen; (3) British—the master, the other two stewards, and the four engineers; and (4) European—the remaining fourteen members, including the donkey-man and the carpenter.

When the *Normanton* struck the rock, the rear part of its hull was crushed. The master ordered the holds sounded. Ten minutes were spent in sounding the holds, and the presence of water was reported to him. Before this report was made, however, he had issued a second order, an order to ready the boats and look after the passengers. To carry out this order, some of the crew at once proceeded to ready the port lifeboat, the port pinnace (a small tender), and the starboard lifeboat. They did not lower the starboard pinnace because one of its side planks had been crushed. Meanwhile, the boatswain went down to the passengers to look after them. He later testified: "No one went with me at that time. I went to the port alley-ways. I tried to describe to the passengers the danger they were in. . . . I did not try to pull them out at that time." He then proceeded to the bridge and set to work clearing out the port lifeboat.

While the crew proceeded with the work of lowering the two lifeboats and the port pinnace, the master ordered the chief mate to get the anchor over the bow. The execution of this order entirely stopped the lowering of the starboard lifeboat. The chief mate, the carpenter, and the boatswain had to proceed to the bow to work on the anchor, which required twenty to twenty-five minutes. When this party returned to the bridge, the remainder of the crew had just succeeded in getting out the port lifeboat and the port pinnace. It was about this time—about half an hour after the steamer had struck the rock—that the master ordered the boatswain to try to get the twenty-five passengers to the boats. "I then went aft through the port alley-way," testified the boatswain. "The carpenter came there afterwards. I made another attempt to get some of the Japanese out. I remained there 3 to 5 minutes. . . . It is my opinion that the passengers knew the danger perfectly . . . could see it."

Once his order to the boatswain was issued, the master took to the port pinnace. The chief mate, the boatswain, the carpenter, and the passengers had no means of escape, for the starboard lifeboat had capsized before it hit the water. (At that time, a seaman named Barnard was lost.) When the chief mate saw the port pinnace leaving the steamer, he hailed the pinnace, asking whether the master and others in the small boat were going to leave him and the others on board. He heard someone answering him but could not make out what was said. Then he, along with the boatswain, cast off one end of the lashings of the starboard quarterboat, then perceiving that the starboard lifeboat had righted. Thereupon he stopped working at the quarterboat and jumped into the lifeboat. Six Hindus and the carpenter joined him in the boat, but not the boatswain, who was washed off the steamer wearing a life buoy. For twelve hours he floated about, and it was not until the next morning that one of the boats picked him up.[5]

The above account shows that neither the boatswain nor anyone else ever made a forceful effort to rescue the passengers. At the trial, the Crown prosecutor asked the boatswain and the chief mate whether the crew could have forcibly compelled the passengers to get into the boats. Each answered in the affirmative.[6] It is beyond doubt, then, that no determined attempt was ever made to get the passengers to the boats. Whatever attempt was made was half-hearted and ineffective.

Evidently, no less half-hearted was the attempt of the passengers to save themselves. In response to the Crown prosecutor's inquiry as to what was the cause of the passengers being drowned, the chief mate replied that "the chief cause was that they would not struggle to save their own lives."[7] The will to survive, or the instinct for self-preservation, is a powerful, instinctual, human drive. One would think, therefore, that such will alone could have driven the passengers to the boats. Apparently, however, it did not. Since none of the passengers survived, the apparent indifference to life which both the passengers and the crew displayed will remain an eternal mystery. No one can ever know why the passengers did not move to the boats.

One might wonder if there was collusion between Captain Drake and his crew, so that the witnesses at the trial did not tell the truth in claiming that the passengers had not struggled to save their own lives. One may not rule out this possibility of perjury. Nevertheless, careful study of the minutes of the proceedings does not suggest that the adjudication of the *Drake* case represented a mockery of justice.

Were there enough boats to save all on board the steamer? The answer is yes. Following the wreck, four boats from the *Normanton* were found on the beach. A retired commander of the British Royal Navy, employed by the Japanese government to locate the whereabouts of the *Normanton*, examined the capacity of the four boats and was a key witness at Captain Drake's trial. Since he was a disinterested party to the trial, one may take, as did the Yokohama Court, his assessment of the capacity as reliable. Of the four boats, he testified, two were lifeboats, each of which could comfortably hold thirty-eight people; a third boat was a square-stern boat which could have held seventeen or eighteen. Altogether, these three boats had the capacity for ninety-three people. Only sixty-one people were on board the *Normanton*. Moreover, there were other boats on board the freighter—for example, six boats on the lower bridge.[8]

The foregoing confirms two observations that have been advanced by Japanese historians. First, prior to the wreck, Drake had not conducted lifedrills as is customary to save lives during a potential crisis, nor did he act aggressively to save the passengers after the *Normanton* had struck the rock. Second, there was no evidence whatever supporting what contemporary public opinion in Japan considered to be the ultimate explanation of Drake's and his Western crew's so-called indifferent attitude toward the lives of the passengers: the Westerners regarded the Japanese in the same light as wild beasts.[9]

On the morning of October 25, Captain Drake and his crew reached the shore, received aid from officials of Wakayama Prefecture, and arrived at Kōbe on October 28. Meanwhile, Drake offered the explanation already mentioned—namely, that he had ordered the Japanese passengers to take to the lifeboats, but none had obeyed the order because they could not understand English. The Japanese gave no credence to his explanation. For one thing, they could not believe what they were told the passengers had done—remained where they were. Major newspapers (*dai shimbun*) like the *Chōya shimbun* and the *Jiji shimpō* expressed disbelief, asserting that, however impossible it was to communicate with the passengers, it was inconceivable that they had not perceived the danger and had declined to take to the boats. Individuals expressed the same disbelief. For example, K. Nabeshima, a Cambridge-trained official of the Foreign Ministry, wrote to each of the five major newspapers in Tokyo, attributing the fate of the passengers to one of two possible causes, as follows: " . . . either they were abandoned to their fate by the so-called 'civilized' Occidentals; or, obeying a chivalrous instinct, they generously sacrificed themselves so as not to obstruct the safety of the Westerners, to whom life is very precious. . . . "[10] For another thing, the Japanese at first found it difficult to comprehend Captain Drake's action: he took to the lifeboat while the passengers were still on board the sinking ship under his command. In the event of shipwreck, pointed out the *Jiji shimpō*, the master is responsible for saving the passengers, the crew, and then his own life in that order; it is neither legally nor morally permissible for the master to leave his ship upon facing a crisis before executing his responsibilities.[11]

The Japanese inquiry into why all of the passengers had perished produced two theories. According to the first, a caging theory, the passengers were unable to take to the lifeboats because the crew had chained and caged them in a cabin. To verify this suspicion, it was necessary to examine both the conditions in which the passengers lay dead and their dead bodies. As a result, the government and civilians alike made a number of plans to send a diver down to the bottom of the sea where the *Normanton* was presumably lying, but these plans had to be abandoned. Sunlight cannot penetrate ocean water too deeply. At that time, the best diver could not distinguish even his own body at 120 *shaku* below the ocean surface. (The *shaku* is equivalent to .995 foot.) The presumed location of the *Normanton* was at about 300 *shaku*. It was, therefore, considered impossible to locate the steamer and examine the corpses of the passengers.[12]

The Japanese then went a step further in their search for an underlying motive that could satisfactorily account for the British seamen's failure. The net result of this search was the second theory, a theory of racial prejudice. In its editorial of November 17, 1886, the *Chōya shimbun* expounded the theory by voicing a might-have-been that every Japanese may have felt upon hearing about the *Normanton* incident. Had the ill-fated ship sunk off the coast of Europe and had the passengers been Europeans, would the crew have abandoned them and taken to the boats to escape from the danger? The editorial answered "No." The crew would have been keenly afraid of two possible consequences: a bitter and uncompromising cry of indignation that would have been raised by a large section, if not the whole, of the European community; and the sanction of strict maritime law enforced by impartial courts. As a result, in spite of the dark night and the tempestuous weather, the crew would have risked their lives to save the passengers. In the crew's eyes, the editorial went on to say, the Japanese people and the Japanese Empire counted for nothing. They would never put their lives in jeopardy to rescue any Japanese passengers. The sinking of the *Normanton* did not simply mean the drowning of the twenty-five compatriots; it meant the death of 37 million Japanese![13]

In one of its November 1886 editorials, the *Jiji shimpō* gave its most lucid and eloquent expression to the theory of racial prejudice. The editorial stated:

It is probable that the want of means of communication was a hindrance to a certain extent, but that the Japanese declined help through ignorance can hardly be credited. . . . Has Captain . . . discharged his trust? We doubt it. Some people may say:—"It is commonly acknowledged all over the world, that the captain of a ship is the last person to leave it in the event of wreck, and in practice this rule is so regularly followed that those who disregard it are not permitted to appear in society with honour. But all this applies only so far as relates to the people of the West, and in dealing with Japanese the rule cannot be observed as a standard. Occidentals think that their religion and laws are different from those of Orientals, and that in dealing with the latter, they need not observe those rules of etiquette which are applicable to the peoples of the West,—that in fact they may treat them like cats and dogs. . . . Those foreign vessels . . . plying on our coasts do not take in Japanese passengers as passengers, but as a class of animate commodities. . . . When a storm rages, these living goods are not allowed to come out of their place of storage, lest they may interfere with the work of the sailors, and the captain and the crew of the ship do not even think of them in finally leaving the vessel. The case of the *Normanton* may be one of these." We neither agree with those who use this language nor do we pronounce Captain Drake guilty of such act. But we have strong suspicions as to the wreck of his ship, and some very unpleasant thoughts are awakened in our minds.[14]

What added oil to the fire of "strong suspicions" and dismay was the finding of the naval court of inquiry held at the British consulate at Kōbe immediately after the *Normanton* wreck. On November 5, 1886, the court, composed of a British consul and the masters of two British ships sitting as assessors, found that the vessel had been seaworthy in every respect, that the conduct of the master and his crew had been blameless, and that their licenses which had been lost were to be reissued.[15]

The Japanese misidentified this finding from a naval board of inquiry with a decision by a court of law. At the heart of this misidentification was the failure to distinguish the court of naval inquiry from a court of law. Responsible only to the Board of Trade, the court of naval inquiry acted only in the name of that board and had power to dismiss any member of the crew, but it had no authority to inflict punishment for any crime at common law. It was only a court of *law* which had power to deal with crime and to mete out punishment. Therefore, the function of any naval court of inquiry was administrative, not judicial.[16] One may see that the inability to make this distinction could result in cloaking a decision from the court of naval inquiry with the authority of a judicial determination. This is precisely what happened. At the time of the *Normanton* tragedy, as Judge Kikuchi Hiroshi points out, Japanese journalists were unable to make the distinction. Consequently, Japanese newspapers simply reported as though reporting the finding of a court of law that the British consul who had presided over the naval court of inquiry at Kōbe had fully exonerated the master and his crew. The result was a frenzy of rage on an unprecedented scale. Newspaper articles, public speeches and letters, circulars and resolutions by legal, commercial, and scholarly bodies, and religious protests, all vented their anger. In the eyes of the Japanese, the finding was but another instance of the Westerners' contempt for the Japanese, as well as of the evils of extraterritoriality.[17]

The Japanese condemnation of Drake's action could not have become so intense without the Japanese press's agitation. The press understood that the government was disposed to regard such agitation with benevolent indifference, if not approval. Apparently, the government assumed this stance because of its pent-up irritation against the aggressive policies of the Western treaty powers. Of particular weight was the disappointment which the government had been experiencing in its attempt to revise Japan's existing unequal treaties with those powers.[18]

Regina v. John William Drake

Under instructions from the central government, Governor Naikai Tadakatsu of Hyōgo Prefecture brought prosecution charges against Captain Drake for manslaughter by negligence, at the British consular court at Kōbe (hereafter referred to as the Kōbe Court). J. F. Lowder, an ex-British consul and now adviser to the Ministry of Foreign Affairs, represented the complainant. The prosecution elicited much support from many Japanese who had been outraged by the *Normanton* incident. A preliminary hearing, begun on November 16, led the Japanese public to further condemnation of Drake. The hearing revealed that he had taken his log and other books from the *Normanton* to the lifeboat and that these books subsequently enabled him to pay his crew's wages accurately. It was evident to the public that before leaving the *Normanton* he had been fully aware of the danger the ship faced. If he had time to fetch his books, why did he not have time to save the lives of at least some passengers? In two days the hearing established a *prima facie* case, and the Kōbe Court decided to commit the accused for trial. A few days later, the Kōbe Court announced that the trial would take place at the Yokohama Court.[19]

In all probability, the change of venue occurred because in the Ōsaka-Kōbe area anti-Drake feelings among the Japanese were running so high that the Kōbe Court feared the accused might not get a fair trial under the circumstances, even though the jurors to be selected were British.

On December 7, 1886, the trial of Captain Drake began at the Yokohama Court. Forty or more Japanese, including several judges of the Tokyo and Yokohama District Courts, attended the trial. The occasion provided an excellent opportunity for the judges to observe directly a criminal trial as conducted in a British court. Edward Robinson, an English barrister who practiced in Shanghai, was counsel for the prisoner at the bar. He contended that there was contributory negligence on the part of the Japanese passengers. Their conduct in refusing to be guided by the crew on board accounted for their fate, he argued, and that exonerated the master. The Court, however, ruled that in criminal cases the law does not allow the contention of contributory negligence. In other words, such negligence does not serve as a bar to conviction. The Crown Prosecutor, Henry Charles Litchfield, together with Lowder, conducted the prosecution. The prosecution asserted that the prisoner's defense might be that he was not invested with the duty of looking after the passengers and that, finding or imagining that they were reluctant to leave the vessel, he was justified in saving his own life. The prosecution argued, however, that although

self-preservation is the first law of nature there are circumstances, times in a man's life, when that law has to be broken. When a man who has taken upon himself the duty that the captain of a ship does, of preserving and looking after the lives of passengers, it is self-sacrifice rather than self-preservation that is the first duty of that man. There was a duty that the captain of a vessel owed to his crew, and there was a duty that the captain and crew owed to the passengers.

More specifically, the prosecution maintained that Captain Drake should have assigned boat stations and conducted lifeboat drills; that he should have ordered someone to look after the passengers while the chief mate went to oversee the anchor; and that he should have directed someone specifically to go to the starboard alleyway to get the passengers to the boats. It was on these counts that the Court directed the jury to deliberate whether or not Captain Drake was guilty of neglecting his duty.[20]

On December 8 the five jurors deliberated an hour and a half and rendered a guilty verdict.[21] At the same time the jury desired to record

their sense of the difficulties of the position in which the captain was placed, aggravated by the fact of the engineers having left the ship in the port life-boat, thereby diminishing the means of saving life at his command, and also by the unwillingness, if not actual resistance, offered by the Japanese passengers to the efforts made to get them out of the alley-way towards the boats.

In short, the jury recommended mercy.

Judge Nicholas J. Hannen then addressed himself to Captain Drake in part as follows:

I am sorry to have to pass sentence upon you. I am not going to aggravate the position in which, no doubt, you are, by making any remarks, beyond this, that it cannot but be a matter of deep regret, not only to us all, but also no doubt, to you now, that you did not take such steps as would have been more effectual towards the saving of life. We have been accustomed to expect from the merchant service of England heroism and devotion to the interests of the crew and passengers, that I am afraid in this case [they] were wanting. It is my painful duty under circumstances, and taking everything that has been said into consideration, to sentence you to three months' imprisonment.[22]

Evaluation of the Sentence

As previously mentioned, the Japanese believed that Drake's sentence, three months' imprisonment, was too lenient. Today's historians also accept this view. One recent work states: "The master and the twenty-five English crew[sic] saved their lives by taking to boats, but every one of the twenty-three Japanese passengers [sic] was left to his [or her] fate. Nevertheless, a British consular trial sentenced the master to a mere three months' imprisonment, and not a penny was paid for loss of the lives."[23] Why did the Japanese public—and why do historians today—consider the sentence to be too lenient? This crucial question is difficult to answer, for there is not a great deal of evidence to suggest an entirely satisfying answer. Even so, an attempt will be made to offer several reasons.

Undoubtedly, the Japanese press's misinformed reporting of the initial finding by the naval court of inquiry goes a long way toward explaining the Japanese view of Drake's subsequent sentence. That finding lent support to the contemporary Japanese opinion that the Yokohama Court failed to mete out a punishment he deserved. As already mentioned, the press erroneously equated the finding with a judgment rendered by a law court, even though the finding was not a judicial determination. (In the light of the subsequent finding of guilty in the Yokohama Court, one can hardly deny that the initial finding was less than accurate and therefore unfortunate and misleading.)

The erroneous reporting created the wrong impression that the British consular court at Kōbe tried Drake and acquitted him. All Japanese conscious of public affairs must have felt that the Court once again had demonstrated what they had long "known"—namely, that all Western consular courts in Japan, as elsewhere in the world, were so interested in protecting their own nationals that they were willing to wink at their wrongdoings and would even bend their laws to shield the nationals from the rigor of impartial justice. The erroneous reporting thus confirmed and reinforced what the Japanese believed to be the partiality of the justice of the Western consular courts, particularly the British consular courts, in Japan. Given this frame of mind, one can conclude that only a drastically severe and even unusually cruel punishment—such as imprisonment for ten years, twenty years, or life—could have satisfied the Japanese public. Therefore, when the Yokohama Court sentenced Drake to three months' imprisonment, every Japanese intellectual must have shrugged his shoulders and exclaimed in disgust, "What else could we expect from the second trial?" Taguchi Ukichi, an articulate contemporary publicist, gave an inkling of these effects following the erroneous reporting. In his *Jōyaku kaiseiron* (On Treaty Revision), published in 1889 and widely read by his contemporaries, Taguchi wrote: "The British judge in Kōbe acquitted Drake of any wrongdoing," but public outrage generated by the acquittal obliged the Yokohama Court to sentence Drake to three months' imprisonment.[24] The fact of the matter is that there was no trial, let alone any acquittal, in Kōbe.

Even today's historians are not free from the hundred-year old error of identifying the naval court of inquiry with a court of law. Shimomura Fujio writes: "All of the twenty-six [*sic*] foreign crew and passengers were rescued; all of the twenty-five Japanese passengers were drowned. But in November the British consular court at Kōbe exonerated the master of any wrongdoing."[25] Speaking of Captain Drake's explanation of why not a single Japanese passenger was saved, Inoue Kiyoshi states: "However speechless the dead may be, how could any Japanese believe such an absurd statement as this one [Drake's]? They could not. Nevertheless, the British consul decided that the master had fully discharged his duties, and adjudged him not guilty (*muzai*)."[26]

Another reason why the Japanese public considered Drake's sentence too lenient appears to have been that they took the view that he should be punished in proportion to the amount of injury he had inflicted—the death of the twenty-five passengers and the incalculable human suffering of their surviving families.

One of the main theories of punishment rests on the principle of retribution. The retributive theory looks to the past, emphasizing either the appropriateness of taking vengeance on the wrongdoer or the necessity of exacting expiation or retribution. The theory implies that "offenders should be punished in proportion to their guilt, or perhaps to the amount of injury they have inflicted, or both together." General public opinion is usually retributive.[27] since the *Normanton* tragedy resulted in the loss of twenty-five lives, the Japanese may have expected the Yokohama Court to impose on Drake a sentence much more severe than three months' imprisonment. During the preliminary hearing, certain Japanese newspapers are alleged to have predicted that he would be sentenced to twenty-years' imprisonment. Historian Tanaka Tokihiko may be said to reflect this old point of view when he observes: "It is evident that this judgment [of the Yokohama Court] did not attach any importance to the fact that none of the Japanese passengers was saved."[28]

The Japanese view that drake's sentence was lenient drew its support also from the long-standing Japanese belief that the Western consular courts habitually had been unfair and unjust to Japanese litigants. The *Chōya shimbun*, for example, reflected this belief when it commented on the finding of the naval court as follows: "It does not commence today that foreign judges in the Orient hand down decisions calculated to protect their fellow countrymen."[29] This comment implied that the finding, mistaken for a decision from a court of law, was no exception to the practice of partial justice.

Given the newspapers' unrealized prediction of twenty years' imprisonment for Drake, one may wonder if the prevailing criminal laws of Japan account in any way for the public view that the sentence was too lenient. The applicable provision of the Penal Code of the time was Article 317, which imposed a fine ranging between ¥20 and ¥200 for manslaughter by negligence (*kashitsu satsushō*). Local law, therefore, provided no grounds for the Japanese indignation. It would be far closer to the truth to point out that the Japanese had long been accustomed to harsh punishment—a legacy of Edo Japan.

This brings us to the fourth, and final, possible reason for the Japanese dissatisfaction with Drake's sentence. The Japanese people had become so accustomed to the concept of punishment by imprisonment (*kinko*) that they probably did not regard Drake's short sentence as a punishment befitting his guilt. The compiler of the Japanese translation of the proceedings of the *Drake* case published in 1887 pointed to the fact that a slip of the tongue to a policeman was punishable by heavy imprisonment (*jū kinko*) ranging between a month and a year, and that a journalist who published another newspaper while the suspension of his newspaper was in force drew light imprisonment (*kei kinko*) ranging between six months and three years. Hence, noted the compiler, it was quite natural and reasonable for the Japanese to be dissatisfied with Drake's light penalty for the twenty-five-fold homicide. At the same time, however, the compiler asserted that those Japanese arguing against Drake's sentence should bear in mind that English cases like the *Drake* case had nothing to do with Japanese law; they were adjudicated according to English law.[30]

So much for the reasons why the Japanese may have felt that Drake's sentence was not severe enough. Let us now turn from this subjective, sympathetic examination to an objective, analytical evaluation. The question is whether today one can assert with assurance that the sentence was indeed too lenient. Perhaps the best way to answer this question would be to compare the sentence with sentences imposed in similar English cases. Unfortunately, however, there have been no similar English cases. As already mentioned, the case seems to have been *sui generis* in the annals of British merchant marine service. The only known case bearing any resemblance to the *Drake* case is the American case of *United States v. Holmes*,[31] a brief account of which is in order to help provide perspective on the *Drake* case.

The American ship *William Brown*, bound for Philadelphia, sailed from Liverpool on March 13, 1841. On board were seventeen officers and crew and sixty-four emigrants. (A sixty-fifth emigrant died soon after embarkation.) Of these emigrants, fifty-nine were Irish and the other five, Scottish females constituting a family. The master, the first mate, and a seaman were American, as were probably two blacks, a steward, and a cook. The other ten crew members were English and European. On the night of April 19, the *William Brown* struck an iceberg in nearly the same position where the *Titanic* was to run into one on April 12, 1912, and in an hour and a half sank with thirty-one of the passengers it carried. Unlike the *Normanton*, the *William Brown* was equipped only with a long boat and a jolly boat, lacking the means, therefore, to save all of the eighty-one crew and the passengers on board. After the ship went down, the master, every member of the crew, and the surviving thirty-three passengers in the two boats totaled fifty persons. Of the two auxiliary boats, the long boat commanded by the first mate carried eight seamen, including Alexander William Holmes, a Finnish crewman, and thirty-two passengers—forty-one persons in all. The jolly boat carried the master, the second mate, six seamen, and one passenger. Before the two boats lost contact, the master ordered the crew of the long boat to obey the first mate's orders as though they were his own. The overloaded long boat began to leak as soon as it was launched. The next day when a storm arose, the mate thought the overloaded and leaky boat was destined to sink. He ordered Holmes and other seamen to throw overboard all unmarried, adult, male passengers to lighten the boat. Sixteen passengers died. The next day the boat was sighted by a passing ship which rescued the remaining twenty-six persons.

In Philadelphia, Holmes was indicted for the crime of "manslaughter upon the high seas" for casting one of the sixteen passengers from the long boat. (Holmes was named in depositions made by two of the surviving passengers as one of the crew who had thrown passengers overboard. Three other members of the crew named in the depositions could not be found. A warrant for the arrest of the first mate was issued but not served.) This crime was punishable by the act of Congress of 1790, with imprisonment not exceeding three years, and by fine not exceeding $1,000. The jury found Holmes guilty as charged, but recommended mercy. Taking into account the fact that he had already been confined in jail for several months, the court sentenced him to six months' imprisonment with hard labor, a fine of $20, and the cost of prosecution.[32]

United States v. *Holmes* was a landmark case in that it sanctioned the legal proposition that a passenger on board a vessel may be thrown overboard to save the others. Stated another way, the seaman has a duty to protect all of the passengers' safety; but if he cannot save all, it is still his duty to save all that he can, even at the expense of the others. This legal proposition is a species of the doctrine of necessity sometimes invoked in defense arguments that hold that homicide sometimes may be excusable under the defense of necessity. The most frequent instance cited by advocates of the doctrine of necessity is that of two shipwrecked persons clinging to the same plank. Upon finding that it will not support both, one of them thrusts the other from it.[33]

There is nothing outrageous or even unfair about the adjudication of the *Drake* case in comparison with that of the *Holmes* case. On the contrary, one may argue that the *Drake* case was adjudicated more equitably and justly than was the *Holmes* case, for four reasons. In the first place, whereas Drake was indicted, tried, and convicted of manslaughter, Captain George L. Harris, master of the *Willaim Brown*, was not even indicted for deserting thirty-one passengers. The doctrine of necessity, of course, might have been employed to render the master's action excusable had he been tried and given a very lenient sentence. In that event, the defense would have been that he had sacrificed some passengers to save the others.

Second, whereas Drake fulfilled the legal duty to equip his ship with a sufficient number of lifeboats and life-preservers to save all aboard in any contingency, Harris failed to discharge his duty in that regard. One writer has commented: "I can't understand how a vessel authorized to carry passengers, and having only two boats and no rafts or life-preservers, could have been allowed to sail with eighty-two persons aboard. That alone was gross negligence amounting to a crime. Such a thing would not be permitted today."[34] Yet, Harris was never tried for this negligence.

Third, Drake was tried for an unintentional killing of twenty-five lives; Holmes was not even indicted for his part in throwing sixteen passengers overboard, an act committed with foreknowledge that that act would result in their death. Instead, he was held accountable for the death of only one of the sixteen. A grand jury declined to return an indictment for murder against Holmes, but subsequently accepted the bills of manslaughter drawn up by a federal attorney. The grand jury decided that he was guilty of manslaughter, but that he was not a murderer.[35] In this regard, what the grand jury did was tantamount to reducing Holmes' homicide from murder to voluntary manslaughter, as contrasted to involuntary manslaughter.

In English criminal law, it has often been the practice to divide the crime of manslaughter into (1) voluntary manslaughter, which makes up only those homicides that are reduced from murder to manslaughter owing to provocation, and (2) involuntary manslaughter, which comprises all other cases.[36] These two categories of manslaughter have traditionally been defined as follows:

Voluntary manslaughter is an intentional killing without malice. It occurs when the homicide is committed in sudden mutual combat and when committed in passion and hot blood induced by great provocation. Such provocation must result from acts and conduct of the deceased and is ineffective to reduce the homicide from murder to manslaughter if induced or sought for by the defendant. Both provocation and great passion must be present and must concur at the time of the homicide. If reasonable time for cooling and for the return of reasoned judgment elapses before the killing then it is murder.

Involuntary manslaughter is homicide unintentionally caused without malice, resulting from the commission of an unlawful act not amounting to a felony, or from negligence, or lack of caution, or absence of skill in the commission of a lawful act, or from failure to perform a legal duty.[37]

Murder has been defined as "the unlawful killing of one human being by another with malice aforethought." Malice aforethought is present "when there is an intention to cause death or grievous bodily harm, or knowledge that one's act will probably result, when committed, in the commission of a felony."[38]

Given these definitions, manslaughter by negligence, the offense of which Drake was convicted, is involuntary manslaughter. On the other hand, Holmes' act of throwing sixteen passengers overboard actually falls into the most serious of the three categories, murder. Since the sixteen gave no provocation, his offense in theory cannot be labeled voluntary manslaughter. But since he had perfect foreknowledge that his act of casting the passengers overboard would result in their death, malice aforethought was present in his act. Nevertheless, his homicide was reduced by the grand jury from murder to manslaughter, and thus became, in point of law, voluntary manslaughter, an offense more serious than involuntary manslaughter. From the viewpoint of retribution, therefore, Holmes deserved a heavier punishment than Drake. Stated another way, Drake deserved a penalty lighter than the one meted out to Holmes. This actually turned out to be the case, since Drake was sentenced to three months' imprisonment and Holmes to six months' imprisonment.

One might argue that Drake's negligence was more serious than Holmes' murderous act because Holmes was merely obeying the mate's order when throwing the sixteen passengers overboard. This argument would not constitute a defense, however. It had been the law of the land prior to 1841 that an inferior was liable for obeying an unlawful order given by a superior.[39]

Fourth, and finally, since the Japanese public imputed the drowning of the Japanese passengers to the racial prejudice of the Western crew of the *Normanton*, it should be noted that both the crew and the passengers of the *William Brown*, unlike those of the *Normanton*, were of the same race—Caucasion; not a single passenger was Oriental. Yet, the conduct of the crews of both vessels produced the same result: the desertion of passengers. This alone—quite apart from the testimonies given in the Yokohama Court to the contrary—casts serious doubts as to the validity of the Japanese opinion that racial prejudice underlay the *Normanton* tragedy. For one thing, while saving their own lives, the master and crew of the *William Brown* deserted the ship with the thirty-one Irish passengers on board. In other words, when facing the choice between their own lives and those of the passengers, the master and crew chose their own at the expense of the passengers. The choice stemmed from the instinct for human survival; it had nothing to do with color. For another, unlike the passengers of the *Normanton*, the thirty-one passengers left on board the *William Brown* struggled to save their lives, but to no avail. They begged the master to stay with them. When he finally got into the jolly boat and began to move away, came the voice: "Captain Harris, come back and get us! Captain Harris, come back, let us all die together."[40]

In response to the fourth reason discussed, one might argue that the crew of the *William Brown* abandoned the thirty-one Irish passengers on board the sinking ship because of their antipathy toward the Irish. (The five Scottish female passengers climbed into the long boat.) This argument assumes that during the hour of frantic excitement and dismay the crew managed to select which Irish passengers should get into the boats and which should remain aboard the sinking ship. The fact of the matter is that there was no selection. The boats filled indiscriminately. The frantic passengers and seamen alike jumped into, fell into, or clambered up into the boats.[41] Hence, the assumption is faulty; the argument is a fallacy.

It seems evident, then, that overall the adjudication of the *Drake* case was more equitable than that of the *Holmes* case.

What about the sentences of the two cases? There was not a great deal of difference between the two. If three months' imprisonment for manslaughter by negligence, a case of involuntary manslaughter, can be regarded as lenient, so can six months' imprisonment with a fine for a homicide reduced from murder to manslaughter.

Before entertaining the three questions raised at the outset of this chapter, it should be emphasized here that of the five publicized cases, the *Drake* case presented the greatest difficulty and uncertainty with respect to the evaluation of the sentence. The difficulty lies in the fact that what has been evaluated as to its fairness is something that cannot be readily measured as to fairness. It is even arduous to secure fair and just punishment for the crime of manslaughter on the high seas—a crime committed in response to the pressure of natural rather than human forces. As George E. Dix and M. Michael Sharlot point out, "the rule of positive law and their rationales, which normally operate quite satisfactorily, seem inadequate to deal with the harsh conflict between the urge for self preservation and our commitment to the sanctity of life."[42]

Conclusion

Do the accounts of the *Drake* case presented here tell both sides of the case? They do not. Like the accounts of the other publicized cases, they are plagued with errors of interpretation and fact. But, on the whole, together they present a fuller and more comprehensive picture of the case than do the accounts of any of the other cases evaluated in this book, primarily because translations of the minutes of the trial proceedings were published in Japan soon after the trial.[43]

Did the Yokohama Court render its decision in accordance with the law applicable? That law was the Offences Against the Person Act, 1861, Section 5 of which read as follows: "Whosoever shall be convicted of manslaughter shall be liable, at the discretion of the Court, to be kept in penal servitude for life or for any term not less than three years—or to be imprisoned for any term not exceeding two years, with or without hard labour, or to pay such fine as the Court shall award, in addition to or without any such other discretionary punishment as aforesaid."[44] Under this provision, the punishment imposed on Drake, however light it may seem, conformed to the law. In England, as in the United States, the approach to trial was objective, but the approach to sentencing was subjective. As a result, as already mentioned in Chapter 2, there was marked

Table 6
Total Number of Persons Committed or Bailed for Trial
at the Assizes and Quarter Sessions in England
and Wales for the Crime of Manslaughter, and the
Result of Proceedings, 1880-1886

Disposition	Number	Number/1,551
For trial	1,551	10.0%
Acquitted	813	52.4
Convicted	738	47.6

****
Acquitted

No prosecution	2
No bill found	130
Found or declared insane	3
Not guilty on trial	675
Acquitted as insane	3
Total	813

Convicted

Penal servitude	
Life	21
Over 15 years	41
15 years and over 10 years	29
10 years and over 7 years	40
7 years	40
3 to 6 years	37

"Imprisonment with,
in some cases, Whipping, fine &c. [etc.]"

Over 2 years	0
2 years and over 1 year	77
1 year and over 6 months	111
(The median sentence falls into this category.)	
6 months and over 3 months	120
3 months and over 1 month	78
1 month and over	106
Fined	43
Total	743

SOURCES: Computed from Great Britain, Parliament (Commons),
Parliamentary Papers, 1881, 95.105, Cmnd. 3088; 1882, 75.105,
Cmnd. 3333; 1883, 77.105, Cmnd. 3763; 1884, 86.105, Cmnd.
4170; 1884-1885, 86.105, Cmnd. 4518; 1886, 72.105, Cmnd.
4808; 1887, 90.109, Cmnd. 5155.

disparity in sentencing. One may, therefore, wonder how severely the English convicted of the crime of manslaughter were punished prior to adjudication of the *Drake* case. Table 6, based on *Judicial Statistics*, shows the number accused and the results of Britain's manslaughter cases in the 1880s.

From Table 6 one may readily calculate that the median sentence for manslaughter, the sentence designating the middle point of the series of 743 sentences (the 372nd sentence), falls in the category of one year and over six months; and that Drake's sentence, three months' imprisonment, was lighter than the median sentence. From this one may not, however, deduce that Drake's sentence was too lenient. To begin with, in sentencing for many crimes, as already mentioned, the English courts lawfully exercised wide discretionary powers with little concern for consistency; as a result, individuals committing like offenses often drew widely disparate sentences. Moreover, the kind of criminal statistics compiled and presented in the table was not available to judges in late nineteenth-century England, let alone to consul-judges in Japan. "Difference in sentencing between courts could not begin to be eliminated until detailed comparative information was made available," and efforts to compile this information have now begun in England.[45]

As for the third question, whether the outcome of the *Drake* case would have been harsher to the defendant if the plaintiff had been English rather than Japanese, there are no sufficient facts, evidence, or precedents to provide a satisfactory answer. One may recall that there have been no English cases similar to the *Drake* case and that there has been but one similar American case, the *Holmes* case. If one were to speculate on the basis of the sentence Holmes received, one would have no grounds to believe that Drake would have been punished far more severely if the complainant had been English rather than Japanese.

The preceding analysis leads to the conclusion that the *Drake* case does not support the interpretation that the Western consular courts in Japan as a rule did not render evenhanded justice.

5

In the Name of the Emperor: The *Chishima* Case (1893–1895)

From the standpoint of international law, *The Imperial Japanese Government v. The Peninsular and Oriental Steam Navigation Company* was the most complex of the five publicized cases with the most far-reaching ramifications. Nevertheless, only a few, most relevant legal issues are dealt with here. They are presented as simply as possible. Every effort is made to minimize legal jargon.

The first part of this chapter describes the collision between the British and Japanese vessels and Japanese reactions. The second part analyzes briefly the resultant long drawn-out court battles. The third part explains why in 1895 the Meiji government, after having litigated the case for over two years, elected to accept an out-of-court settlement. This apparently unsatisfactory compromise was, and still is, largely responsible for one of the most vociferous criticisms leveled against the *Chishima* case. The criticism contends that, since the Meiji government expended more on the litigation than it finally recovered from the Peninsular and Oriental Steam Navigation Company (the P & O), the out-of-court settlement was unfair. The fourth and final part answers the three questions raised in evaluating the adjudication of each of the other four major cases examined in this book.

The Chishima-Ravenna Collision

In November 1887 the Japanese government ordered the construction of the *Chishima*, a torpedo boat (*suirai hō kan*), in a French boatworks, for a cost of about £670,000. With a displacement tonnage of 750, the man-of-war measured seventy-one meters in length and was equipped with three masts, eleven torpedo-firing guns, and four torpedo-firing tubes. The boat was launched in November 1890 and embarked for Japan in April 1892. En route it encountered three severe storms between the Indian Ocean and Nagasaki, but weathered them all. Then at 4:58 A.M. on November 30, 1892, between Gogo and Mutsuki Islands off the present-day city of Matsushima, Ehime Prefecture, the *Chishima* collided with the *Ravenna*, a steamship owned by the P & O, a British firm. Split into two, the *Chishima* sank almost immediately, taking with her seventy-four of the ninety on board. The *Ravenna* sustained some damage, but no one died.[1]

The loss of the *Chishima* came as a real blow to the Japanese public, who felt its loss all the more keenly because another naval vessel built abroad had mysteriously disappeared recently prior to reaching Japan. At the time of the *Chishima* incident, the Japanese Navy had only thrity men-of-war on commission, not all of them seaworthy. Even as of March 1894, shortly before the First Sino-Japanese War, the fleet included only thirty-two men-of-war on commission. At the time, Japanese naval architecture was not yet advanced enough to undertake the construction of warships in Japanese shipyards. In early December 1892, Aoyama Hogaru, a member of the House of Representatives, the Shūgiin, expressed the general feeling of the Japanese public when he said on the floor: "By what means did we have these two vessels [the *Chishima* and the other warship] built? Of course, the people's—we first sucked the lifeblood of our forty million fellow countrymen and then had these warships built."[2]

After the *Chishima* disaster, many asked whether the naval vessel had been insured. No vessels of the Imperial Japanese Navy were insured. Since the *Chishima* had been turned over to the Navy in France and was manned by Japanese naval officers and sailors, it was not insured for its homeward voyage. Undoubtedly, the loss of the *Chishima* was not only a strain on the national budget but also a severe blow to the pride and honor of the Imperial Japanese Navy. The headline of a newspaper report on the collision read: "Alas! Warship Sunk by Merchant Ship." Even four years later, Representative Moriya Konosuke bitterly remarked before the Shūgiin:

A warship of a nation sank following a collision with a merchant ship of another, and one nation had to sue the other for damages at the latter's court. This, as many people have pointed out, is like a samurai who, having been struck by an ordinary townsman in the middle of a road, then begs of him some money for plaster. What an awful shame![3]

After the collision a number of inquiries were immediately launched to determine the cause of the accident, the most important of which was the naval court-martial to determine if there was any negligence on the part of Lieutenant (*taii*) Kaburagi Makoto, acting commander of the *Chishima*. On January 25, 1893, the following verdict was announced: "Commander Kaburagi adopted all precautions necessary to secure the safety of the *Chishima kan* and . . . no act of negligence has been proved against him. He is, therefore, acquitted of all blame and released."[4]

Moreover, the Japanese District Court at Nagasaki tried Kitano Yohibei, the Japanese pilot in charge of the pilotage of the *Ravenna* at the time of the collision, on a charge of "involuntary homicide and wounding." On February 24, 1893, the Court found him guilty as charged—guilt arising from error in the steering of the *Ravenna*—and sentenced him to a fine of $200 under Article 317 of the 1880 Penal Code. This finding of fault resembled that of a British court of inquiry that had the *Ravenna* engines been instantly stopped and reversed when the catastrophe was imminent, the effect of the collision might have been modified.[5]

It was only a short step from these verdicts to the inference that, since the *Chishima* was not to blame for the collision, then the total blame lay with the *Ravenna*. This inference led to Japan's decision to commence an action against the P & O.

The Japanese press had jumped to this same all-or-nothing conclusion even before the verdict of the court-martial was announced. For the next three years, this view of the case remained the intellectual framework within which the Japanese evaluated all information about the proceedings of the *Chishima* case.[6]

The Imperial Japanese Government v. The Peninsular and Oriental Steam Navigation Company

After failing in an attempt to arrange for an out-of-court settlement,[7] the Imperial Japanese government on May 6, 1893, brought an action against the P & O for damages at Her Britannic Majesty's Court for Japan in Admiralty at Kanagawa. (Hereafter this court will be referred to as the Yokohama Court.) The petition filed by the plaintiff, the Japanese government, alleged that the collision was due to the default and negligence of the crew on board the *Ravenna*, that no fault could be attached to any one on board the *Chishima*, and that the damage occasioned to the plaintiff was $850,000.

The defendant, the P & O, in its answer alleged that the blame for the collision had to be put solely on the crew of the *Chishima*, that no blame was attributable to the *Ravenna*, and that they had sustained damage due to the collision amounting to $100,000.[8]

Counsel for the British defendant was J. F. Lowder, who had previously represented the Japanese plaintiffs in the *Hartley* and the *Drake* cases. A. B. Walford, another British barrister, represented the Japanese plaintiff. It was, however, Montague Kirkwood, an experienced British lawyer who had long practiced in the Yokohama area and while serving as an adviser to the Japanese Ministry of Justice, who was entrusted with the task of overseeing the entire litigation on behalf of the Japanese government.[9]

By and large, the *Chishima* case owed its extraordinary character to two issues raised by the case. One was the fact that the Japanese government was forced to litigate in the name of the Emperor. The other issue, which was resolved only at the end of the case, was the legal question of whether a counterclaim against a Japanese plaintiff could be filed in a British consular court. Both of these issues require amplification before proceeding to an examination of the case.

The *Chishima* case was probably the only action in the entire annals of the foreign consular courts in Japan in which the Emperor actually became a plaintiff. The reason why he was named the plaintiff is tied to a legal principle known as the master-servant doctrine. This doctrine states that under the law a master is held responsible for any wrong committed by his servant within the scope of his employment.[10] A crucial issue was whether this doctrine was applicable to the Emperor of Japan as the owner of the *Chishima*. The formal theory of sovereignty—that is, the state is superior to and creates law—held that a suit against a sovereign was a contradiction in terms. In England as in Japan, the maxim "the King can do no wrong" was thought to provide a practical bar to a suit against the Crown.[11]

The second issue, that of counterclaim, was related to the nature of British consular jurisdiction in Japan. From the standpoint of international law, the right to establish British consular courts in Japan was granted by the Emperor through the 1858 treaty between Japan and Great Britain. In turn, the authority of the courts thus established was derived from the Foreign Jurisdiction Acts (1843–1890) and the Orders in Council passed to execute these acts.[12] In other words, the acts and the orders prescribed how consular jurisdiction was to be exercised, but it was the treaty which defined the boundaries of that jurisdiction.

Furthermore, both the British consular courts in Japan and the territorial courts of Japan had exclusive jurisdiction. The principle was that each defendant, whether Westerner or Japanese, was entitled to be tried in the court of his or her own nationality. This stipulation was most precisely stated in the 1869 treaty between Austria-Hungary and Japan, a treaty that was more comprehensive in coverage and more exact in wording than any other unequal treaty Japan concluded with the Western powers. Article 5 read in part as follows: "If an Austro-Hungarian citizen has a complaint or grievance against a Japanese subject, the case shall be decided by the Japanese authorities. If, on the contrary, a Japanese has a complaint or grievance against a citizen of the said monarchy, the case shall be decided by the Japanese authorities. If, on the contrary, a Japanese has a complaint or grievance against a citizen of the said monarchy, the case shall be decided by the Imperial and Royal authorities." Since the British treaty of 1858 accorded most-favored-nation treatment to Great Britain, the provision quoted from the treaty with Austria-Hungary applied to all British subjects as well, with the result that British defendants were tried in British consular courts and Japanese defendants in Japanese courts.[13]

On the issue of counterclaim, the Japanese government maintained that a Western consular court could not entertain a counterclaim against a Japanese without a violation of the existing treaties. In an 1879 mixed case, a Japanese court did not allow the Japanese defendant's counterclaim against the American plaintiff on the ground that the American court alone had jurisdiction in a complaint against an American. The issue of counterclaim arose in 1891 when the French consular court at Yokohama acknowledged a French defendant's demand for a cross-action against the Japanese plaintiff. Considerable correspondence ensued between the Japanese government and the French, the Japanese denying and the French affirming the rights of the French court to entertain a counterclaim against a Japanese. The issue remained unresolved when the *Chishima* case arose.

In his dispatch to the foreign secretary, the Earl of Rosebery, dated July 1, 1893, Maurice William Ernest de Bunsen, of the British legation at Tokyo, later to become a prominent diplomat, stated that the German and the Dutch legations took the same view on this subject as the French, but that the Americans upheld the Japanese.

De Bunsen went on to say:

It appears to have been the custom of the British Courts not to entertain counterclaims against Japanese for fear that the Japanese would entertain counterclaims against British plaintiffs; and in a case in which the British Court did entertain such a counterclaim the decision given was in favor of the Japanese plaintiff, and the question [of counterclaim] was not raised.[14]

But the *Chishima* case raised the question, and British judicial authorities had to deal with it.

Before returning to analysis of the court battles, one final item of explanation concerns the term "appearance," a coming into court as a party to a suit, in person or by attorney. Appearance may be either general or special. A general appearance is an unqualified or unrestricted submission to the jurisdiction of the court. A special appearance is a submission to the court for some specific purpose only, not for the purposes of the entire suit.[15]

Despite the formal name of the case, *The Imperial Japanese Government* v. *The Peninsular and Oriental Steam Navigation Company*, to all intents and purposes, this case was converted into "The Emperor of Japan v. The Peninsular and Oriental Steam Navigation Company" on May 25, the first sitting day of the trial of the case. On that day the defendant moved for a demurrer for dismissal of the case on the ground that "an unknown and undefined body such as the Imperial Japanese Government cannot sue in this Court by name." He argued further that the *Chishima*, being a public vessel of the state of Japan, was owned by the sovereign, the Mikado, and that the Court should recognize this fact. What the defendant had in mind was to effect the amendment of the petition by substituting the name of the actual plaintiff, so that the master-servant doctrine might be utilized to the advantage of the defendant. In an answer to this motion, an affidavit was filed and a guarantee given that "the actual plaintiff [the Emperor] is suing, but elects to sue under the name of the Imperial Japanese Government." Satisfied with this guarantee, the defendant withdrew the motion. Henceforth, the case was so treated by all of the three courts involved, as well as by the litigants themselves.

Considered in retrospect, what the plaintiff did in response to the motion for demurrer was a critical move, for the motion could have resulted in putting an end to the case. Demurrer, now a defunct procedure in common law, was "an objection made by one party to his opponent's pleading, alleging that he ought not to answer it, for some defect in law in the pleading." Once having demurred, the objecting party would not proceed, but would await the judgment of the court as to whether he was bound to proceed.[16] What the P & O was objecting to was that the other party failed to state the actual plaintiff, the Emperor of Japan. Had the plaintiff failed to meet the demurrer in the way he did, and had the Yokohama Court sustained the demurrer, the case would have been thrown out of court and could never again have been instituted. Hence, all chances of ever recovering damages by the plaintiff would have been lost. Thus viewed, it must be said that the plaintiff had taken a prudent step by recognizing that the actual plaintiff was the Emperor, while maintaining the fiction that the nominal plaintiff was the Imperial Japanese government. However, the Japanese public did not comprehend this when they learned of the use of the Emperor's name, perhaps because they knew nothing about the legal intricacy and implication of the motion for demurrer.

On June 6 the case took a new turn when the defendant made another motion, this one asking the Court for (1) leave to file a counterclaim for the recovery of $100,000 in damages from the plaintiff, (2) an order that the suit and the counterclaim should be heard together, and (3) an order that the plaintiff should be required to give a security to abide by and perform any decision of the Court on the counterclaim. Since these two orders depended on the prior granting of leave for a counterclaim, the defendant's whole motion boiled down to one issue, the very issue for which the *Chishima* case became a *cause célèbre*: "May the British consular court entertain a counterclaim by a British defendant against a Japanese plaintiff?"

The defendant, the P & O, eager to have the Court hear its counterclaim as part of the action brought by the plaintiff, not as a separate cross-action brought by the defendant, was in essence insisting that the plaintiff, the Emperor of Japan, made a general appearance, as opposed to a special appearance, when he brought the action against the defendant and must, therefore, abide by all the decisions of the British court on the claims of both parties arising out of the collision. The plaintiff, on the other hand, insisted that his appearance was special, that is, only for the purpose of having the Court decide on his claim and not the claim of the other party. The plaintiff further argued that the treaties from which the jurisdiction of the British consular courts was wholly derived empowered the courts to determine the claims of Japanese subjects only, not the claims of British subjects. Cognizance of British claims was reserved exclusively to the territorial courts of Japan.

The difference between the above positions lay in the question of whether

the Emperor of Japan waived his dignity when he submitted himself to the jurisdiction of the Yokohama Court. The plaintiff took the view that even when
the Emperor recognized the competence of that court he was still a sovereign,
and, therefore, the principle "the King can do no wrong" still applied. But the
defendant disagreed, saying that, while he admitted the validity of the principle
cited, it was a very different thing indeed when the sovereign

divested himself of the dignity of his Crown and descended to place himself in the position of a suitor in a foreign court. . . . When he became a plaintiff he dropped his
dignity as Sovereign and had to take the humble position of a suitor in the courts, and
he could ask nothing more than a suitor in our [the British] Courts could ask.[17]

The court battle between the two parties was waged on another front—the
law applicable. The plaintiff maintained that, even if the Emperor were to submit himself generally to the jurisdiction of the Court, there could still be no
remedy for a counterclaim there. Since the collision unquestionably took place
within the Japanese domain, Japanese law applied, and by that law the Emperor was not liable for the negligence of his servants. Hence, argued the plaintiff, in a counterclaim the defendant should sue the wrongdoer—the master,
officers, or any crew member of the *Chishima*. By sharp contrast, the defendant
claimed that the place of the collision was undoubtedly of the high seas where
maritime law applied and that under that law the owner of a vessel doing damage to another was liable for the negligence of his servants.

The response of the Yokohama Court to the move to file a counterclaim was
not long in coming. On June 29, 1893, the Court refused to grant the permission on the ground that the collision had occurred within the three-mile limit
of the Japanese coast; that, accordingly, the law of Japan was applicable to the
collision; and that, as by that law the Emperor of Japan was not liable for the
negligent acts of his servants, he could not be sued in a British consular court
for damages resulting from the collision.

In applying Japanese law to its judgment, the Court relied on the expert testimony of Hozumi Nobushige, chief professor (*kyōtō*) of the College of Law,
Imperial University (now Tokyo University), who had been called to the English bar in 1879. He was to remain important to the case in the months that
followed. At this point he testified: "According to Japanese law the Emperor of
Japan can do no wrong. His Majesty is sacred and inviolable. He cannot be
sued in person or by representation for damages for any misconduct or negligence of an official in his service, whether in the discharge of such official's
duties or otherwise."[18]

The P & O took exception to the decision of the Yokohama Court and filed
an immediate appeal. To Japan's chagrin, Her Britannic Majesty's Supreme Court
for China and Japan at Shanghai in October 1893 reversed the decision of the
lower court, and issued the orders sought by the defendant. The Supreme Court
based its decision on the following grounds. First, the Court's Rules of Proce-

dure and the Orders in Council justified an order giving leave to file the counterclaim, and those rules and orders did not exceed the provisions of the treaties between Great Britain and Japan. Second, the respondent, the Emperor of Japan, having originally invoked the jurisdiction of the Yokohama Court, submitted himself generally to its jurisdiction. Since the counterclaim arose out of the same transaction as did the action, complete justice could not be done unless the Court could deal with the mutual claims of the parties against each other. Third, the collision did not occur within the limits of the Japanese Empire, but on the high seas, where the Courts of Admiralty had jurisdiction and maritime law applied.

With respect to the last of the three reasons cited, the Supreme Court asserted, in an obvious reference to the Shimonoseki Bombardment of 1864:

The place of collision was undoubtedly upon the highway of nations. We know that at the present time almost every mail steamer going from China to the western side of the Continent of America passes the spot where the collision took place, and we know as a matter of history that when the entrance to the Inland Sea was stopped the right to enter and pass through it was asserted by force of arms by England, France, Holland, and America, and such right was admitted by the Government of Japan.[19]

The assertion of the Supreme Court that the Inland Sea was "the highway of nations" drew immediate and sharp reaction. Newspapers deplored the Court's position, lawyers met to discuss and debate the question, and meetings were held to denounce the claim.[20] In addition, the Japanese government itself, which had declared a good many times that the Inland Sea was part of the Japanese domain, quickly responded. On November 13, 1893, through the British legation in Tokyo, the government sent to the Court of St. James a new declaration that, although the vessels of all friendly nations were permitted to ply the Inland Sea freely, the Imperial Japanese government took exception to the view that the Inland Sea was "the highway of nations," and that the sea, being land-locked by the territories of Japan, constituted an integral part of the territorial waters of the Japanese Empire.[21] It would seem from the viewpoint of today that the Supreme Court's position was a reflection of nineteenth-century imperialism.

The most vociferous of all public criticisms that arose in response to the Supreme Court decision was the use of the Emperor's name. The reason why this became such an issue at this time rather than immediately after the rendering of the Yokohama Court decision was probably that, since this decision was in favor of the plaintiff, no Japanese paid much attention to the Court's records which clearly indicated that the Emperor was the actual plaintiff. The public was convinced that the name of the Emperor had been shamed and the honor of the Empire impaired. The political opposition in the Fifth Diet was quick to exploit this cry politically and, as a result, helped intensify the criticism. The secretive conduct of the government also contributed to the agitation. The government neither acknowledged the fact that the Emperor had become the plaintiff nor explained to the public why it had been forced to acquiesce in this in order to carry on the litigation.[22]

This government policy of secrecy has had a far-reaching impact on the historiography of the *Chishima* case, for some historians would not believe that the Emperor was ever a party to the action. For instance, Osatake Takeshi, the great judge-historian, took for granted that the report that the Emperor was the suitor was just a "rumor." To quiet the public indignation over the report, the government had announced that, although the Emperor had been referred to as sovereign or the head of state in the trials, he had never been regarded as the suitor. Osatake took this prevarication at face value.[23] Evidently, Hanabusa Nagamichi accepted Osatake's erroneous conclusion; he, too, has written that the use of the name of the Emperor as plaintiff was "contrary to fact" (*jijitsu sōi*).[24]

For all its intensity and unfortunate consequences, this particular criticism, that the name of the Emperor was shamed, had nothing to do with the question of whether or not the actions of the Court were fair. But the issue did stir up new resentments against the whole regime of extraterritoriality, which the public felt was to blame for the disgrace of having the Emperor named a party to a lawsuit.[25]

On November 15, 1893, in order to map out Tokyo's next move following the Supreme Court decision, Minister of the Navy Saigō Tsugumichi appointed a six-man Committee for the Examination of the Chishima Collision Case. The guiding spirit of the committee was Hozumi Nobushige, the lawyer mentioned earlier who had given testimony to the Yokohama Court concerning Japanese law. By this time he was dean of the College of Law at Imperial University. The committee studied the case and on December 2 recommended to Saigō: (1) that an appeal be made to the Privy Council in London; (2) that the British lawyers to be retained be ordered to plead only in the name of the Imperial Japanese government, the plaintiff so designated in the petition, and to refrain from referring to His Majesty; and (3) that in the event that Tokyo lost the suit, Tokyo be prepared to convert it into a diplomatic issue, first withdrawing the original action and announcing that Tokyo would not abide by the decision of the Privy Council. If negotiations between the two countries were to fail to yield an amicable understanding, the committee further recommended, Tokyo should be resolved to resort to international arbitration.[26]

Another important recommendation made by the committee was that Montague Kirkwood, who was responsible for the compromise that saw the substitution of the Emperor as the actual plaintiff, be relieved of his duties as the lawyer in charge of the litigation. The committee made this recommendation both because it blamed Kirkwood for conducting the litigation in the name of the Emperor and because it disapproved of his uncompromising stand on the issue of sovereign immunity, that is, whether the maxim "the King can do no wrong" applied to the Emperor of Japan in the British consular court.

The committee considered that the litigation in the name of the Emperor had contravened Article 14 of the Code of Civil Procedure and Imperial Ordinance No. 3 of 1891 passed in pursuance of that article. Under these statutory provisions, the plaintiff should have been the minister of the Navy or a subordinate designated by him. The committee felt strongly that, although it was too late to designate a minister of state as plaintiff, His Majesty's name must not be permitted to be heard in any further proceedings.[27]

Moreover, in the committee's opinion, Kirkwood's unyielding stand on sovereign immunity might prove unacceptable during the forthcoming trial in the Privy Council. During his appearance before the committee, Kirkwood had argued that the Emperor of Japan had delegated the jurisdiction of the Yokohama Court and that, like the queen of England, the Emperor could not be sued in that court. This argument had already been rebutted by the Yokohama Court and by the P & O at the Shanghai trial. It would seem that the committee disagreed with Kirkwood in this and other arguments because it was afraid that his point of view would not be well received by the Privy Council. Furthermore, given his stand on sovereign immunity, the committee judged that, however he might try, it would be impossible for him to direct the litigation in such a way as strictly to avoid the mention of the Emperor as plaintiff. Hence, the committee recommended that a Japanese be selected to take charge and proceed to London. (The Japanese sent was Okamura Teruhiko, a practitioner in maritime law. Trained in England along with Hozumi, he had assisted Kirkwood in directing the litigation.)[28] The irony of this whole affair was that, even though the committee's recommendation for the selection of a Japanese was made in an attempt to keep the name of the Emperor out of the courtroom, the trial in the Privy Council proceeded as before when the Privy Council chose to identify the Emperor as plaintiff.

On July 3, 1895, almost two years after the decision by the Shanghai Court, the Judicial Committee of the Privy Council—the court of ultimate resort for all British consular courts, as well as all courts in the British colonies—reversed the order of the Shanghai Court, restored the order of the Yokohama Court, and further ordered the respondent, the P & O, to pay the court costs in both the Privy Council and the Shanghai Court suits.

Behind this decision lay a desire to maintain the basic tenet of British consular jurisdiction in Japan—the British subject's immunity from proceedings in the territorial courts of Japan. If British consular courts were permitted to hear counterclaims against Japanese subjects, it should follow that Japanese courts were entitled to entertain counterclaims against British subjects as well. The result would be to render British subjects amenable to the jurisdiction of the courts of Japan and thereby deprive the British of the privileges granted by the existing treaties. Consequently, it was held that it would be beyond the jurisdiction of the British consular court to entertain a British defendant's claim against a Japanese plaintiff; therefore, the counterclaim at issue could not be entertained.

The issue of counterclaim thus disposed of, the way was cleared for the original action to be adjudicated at the Yokohama Court. What followed came as an anticlimax. In early September 1895, before the hearing got under way, the P & O asked the British Foreign Office to mediate an out-of-court settlement with a payment to Japan of £10,000, and the Foreign Office succeeded in doing so. As a result, the plaintiff received from the defendant £10,000, or ¥91,866, plus the counterclaim costs of ¥12,176, in full satisfaction of all its claims. The aggregate of the litigation expenses incurred by Tokyo stood at ¥124,378, and, therefore, exceeded the amount of recovery. On September 19 the case was officially withdrawn from the Court.[29]

Evaluation of the Settlement

So much for the *Chishima* case itself. Of all the outcries raised in connection with the *Chishima* case, by both the contemporary public and later historians, there is only one criticism germane to our inquiry: that, since Tokyo had to expend more on the litigation than it finally recovered from the P & O, the out-of-court settlement was unfair. Let us now turn to an evaluation of this criticism to find out to what extent it bears out the view that somehow the case mirrored the basic injustice of the decisions rendered by the consular courts in Japan.

The sense of puzzlement and disappointment over the final outcome of the *Chishima* case was poignantly felt by many contemporaries. On February 6, 1896, in the Ninth Diet, for example, Representative Moriya Konosuke raised the following question: "Our claim was ¥800,000. Why did we settle for such a small sum as ¥90,000. If the cause of the action was just, why did we not take all necessary measures to realize the claim and thus recover the damages? If, on the other hand, the cause was not just, why did we not abandon the claim and thus maintain the honor of our Empire?"[30]

On March 9 Minister of the Navy Saigō, on behalf of the government, supplied the Shūgiin with a written reply to Moriya's questions. He stated that, if Tokyo had declined to accept the compromise, the P & O would have defended itself to the best of its ability and, consequently, that the outcome might not have been what the public had expected it to be. He further stated that it would have required an enormous outlay of sums for Tokyo to have continued the litigation and that, even if Tokyo had won the case, the damages to be recovered would have been too small to justify continuing the litigation. He then explained that a provision of the British Merchant Shipping Act (*Eikoku kaisen jōrei*) stipulated £8 to be the maximum liability of shipowners for every ton of their ship's gross tonnage. Since the *Ravenna* had a gross tonnage of 3,265 tons, even in the event that Tokyo had won the case, if the courts had decided that "the amount of damages should be governed by this provision of the Merchant Shipping Act," Tokyo would have recovered no more than £26,048 (£8 × 3,256 tons).[31]

The statute referred to by Naval Minister Saigō was the Merchant Shipping

Act of 1894, which went into effect on January 1, 1895.[32] Both the cause of action and the trial had occurred before the 1894 act went into effect. Therefore, the crucial question to be raised here was whether or not the £8-per-ton provision applied retroactively to the *Chishima* case. To answer this question, one should bear in mind three developments in English legal history. One is that by the midnineteenth century the English courts were beginning to make a distinction between (1) matters of substantive rights and obligations and (2) matters of procedure, with respect to retrospective effect. Since then, it has been the firmly established law of England that, as long as they do not deprive the parties of their rights, alterations in matters of procedure are retrospective; alterations in matters of substantive rights are *not*.[33] A second development is that until 1972 there had been no case in which an English court pointedly decided into which category, substantive law or procedure, alterations in the mode of assessing damages fell.;[34] In that year the Court of Appeal in England held that the measure of damages affects substantive rights. By virtue of this decision, the measure of damages is now regarded as a matter of substantive law and not of procedure.[35] The third development is that in a number of cases over the years the English courts have ruled that provisions introducing new remedies—a remedy being a legal mode for enforcing a right or redressing or preventing a wrong—are procedural in character with regard to retrospectivity. But in 1895 there had been only one case which 'delivered a decision of this sort.[36]

Until 1895, therefore, no cases had provided any answer to the question of whether the measure of damages was a matter of substantive rights or procedure. Hence, all that could have been done in 1895 was to ask whether or not the measure of damages was a remedial matter affecting no substantive rights and, if so, to predict that in the future an English court might very well pronounce the measure of damages as a matter of procedure. It appears that this was precisely what both the Meiji government and the P & O did. Once the £8-per-ton provision was accepted as a matter of procedure, it followed that the provision was retrospective and hence applied to the *Chishima* case.

It would seem therefore that in March 1896 Naval Minister Saigō was telling the Shūgiin the truth about the main reason why the Meiji government had opted for the compromise rather than for continued litigation. That reason was a matter of simple arithmetic—the cost of litigation might have exceeded the amount of damages which could have been awarded to Japan.

The evidence available enables us to reconstruct the calculations made by Tokyo which influenced the government to accept the compromise. As background, it is necessary both to enumerate all possible outcomes of the case and to explain two notions: (1) the mode of recovery under the equal division rule; and (2) the limitation of the liability of shipowners.

In the event of a maritime collision between two or more vessels, where the blame lay on both sides, the English Courts of Admiralty at that time followed a rule, known as *judicium resticum*, which required an equal division of loss.

Consequently, if Ship A sustained damage worth $850,000 and Ship B $100,000, Ship A would recover $375,000 from Ship B, being one-half of the difference. Substituting the *Chishima* and the *Ravenna* for Ship A and Ship B, respectively, the recovery under the equal division rule may be illustrated as follows:[37]

```
Assumed facts

   The Chishima held one-half to blame--damage      $850,000
   The Ravenna held one-half to blame--damage        100,000

Recovery
   The Chishima would recover from the Ravenna
      one-half of $850,000                          $425,000
   The Chishima would have to pay the Ravenna
      one-half of $100,000                          -50,000(38)

   The Chishima's net recovery                      $375,000
```

The statutory limitation of the liability of shipowners stems from a public policy calculated to encourage the expansion of the merchant marine. This legal protection enables the shipowner to limit any liability that might be incurred by the crew during the performance of their duty. To entitle him to such protection, marine accidents must have taken place without "his actual fault or privity." The fault of the owner may take two forms: "the direct form of supplying a fault system of working or deficient equipment, or the indirect form of failing to instruct those who have to use the equipment, or see that they are instructed in the proper method of using it."[39]

The 1894 Merchant Shipping Act, the statute referred to by Naval Minister Saigō, was generous in that it allowed the shipowner to limit his liability to £8 for each ton of the gross tonnage of his ship, when the ship caused loss of or damage to another vessel. This was the amount regardless of whether or not there was, in addition, loss of life or personal injury, provided the liability was incurred without his actual fault.[40] By way of example, consider the mode of recovery illustrated earlier. It may be recalled that the *Chishima's* net recovery, $375,000, was contingent upon the eventuality that the crew of both ships would be found to blame. Suppose, for its part, the P & O had allowed the *Ravenna* to put out to sea despite the fact that it had a defective hull, and suppose the collision had been due in part to this defect. It could then have been said that the P & O was partly to blame for the collision. Therefore, the company would not have been able to limit its liability and would have had to pay Tokyo $375,000. On the other hand, suppose the P & O had been able to prove that the defective hull did not contribute to the collision. Then the Court would likely adjudge that the collision took place without the P & O's actual fault. In that case, the P & O would have been able to limit its liability under the £8-per-ton provision and pay Tokyo only £26,048, or $123,233.

Table 7 illustrates all the possible outcomes of the *Chishima* case under the

Table 7
Possible Outcomes of Chishima Case

Case	Chishima Negligence of Crew	Chishima Fault of Owner	Ravenna Negligence of Crew	Ravenna Fault of Owner	Recovery by Chishima	Recovery by Ravenna
1			x	x	$850,000	
2	x		x	x	375,000	
3	x	x	x	x	375,000	
4	x		x		123,233(a)	
5	x	x	x		123,233	
6			x		123,233	
7	x					$100,000 w/limitation(b)
8	x	x				100,000

(a)This amount is arrived at by taking a pound as equivalent to $4.37. See note 45.

(b)In Case 7, the amount of recovery would be either $100,000 or the amount to be determined by multiplying £8 by the "gross tonnage" of the Chishima, whichever was smaller. This gross tonnage was not only unknown; it was also unknowable as the naval vessel was (and still is) measured by displacement tonnage, not by gross. Hence, if the Chishima had been found entirely to blame, the search for the "gross tonnage" of the Chishima would have enhanced the drama of the courtroom battle.

hypothetical application of the 1894 Merchant Shipping Act.[41] Cases 2 and 4 correspond to the two examples given in the preceding paragraph. Since Tokyo considered that neither party would be adjudged entirely at fault, it appears that it did not take into account Case 1, 7, or 8, weighing only the remaining five cases. In Case 2 or 3, a collision occurring with the P & O at fault, Tokyo could have recovered $375,000 plus interest. On the other hand, in Case 4, 5, or 6, examples of collisions without the P & O at fault, Tokyo could have recovered only $123,233, plus interest.

When in August 1895 London broached the subject of the compromise, Tokyo's crucial question was, "Will it be possible for the P & O to prove that the collision took place without its actual fault or privity?" Saigō repeated this very question in his reply to the Shūgiin of March 1896 that, even in the event that Tokyo had won the case, if the courts had decided that "the amount of damages should be governed by this [the £8-per-ton] provision of the Merchant Shipping Act," Tokyo could recover no more than £26,048. One more piece of evidence that Tokyo considered the question to be crucial will be adduced here. Upon learning through London of the P & O's interest in a compromise, Saigō sent a telegram proposing £25,000 as settlement, and he instructed Katō Takaaki, the Japanese minister at the Court of St. James, to lower this amount to £20,000 if the P & O found the £25,000 amount unacceptable. Saigō insisted that the "English statute limiting liability of British ship-owners to £8 sterling per ton of gross tonnage should apply to their case, and consequently contend that £26,048 sterling plus interest is the full sum they would have to pay even in the event of their losing the case."[42]

If the original action had been litigated, both parties would most likely have been adjudged to be partly at fault. This might-have-been rests on the evidence that all those involved—the plaintiff, the defendant, the Yokohama Court, and the Privy Council—saw no prospects of either party being found exclusively to blame. Tokyo accepted the compromise precisely because it saw no chance of obtaining a judgment exonerating its side.[43] Likewise, the P & O did not believe it could completely defeat Tokyo's claim either. A letter of September 4, 1895, which the secretary of the P & O addressed to Foreign Secretary Salisbury, contains the following statement: "If the case had proceeded, [in the opinion of the Board of Directors] it would in all probability not have been brought to a termination for another two years and the issue [*sic*, outcome] would have been little satisfactory to either side."[44] Moreover, the judge of the Yokohama Court twice expressed the opinion that both parties would be found at fault when adjudged, even mentioning once that Tokyo's recovery would likely be $375,000. Finally, the Privy Council devoted the last part of its judgment in the *Chishima* case—rendered after the commencement of the Merchant Shipping Act of 1894—to detailing how the equal division rule might apply to the case in the event both parties were found to blame. It is, therefore, clear that the Imperial Japanese government knew in 1895 that, had the original action been litigated, both parties would most likely have been found at fault.

Undoubtedly, Tokyo thought there could be one of two possible outcomes in such a mutual-fault case: (1) it might recover $375,000 if the P & O should either not attempt or attempt unsuccessfully to prove that the collision took place without the actual fault of the P & O, or (2) it might recover only $123,233 if the P & O should prove that the shipowners themselves were not at fault.

The Board of Directors of the P & O, as already noted, surmised that if the case had proceeded it would have lasted another two years. Given the fact that the plaintiff's expenditure on the litigation for the period from May 1893 through August 1895 had been slightly less than $62,000,[45] another two years of litigation might have cost the plaintiff an additional $60,000. Assuming that the annual interest accruable to damages was a simple 5 percent, the interest on $375,000 for four years would have been $75,000, with the interest on $123,233 for the same period $24,647. Hence, Tokyo probably estimated that, after subtracting an estimated four-year litigation expenditure of $122,000, the plaintiff could have retained approximately $328,000 in one case, or about $25,880 in the other. The $328,000 figure was not a small sum in itself, representing almost three times as much as the estimated expenditure on the litigation. But the $25,880 total was insignificant especially if, in order to get this inconsequential sum, Tokyo were forced to spend almost five times that amount to pay for the litigation. No wonder then that it was this smaller of the two possible recoveries which concerned Tokyo. Obviously, the amount was not worth the trouble. Precisely because of this possibility, Tokyo decided not to proceed with the original action and accepted the compromise.

Looking back to the year 1895, one may find that certain conditions reinforced Tokyo's reluctance to face this costly outcome. First, from the very outset of the *Chishima* incident, the Japanese government and the public alike were deeply committed to an all-or-nothing stand, that is, the entire blame for the collision lay with the *Ravenna*, with no fault attributable to the *Chishima*.[46] Because of this long-standing commitment, Tokyo probably found itself unwilling to face the probability of carrying on the litigation in a "lowly" British court only in the end to share the blame with the defendant, a foreign commercial firm. Undoubtedly, Tokyo anticipated that such a probability would be quite demeaning. Proof of this is that, since the P & O initiated the negotiations for the compromise, both the Japanese government and the public believed that the fact somehow vindicated their belief and demonstrated that the blame for the collision lay with the *Ravenna*.[47] In short, the probability of the suit turning out to be a mutual-fault case was alarming enough, but even more disturbing was the possibility of receiving a net recovery that was only slightly more than one-fifth of the total costs of litigation.

Second, after the First Sino-Japanese War, Tokyo seems to have placed a high value on the goodwill of the mediator, the London government, as evidenced by the recommendation that Katō, the Japanese minister to London, made to Tokyo concerning the P & O offer of £10,000. He argued that, quite apart from the factors of money, time, and waste of energy, Tokyo should consider the consequences that might result from its failure to reach a compromise with the P & O. Since the defendant was a leading English firm with considerable interests in the Orient, claimed Katō, continued litigation against the firm would likely unfavorably affect Anglo-Japanese relations.[48] At that time, one vital area of Japanese concern for relations between the two countries was the revision of the unequal treaties. On July 16, 1894, London and Tokyo had signed a new treaty intended to supersede the existing unequal treaty in 1899 or thereabouts, and the other Western treaty powers were following Great Britain's lead. Consequently, in 1895 the completion of treaty revision was still four years away; Japan could not afford to strain its relations with Great Britain, the foremost treaty power. Besides, the fact that Japan was starting to order battleships from British yards at this time may have made the Ministry of the Navy all the more anxious not to reject the compromise, the fruit of London's mediation efforts.

Third, and finally, Japan wanted to dispose of the *Chishima* case. In addition to the acquisition of Formosa and the Pescadores Islands, Japan had just made large profits on the First Sino-Japanese War. In early June 1895, Naval Minister Saigō ordered Vice Admiral Yamamoto Gonnohyōe, chief of the Naval Affairs Bureau (*Gummukyoku*) of the Naval Ministry, to lay plans for the postwar expansion of naval armaments, with Russia regarded as Japan's primary potential enemy. At that time, Saigō informed Yamamoto that Japan, after subtracting war expenditures of ￥200 million, still had a net gain of ￥165 million, or approximately $82,090,000, and that Yamamoto should not overly be concerned with the budget.[49] Because of the war profits coupled with such postwar tasks as the development of Formosa, Saigō and his fellow Meiji leaders were probably well disposed to put an end to the drawn-out, costly litigation by accepting the out-of-court settlement.

Out of these financial, emotional, and diplomatic considerations came the conclusion of the case, a compromise, which was a deliberate choice of the government and had nothing to do with the justice or injustice of the British consular courts in Japan. For this reason, the criticism which has long been leveled by Japanese historians—that Tokyo had to expend more on the litigation than it finally recovered from the P & O and that this was indicative of the inequity of the Western consular court decisions—misses the mark.[50] Basically, it is unreasonable and unfair to compare the Japanese government's litigation expenditure, that is, both the court costs and lawyers' fees, with the court costs recovered by the government—for three reasons. First, the P & O also had stiff lawyers' fees to pay. Can anyone assume that their lawyers charged the P & O substantially less than the lawyers retained by Tokyo charged? Certainly not. Second, since the P & O paid the costs in the Yokohama Court and also paid the costs in the two higher courts, Tokyo had nothing in the way of court costs to pay for the two-year-long litigation.

Third, and finally, lurking behind this criticism is the sense of disappointment, if not resentment, voiced by contemporaries like Representative Moriya,

116   Justice of the Western Consular Courts in Nineteenth-Century Japan

that Japan settled for a small fraction of its prospective damages, $850,000. But this feeling stems from ignorance of the principle of burden of proof—that is, the duty of the Meiji government to establish the truth of its claim by overwhelming evidence. In a maritime collision case, the defendant often contests the amount of the plaintiff's damages. It is, therefore, safe to assume that the P & O would have put up a spirited fight over the amount of the Japanese claim if the original action had been litigated. Although the actual limitation figures under the 1854 and 1894 statutes would have differed, the Meiji government should have been conscious of the statutory limitation of the liability of shipowners inasmuch as Great Britain had been enforcing such limitations since 1734.[51] Through the £8-per-ton provision, therefore, Great Britain did not initiate any new policy, but simply adjusted the amount a shipowner had to pay. All the possible outcomes under the 1894 statute have already been discussed. Even under the 1854 statute, which was in force when the action began, the P & O would have been allowed to limit its liability to the value of the *Ravenna* and its freight carried on the voyage during which the collision occurred if the P & O could have proved that the collision had occurred without its actual fault. In order to proceed with the action, therefore, Japan would have had to show from the outset that the value of the *Ravenna* plus its freight was worth enough to cover its damages. Nevertheless, making allowance for the fact that the issue of counterclaim diverted the attention of the Meiji government from the original action, it would seem that the government failed to give any serious thought to the question of proof until after the rendering of the Privy Council decision on the issue of counterclaim. It is evident, then, that the government was ill prepared to discharge its burden of proof; it could not have recovered all of the damages claimed under any circumstances. Hence, it is meaningless to make any comparison between the compromise and the damages.

Conclusion

An attempt will now be made to answer the three questions used to evaluate the fairness of every publicized case. They are: (1) Do the accounts of the case hitherto presented tell both sides of the story? (2) Did the British courts involved render their decisions in accordance with the law applicable? (3) If the Japanese plaintiff had been English, would the decisions have been more favorable to him?

To answer the first question, the case has almost always been recounted from the viewpoint of the Japanese plaintiff alone, for three reasons. First, the writers have uncritically accepted contemporary versions of the case. Second, they have failed to utilize the full, English records of the court hearings and judgments. Finally, since an adequate analysis of these law reports calls for a conceptual understanding of law—both present and past—which is not ordinarily expected of historians, the writers have been unable to detect the significance of certain facts and to interpret them properly—for example, Tokyo's citation of the 1894

Merchant Shipping Act as a basis for withdrawing the original action. Here the attempt has been made to correct the usual lopsided account of the case by reciting some of the technically legal aspects of the case, at the risk of making the reading of this chapter somewhat heavy.

With regard to the second question, it would seem that each of the British courts did render its decision in accordance with the law which in its view was the only one applicable, although the three courts made two diametrically opposed decisions on three separate grounds. The first court applied Japanese law; the second court applied maritime law; and the Privy Council upheld the existing treaties. The judgment of the second (Shanghai) court alone might in any way be viewed as unfair, since it seems to have reflected the then prevailing attitude of Westerners in China toward the East Asian peoples which was, on the whole, more condescending than that of most of the Westerners in Japan. Of course, what counted was the decision of the Privy Council. Fortunately for posterity, both British and Japanese, that decision rested on what appears to us today to have been the only just ground. It reaffirmed the provision of the treaties that the British consular courts and the territorial courts of Japan had exclusive jurisdiction over claims against British and Japanese subjects, respectively. Hence, it can be asserted that the final decision was rendered in accordance with the only "law" that supposedly applied, the treaty provision mentioned.

As for the third question, whether the outcome of the case would have been more favorable to the plaintiff if he had been English rather than Japanese, it should be recalled that all of the three decisions mentioned were rendered on the issue of counterclaim and that the original claim was never litigated. Nevertheless, the answer to the question is a resounding *no*. There is ample evidence that, if the original action had been tried, both Tokyo and the P & O would have been found at fault. From 1824 through 1910, the courts of England unswervingly adhered to the equal division rule,[52] under which the outcome of such a mutual-fault case as the *Chishima* was quite predictable. On account of this predictability, no British court could have altered the *Chishima*'s net recovery even if it had been tempted to do so.

The foregoing analysis leads to the conclusion that the *Chishima* case fails to buttress the interpretation that the Western consular tribunals in Japan as a rule did not render evenhanded justice.

6

How Many Unfair Cases?

Unlike the social scientist, the historian is at the mercy of the accidental survival of evidence. The social scientist formulates a problem and attendant hypotheses, and then gathers data necessary to test those hypotheses. Since, however, the historian in general has to work with data that accidentally have survived, his formulation of problems and attendant hypotheses is, of necessity, constricted by the availability of historical data. This inherent limitation on historical craftsmanship is evident in this chapter.

This chapter shows briefly how an estimate of the mixed cases adjudicated by the Western consular courts was arrived at. It also discusses how many unpublicized cases may be said to have been adjudicated unfairly and unjustly.

Estimating

A major finding of this study is that the sweeping hundred-year-old interpretation that as a rule no Japanese could expect justice from the Western consular courts in Japan rests on an infinitesimal fraction of the total number of mixed cases adjudicated by the Western consular courts in Japan. Therefore, it is of crucial relevance to determine how many mixed cases there were. But, as Robert William Fogel aptly points out, "counting is rarely an easy task in historical work."[1] What was possible here was to arrive at an estimate of the number of mixed cases.

Every effort was made to be conservative in obtaining the estimate. Whenever it was uncertain whether a given case was mixed or nonmixed, it was counted as a nonmixed case. The estimate does not include cases withdrawn by the plaintiffs or dismissed by the trial courts. These cases, though recorded in the extant records of the courts, are excluded from counting and estimating, since evaluation of the fairness of adjudication calls for examination of those cases actually adjudicated. Also excluded are a small number of appeal cases since they have been recorded previously by the trial courts. Similarly, the cases recorded in the surviving Ōsaka records of the British consular court at Hyōgo and Ōsaka are also excluded, for it was not known how long the Ōsaka vice-consulate maintained dockets separate from those of the Hyōgo consulate.

Another category of cases excluded from the count and estimate is composed of mixed cases adjudicated by the following two consular courts: the British court at Niigata, which existed from 1868 to 1882; and the U.S. court at Edo, which existed from 1869 to 1872. Since it was not possible to find any of the returns of these courts, these cases were excluded in arriving at the estimate.

Also excluded are all mixed cases adjudicated by Western consular courts in Taiwan after 1895 when the island became an integral part of the Japanese Empire as a result of Japan's victory in the First Sino-Japanese War. One may safely assume that most of a small number of "Japanese" plaintiffs who appeared at these courts actually were Taiwanese. More importantly, by 1895 Japan had succeeded in having Great Britain sign a new commercial treaty which was to supersede the 1858 Anglo-Japanese Treaty, an unequal treaty. Consequently, the era of extraterritoriality was about to witness its dusk. Again, one may assume that the justice of the consular courts in the newly acquired, backward, and remote colony of Taiwan was of no particular concern to the Japanese. One may, therefore, be justified in asserting that these Taiwanese cases have no meaningful bearing on the subject of the justice of the Western consular courts in Japan.

Except for these exclusions and inadvertent omissions that may have occurred, the aggregate of mixed cases adjudicated between 1859 and 1899 in Japan by the Western consular courts can be estimated at 3,500. This number is a sum of two smaller estimates: the estimated number of mixed cases adjudicated by the British and U.S. consular courts in Japan, added to the estimated number of cases adjudicated by the consular courts of the other fourteen treaty powers in Japan.

British and U.S. Cases

In contrast to practically nonexistent records of the consular courts of the other treaty powers, large numbers of the British and American consular courts have survived. Yet counting the mixed cases decided by even these courts is not easy. Many of the returns of cases were lost, because they were filed separately from their letters of transmission after being received by the British Foreign Office or the U.S. Department of State. Normally, British letters of transmission contain a sentence similar to the following: "I have the honour to transmit to you herewith the Returns of Civil and Criminal Cases tried in this Court during the half year ending 30th. . . . " But quite often one finds no such returns attached. Some of these separated returns of British consular courts in Japan may be found among the records of both the Supreme Court for China and Japan at Shanghai and the Court for Japan at Kanagawa.[2] In the case of

American returns, from 1870 onward State Department policy was not to file American consuls' letters and their enclosures together but to forward the enclosures to appropriate federal agencies.[3] Today no one knows whether any of the returns of cases thus separated from the general records of the American consulates in Japan are still extant. Fortunately, however, this policy must have not been carried out to the letter, for from time to time the records of the American consulates contain some of the returns supposedly filed elsewhere.

Table 8 indicates a breakdown of the estimated 2,798 cases adjudicated by six British and five U.S. consular courts in Japan. As shown in the table, the *estimate* of mixed cases adjudicated by the U.S. consular court at Ōsaka-Hyōgo is identical with the number of mixed cases found recorded. This congruence arises from the fact that no extrapolation was required to arrive at the estimate since cases were found to cover all of the years during which the court was in operation. The estimate is, therefore, virtually the same as a count—"virtually" because the recorded number 79, not the estimated 79, includes a small estimate. The total number of cases adjudicated by the court is 444. Of these, 304 are criminal cases and the other 140, civil cases. Of the 140, eleven cases adjudicated during the years 1875 and 1876 are not fully recorded in the extant dockets. Therefore, the number of mixed cases is estimated among the eleven. The result is that the count 79 contains four estimated cases. Nevertheless, since the bulk of the estimate of the number adjudicated at the U.S. court at Ōsaka-Hyōgo, unlike all of the other estimates given in Table 8, constitutes a count, it would be a distortion to assert that the estimated 79 is an estimate in the sense that the other subtotals are estimates.

In Table 8, one may note omission of the first U.S. consulate established in Japan: the U.S. consulate at Shimoda. The omission is intentional. Explanation of the omission probably affords the best place to define a phrase to be mentioned occasionally throughout the rest of the book: the Age of Extraterritoriality in Japan. This age is defined as the approximately forty years from 1859 to mid-1899, when extraterritoriality was abolished. Table 8 indicates that four of the ten consulates listed were opened in 1859. But, of course, those four were not the earliest Western consulates. Consul General Townsend Harris was the first Western consul ever to be credited to Japan; the consulate he established at Shimoda in 1856 was the first Western consulate. But there is no evidence that he ever formed an extraterritorial court at Shimoda. The caldendar year 1859 is, therefore, taken in this book as the beginning of the Age of Extraterritoriality.

The estimated total of 2,798 cases was extrapolated from the 668 cases recorded in the returns of cases I was able to locate. Since only one in every four cases is found recorded, it is necessary to explain how the estimate was obtained. The Appendix presents the procedure. The explanation, full of figures, arithmetic calculations, and tables, is relegated to the Appendix because it is unlikely to hold the average reader's interest. For the benefit of those who may skim through the Appendix instead of reading it, it should be pointed out that

Table 8
Estimate of Mixed Cases Adjudicated in British and U.S. Consular Courts in Japan, 1859–1899 (Adapted from Appendix Table 1)

	Consulate	Year Established	Number of Mixed Cases Found Recorded	Estimate of Mixed Cases
BRITISH	Edo (Tokyo)	1859	44	118
	Hakodate	1859	30	74
	Hyōgo and Ōsaka	1868	97	538
	Kanagawa (Yokohama)	1860	36	1,197
	Nagasaki	1859	174	212
	Niigata	1868	--(a)	--
	Subtotal		381	2,139
UNITED STATES	Edo	1869	--	--
	Hakodate	1865	0(b)	0
	Kanagawa	1861	149	507
	Nagasaki	1859	59	73
	Ōsaka-Hyōgo	1868	79	79
	Subtotal		287	659
	Total		668	2,798

SOURCES: Same as for Appendix Table 1.
 (a) The dash(--) indicates "not found" or "not applicable."
 (b) Examination of the records of the Hakodate consulate reveals that none of the consuls ever filed a return of cases, although they filed other kinds of returns. It would seem, therefore, that none of the Hakodate consuls ever formed a consular court.

Appendix Table 1, which represents a distillation of the fruits of ten years' research that went into collecting the data, provides a synopsis of the estimating process.

Other Western Cases

Since the Western residents in nineteenth-century Japan, exclusive of the British and American, constituted only a small portion of the Western population there, the total number of mixed cases decided by the consular courts of the Western treaty powers other than these two must have been very small indeed.

In the absence of actual returns, however, it is exceedingly difficult to assert how small that number may have been. One possible basis for estimating the number is to use the number of cases reported in the *Japan Weekly Mail*, the weekly English newspaper published in Yokohama, the largest of Japan's open ports at the time. The newspaper published the judgments and sometimes even the minutes of the proceedings of cases, both mixed and nonmixed, adjudicated by Western consular courts in Yokohama and Tokyo. The total number of mixed cases adjudicated by the British and U.S. consular courts and reported by the *Japan Weekly Mail* for these two cities in 1875, 1876, 1884, 1886, 1893, and 1896 was 52, and the number decided by the other Western consular courts and reported likewise was 13. In other words, the ratio between the two groups of cases reported by the weekly newspaper is 4 to 1. By sheer coincidence, this ratio is also identical with that between the numbers of British and U.S. merchant seamen who visited Japan in 1885 and the European merchant seamen who did the same in that year. As mentioned in Chapter 1, according to American Minister Hubbard, the British and U.S. seamen accounted for 80.1 percent and the European, 19.9 percent of Western sailors who went ashore. The total number of mixed cases adjudicated by the treaty powers other than Great Britain and the United States may be taken as one-quarter of that of British and American cases. Since the British and American cases are estimated at approximately 2,800, a reasonable estimate of the other number may be 700. These estimates together place the aggregate number of mixed cases adjudicated by the Western consular courts in Japan at 3,500.

How Many Unpublicized Cases May Have Been Decided Unfairly?

The Preface states that in evaluating the unpublished, mixed cases one should ask how many unpublicized cases there were and how many of these, if any, were decided unfairly and unjustly against the Japanese litigants. The first question has already been dealt with in this chapter; let us now turn to the second question.

With regard to inquiring into fairness of adjudication, one must evaluate the evidence in each case. No one is in a better position to evaluate and determine the admissibility, relevance, and sufficiency of evidence adduced at a trial than is the presiding judge of the trial court who can observe witnesses face to face. For this reason, an ordinary appeal is based on the records of the trial court, the court of the first instance; no new evidence is introduced.[4] Hence, it would be meaningless, if not presumptuous, to try to duplicate what the trial judge did as if one had been present in the trial room. To be sure, it is necessary to sift the *extant* evidence, but sifting it is only part of the evaluation. In addition, it is necessary to ascertain whether any miscarriage of justice occurred stemming from biases and prejudice peculiar to the nineteenth-century West. More specifically, an attempt is made here to detect whether the nineteenth-century Europocentric framework in any way played havoc with carrying out impartial justice by the Western consular courts in Japan.

Obviously, it would not have been feasible to have evaluated the records of all mixed cases, even if all the records had survived. Therefore, all the cases that could be identified were taken as a sample. The research involved reading not only the briefly stated decisions of the 668 cases recorded in the returns of cases that were located, but also the judgments, that is, statements containing both the decisions and the reasons behind the decisions, or both the judgments and the lengthy minutes of the proceedings of more than 200 mixed cases. As with almost any sample of historical evidence, these cases do not constitute a random sample of the 2,800 cases but, since they represent almost a quarter of the 2,800, they do constitute a fairly large sample. Therefore, they have been used here as the basis for estimating the total number of mixed cases that may have been decided unfairly against Japanese litigants.

Among the 668 cases, there are 5 British cases that appear to have violated the treaty terms, but that were adjudicated in perfect harmony with an accepted rule of international law. These cases involved seven Japanese seamen employed on board British vessels who were accused of insubordination, desertion, or refusal of duty.[5] The cases in themselves were minor ones as is evidenced by the fact that British and U.S. consular courts, which grouped all cases into three classes—civil, criminal, and police cases—classified such cases as police cases. They are, however, significant from the standpoint of this study. To begin with, the new issue involved was a highly important, sensitive one: which country, Britain or Japan, had jurisdiction over cases of disciplinary offenses involving Japanese seamen in the employ of British merchant vessels lying in Japanese waters? Furthermore, the five cases apparently constitute the only unpublicized cases that might mislead one to believe that they should have been adjudicated by Japanese courts and that, as a result, the Japanese litigants had not been treated justly. For these reasons, Japan's response to the first of the five will be discussed in some detail.

Russel Robertson, the British consul at Kanagawa, on February 24, 1883, sentenced Hosoi Isami, a Japanese seaman serving on a British vessel, to a week's imprisonment for desertion. The Japanese government questioned Robertson's right to exercise jurisdiction over the Japanese seaman. Article 5 of the Anglo-Japanese Treaty of 1858 stipulated that Japanese committing offenses be amenable exclusively to Japanese jurisdiction, and British committing offenses be subject to British jurisdiction only. On account of this stipulation, argued Foreign Minister Inoue Kaoru, the seaman was amenable to Japanese jurisdiction only and not to that of the flag under which he was serving. Sir Harry S. Parkes, Her Britannic Majesty's representative to Japan, "while avoiding any express disapproval of the Consul's action," admitted that

much might be said in favour of his Excellency [Inoue]'s view, that such cases should be governed by the express provisions of the Treaty rather than by the general principle of international law under which Mr. Robertson acted, namely, that jurisdiction in cases of offenses against discipline follows the flag of the vessel under which the seaman is serving.

Foreign Minister Inoue on May 15 informed Parkes that, even though principles of international law justified British consuls in punishing Japanese seamen serving on board British vessels for offenses of a purely disciplinary nature, these principles were overridden by the express stipulation contained in the Anglo-Japanese treaty of 1858. He contended that, by virtue of the stipulation, the Japanese seamen ought to have been dealt with by Japanese authorities, even supposing no Japanese regulations existed for the punishment of such offenses—and such regulations had in fact been in force. Inoue contended further that, if London did not assent to his view, following the principle of reciprocity, cases of a similar nature involving British subjects serving on Japanese vessels should be dealt with by Japanese authorities.[6]

From the perspective of today, it would seem, the British consul had jurisdiction over the disciplinary offense at issue. In other words, the prevailing rule of international law referred to by Parkes should have taken precedence over the treaty stipulation, as it actually did. Even Yamamoto Sōji, an eminent Japanese authority on maritime law, is of the opinion that British authorities in Japan had jurisdiction over Japanese seamen serving under the British flag, for disciplinary offenses like desertion.[7] The key to this opinion hinges on the old, well-established rule that "prima facie the 'law of the flag' governs everything which occurs on board ship."[8] This rule is so well established that even offenses occurring on board a *private* vessel in the internal waters of a foreign state, if they are purely disciplinary infractions like desertion, are not normally interfered with by that state but are left to the jurisdiction of the flag state.

The practice of excepting disciplinary and minor offenses from the complete jurisdiction of the state of the port over offenses committed on board foreign vessels within its ports is French in origin.[9] Until the 1870s England did not accept this usage at all. For example, when in 1817 the commander of a British man-of-war had arrested a deserter at New Orleans, the king's advocate-general (until 1872, the advocate-general was a third law officer who served as standing adviser to the government on questions of international, maritime, and ecclesiastical law[10]) reported that "the arrest of a deserter in a foreign port by a British naval commander is a violation of foreign territory."[11] But the British point of view underwent change, and by the 1870s, the criminal law of England came to accept the state of the port waiving its jurisdiction over disciplinary offenses committed on board foreign vessels in its ports. In 1877—six years prior to the adjudication of the case in question—the then law officers, the very ones who were later to render the four opinions on the *Hartley* cases (see Chapter 3), expressed Britain's full acceptance of the Continental practice of excepting from local jurisdiction offenses against discipline and of leaving them to the jurisdiction of the flag state. On July 20, the officers reported that British consuls "in China and Japan may claim jurisdiction over offences committed by British seamen belonging to foreign (private or merchant) ships within the territorial waters of those countries, except in those cases where the offence is against the discipline of the ship to which the British seamen may belong."[12] Stated another way, the law officers were of the opinion that, with the *exception* of disciplinary infractions, all offenses committed by British seamen on board foreign merchant vessels in Japanese waters were amenable exclusively to the extraterritorial jurisdiction of Britain.

Notwithstanding its protest over Consul Robertson's trial of the Japanese seaman, the Japanese government shortly subscribed to the notion that the coastal state should waive its jurisdiction over foreign merchant vessels within its ports, in matters that concerned the internal order of such vessels, in favor of the respective consuls. In response to a series of British proposals relating to the unequal treaties, on August 4, 1884, Foreign Minister Inoue made a number of counterproposals, one of which read: "His Imperial Majesty's Government desires that the disciplinary power on board ship shall belong to its Captain, whether the vessel be Japanese or Foreign, and without regard to the nationality of the crew."[13]

The foregoing makes it evident that, in spite of Parkes' doubt about Consul Robertson's exercise of jurisdiction over the Japanese seaman for desertion, the consul's authority in the case hinged on the well-established rule of international law that jurisdiction in cases of disciplinary offenses follows the flag of the vessel under which the seaman is serving. Great Britain had fully subscribed to that rule prior to the adjudication of the case discussed. Japan, too, fully accepted the rule shortly after its temporary denunciation of the adjudication. This suggests that in the 1880s the rule was enjoying something of universal acceptance. Therefore, Robertson's trial of the Japanese seaman did not represent an unlawful extension of his judicial competence in a deliberate violation of the express provision of the Anglo-Japanese Treaty of 1858. The trial wrought no injustice; it did not constitute an unfairly adjudicated case.

In addition to the 1883 case discussed, there may have been other cases, adjudication of which initially ruffled but ultimately satisfied the Japanese government. In consequence, contemporary Japanese newspapers and later historical works never reported on such cases. One may learn of them only in the dusty archival records. To all intents and purposes, such cases are the same as the numerous ones of which nothing has ever been heard because the Japanese considered them to have been adjudicated fairly.

Only one case of the kind that initially upset but eventually satisfied Tokyo has been uncovered. In 1884 the boatswain of the British vessel *Emily* was tried before British Consul James Troup at Kōbe for breaking the seals placed on the hatches of the vessel by Japanese customs officers. He was acquitted by Troup on the grounds that there had been no intentional breaking of the seals. Troup justified his decision by quoting from the Japanese text of trade regulations attached to the Anglo-Japanese Treaty of 1858. The Japanese government protested the decision as contrary to the treaty's Article XXI which stipulated that the Dutch version should be considered the authoritative one. In response, British Foreign Secretary Granville had Plunkett, the British minister to Japan, respond to the protest. Prior to sending his instructions, however, Granville had the two law officers of the Crown and Dr. J. Parker Deane—the three who were to render the opinions on the adjudication of the *Hartley* cases (see Chapter 3)—examine his draft of instructions to make sure that the draft was legally sound and proper. On March 3, 1885, the law officers reported that they concurred in substance with the draft, and suggested only a few alterations in wording. The draft read in part as follows:

I have to state to you [Plunkett] that Her Majesty's Government concur with the Japanese Government in the view that the Dutch version is in case of difference to be deemed the original, and that any wilful breaking of the seals, even though no fraud may have been contemplated, renders the person committing the act liable under the Regulations.

But if it were clearly proved that the act was purely accidental and unintentional it would be contrary to the first principles of justice to hold that a criminal offence had been committed.

If a similar case should occur again and the Japanese Government should be dissatisfied with the decision of the Consul, it will be open to them to appeal.

I have to request you to inform the Japanese Government in the above sense.[14]

Nothing was ever reported on this case in the newspapers examined for this study. One may, therefore, conclude that the Japanese government either found the rationale of the judgment as explained in the foreign secretary's draft eminently satisfactory or acquiesced in the rationale. In any event, such a case must be regarded as being not unfairly, even if not fairly, adjudicated, in the eyes of the Japanese government.

One more question remains in dealing with the broader subject of how many unpublicized mixed cases may have been unfairly or unjustly adjudicated: were there cases which, when adjudicated, outraged the Japanese public as did the five publicized, but which have since then been forgotten by historians and other writers? If there were such cases, they should be examined to determine whether their adjudication may have wrought injustice to the Japanese litigants involved.

One may deal with this knotty point by raising two more specific questions. First, are there any cases, other than the five mentioned, in the Japanese-language literature on the subject of consular jurisdiction or, more broadly, of treaty revision? As stated in the Preface, the answer is no. Second, is it possible that the historians and other writers somehow have overlooked other cases that at the time received as much publicity as the five publicized during the second half of the nineteenth century? There is no easy answer to this question. But it must be sought. Should it be yes, undoubtedly cases of the sort would be cited, discussed, and commented upon as extensively as the five in contemporary Japanese newspapers.

To test this hypothesis, I read two major daily Japanese newspapers: the *Chōya shimbun* and the *Jiji shimpō*. Western-language newspapers in Japan once regarded these two papers, along with the *Tokyo nichinichi shimbun*, as the three most "famous" newspapers in Tokyo.[15] Ideally for purposes of this inquiry, the two newspapers should have been published throughout the Age of Extraterritoriality (1859–1899); unfortunately, however, they were not. The *Chōya shimbun* began to be published in 1874, but the Tōdai holdings, microfilmed for the Library of Congress, to which I had access, lack the December 1893 through mid–1900 issues. To make up for this hiatus, I read two other newspapers in the possession of the Library—the *Niroku shimpō* and the *Nihon*. The *Jiji shimpō*, on the other hand, did not commence publication until 1882. To compensate for the absence of pre–1882 years, I examined the *Yūbin hōchi shimbun*, the first issue of which was published in 1872, for the years 1872 to 1882. Moreover, neither the *Yūbin hōchi shimbun* nor the *Chōya shimbun* was published during roughly the first two decades of the Age of Extraterritoriality. Filling this gap for both sets required the reading of *Bakumatsu Meiji shimbun zenshū* (the Collected Works of Bakumatsu and Meiji Newspapers) and the newspaper volume of *Meiji bunka zenshū* (the Collected Works on Meiji Culture) which includes Japanese-language newspapers of the Bakumatsu period as well as of the Meiji. These two sets of newspapers, together with their chronological coverage, are tabulated in Table 9.

The two sets together provide dual coverage of the years from 1861 to 1899. How many publicized cases possibly overlooked by the historians did these newspapers report? To answer this question, it is necessary to find out how extensively those newspapers covered the five publicized cases. The extent of coverage is illustrated in Table 10 which shows the specific dates or the period during which the five cases, along with incidents associated with or caused by them, continued to be reported, criticized, or condemned.[16]

The findings in Table 10 make it possible to devise a functional definition of the expression "publicized case." Of the five cases, the earliest, the *King* case, received the least publicity. During the four-day period indicated in Table 10, June 20–23, 1875, the *Chōya shimbun* not only reported the incident, but

Table 9
Two Sets of Japanese Newspapers Published During the Age of Extraterritoriality, 1859-1899, That Were Examined

Decade	First Set	Second Set
1859-1869	Bakumatsu Meiji shimbun zenshū (1861-1872)(a) Meiji bunka zenshū 4: shimbunhen (1862-1874)	Bakumatsu Meiji shimbun zenshū (1861-1872)(a) Meiji bunka zenshū 4: shimbunhen (1862-1874)
1869-1878	Chōya shimbun(b) (July 1874-November 1893)	yūbin hōchi shimbun(c) (June 1872-December 1882) Jiji shimpō (March 1882-August 1899)
1879-1888	Chōya shimbun (July 1874-November 1893)	Jiji shimpō (March 1882-August 1899)
1889-1899	Chōya shimbun (July 1874-November 1893) Niroku shimpō(b) (October 1893-June 1895) Nihon (July 1895-August 1899)	Jiji shimpō (March 1882-August 1899)

(a)Reprint ed., 8 vols. (Tokyo, 1961).
(b)The holdings of Tōdai Meiji shimbun Zasshi Bunko microfilmed for the National Diet Library, Tokyo.
(c)The holdings of the Yomiuri Shimbunsha microfilmed for the Asian Library, the University of Michigan, Ann Arbor, Michigan.

Table 10
Press Coverage of the Five Publicized Cases

Case	Newspaper	Reporting Period
King	Chōya	June 20-23, 1875; September 24, 1878
Hartley (2 cases)	Chōya	March 18, April 4, 1879; September 28, 1880
	Yūbin hōchi	September 1, 1878 (an editorial)
Drake	Chōya	November 3-December 31, 1886; March 2, April 23, 1887
	Jiji	October 30, 1886-January 27, 1887; May 16 and 28, 1887
Chishima	Chōya	December 1-24, 1892; February 9, 1893; April 5-November 14, 1893
	Jiji	December 7, 1892-December 26, 1893; April 25, 1894; July 4-August 14, 1895
	Niroku(a)	November 5, 1893-January 11, 1894

(a)No issue of the Niroku shimpō published prior to October 1893 was examined, since the examination was occasioned by the fact that I had no access to Chōya shimbun issues published after November 1893.

also printed a reader's opinion about the length of the sentence and two editorials maintaining that six months imprisonment in Japan was equivalent to a year and a half of imprisonment in England. For purposes of this study, therefore, one may safely define a publicized case as one reported, analyzed, and evaluated in newspapers over a period of two days or more with regard to the facts, the decisions rendered, or even the proceedings.

If one applies this definition to nine mixed cases reported in the newspapers, none of them qualifies as a publicized case. On the whole, the newspaper accounts are sketchy, imprecise, and lacking in certain essential details. The accounts given below paraphrase or summarize the newspaper accounts and are, of necessity, incomplete in details or at times even incoherent and, therefore, may be found unsatisfactory as to factuality.

CASE 1. *Chūgai shimbun*, May 27 and June 6, 1869 (April 16 and 26 according to the lunar calendar). In May 1869, a Japanese couple residing in a village near Yokohama preferred a charge of assault and battery against three British soldiers for assault against the wife's younger sister who had been to Yokohama to visit the wife, Ko, and her husband. While walking on the street of Yokohama, the sister was alleged to have been beaten and injured by the three soldiers without provocation. By the time a hearing was held in late April, the younger sister, the subject of the alleged attack, had returned to her distant home; the allegation could not be verified. Moreover, Ko's description of the clothing of the three assailants in no way matched the navy blue uniforms of the accused. So, the alleged charge could not be proved beyond reasonable doubt. It was, the court decided, "an error of hearsay" (*fūbun no sakugo*).

CASES 2 AND 3. *Chōya shimbun*, November 8, 1878. A merchant of British India who resided in Yokohama tried in vain to get through customs an unspecified amount of pearl and saffron by wrapping them up in an old cloth stamped with a seal of approval. The superintendent of Japanese customs sued him at the Yokohama Court. At its hearing, however, the Court decided that the superintendent had no case against the merchant, a decision which the superintendent appealed to the Supreme Court at Shanghai. Meanwhile, the *Japan Weekly Mail* reported that the customs officials had pretended not to recognize the attempted smuggling, even though they had known of it. A libel suit was brought against the *Japan Weekly Mail*, presumably by the superintendent of Japanese customs. The *Chōya shimbun* quoted the *Tokyo nichi nichi shimbun* as reporting that the defendant was found not guilty by the jury. This libel suit will be referred to as Case 3.

CASE 4. *Chōya shimbun*, September 24, 1880. The defendant was an American who had for six years rented land in the foreign settlement in Tsukiji, Tokyo, and for five years had not paid ground rent. The municipal government (*fu*) of Tokyo instituted proceedings against him at the U.S. consular court, presumably at Tokyo. There the defendant argued that treaty prevented the Japanese government from allowing foreigners to reside outside the settlement, but that the government had allowed them to do so in contravention of the treaty terms. Because of this infraction of the treaty prohibition, the defendant had been unable to rent out the land to other foreigners and had sustained a loss; he could not pay the ground rent. Upon hearing the argument, the court decided the case in favor of the defendant. The municipal government considered the decision unfair and was contemplating an appeal against the decision when the defendant notified the government that he would pay the rent deficit. The payment was accepted at once, and legal action was discontinued.

CASE 5. *Chōya shimbun*, December 16, 1882. A Chinese tried to smuggle out of Kōbe three boxes containing gold bars by unsuccessfully claiming that the contents of the boxes were something other than gold. The customs authorities confiscated the boxes. A few days later, a Chinese bank in Hong Kong claimed ownership of the boxes, asserting that their contents were of such a nature that they were not subject to confiscation. The customs authorities brought an action against the bank at Her Britannic Majesty's Court at Kōbe. One may assume that the authorities declared the bank had attempted a smuggling. On December 6 the Court found the plaintiff's declaration "unsound and insufficient," and ordered the boxes returned to the defendant. The lengthy editorial in which the above account was given cited this case as a typical example of the long-standing abuse of extraterritoriality by all Western consuls.

CASE 6. *Chōya shimbun*, August 1, 1884. A group of Japanese lumber merchants brought a suit against a U.S. citizen at the U.S. consular court at Kōbe pleading for a restitution of the lumber he had carried away from Ūllyung Island off the east coast of Korea. A hearing was held at the court on July 26, George H. Scidmore, the American consul, presiding.

CASE 7. *Jiji shimpō*, June 21, 1888. The defendant was an Englishman alleged to have committed an arson in a village west of Yokohama on May 26, 1888. The newspaper simply reported that he was to be tried soon.

CASE 8. *Jiji shimpō*, August 12, 1892. A foreigner who had struck a Japanese failed to appear at his country's consular court at Kōbe. The court rendered a judgment by default, imposing on him one month's "heavy punishment" (*jū kinko*).

CASE 9. *Jiji shimpō*, August 17, 1893. A U.S. citizen who shot at a Japanese groom was tried at a U.S. consular court—presumably, at Yokohama—which found him not guilty and acquitted him. Thereupon, through the U.S. consul, the defendant sued the groom on a charge of attempted murder at the Japanese District Court at Yokohama.

Given the definition of publicized cases, none of the above cases was publicized, since none was ever reported over a period of time as were the five publicized cases, nor were they reported in more than one major newspaper. But each of them may be referred to as a semipublicized case, for it was covered once in a major newspaper whereas most mixed cases were not.

The foregoing suggests that there were *no* cases which, when adjudicated, outraged the Japanese public as much as did the five publicized cases and since have been forgotten by historians and other writers alike.

If any given case, publicized or semipublicized, was unfairly adjudicated, that fact must be conceded. Therefore I now turn to the evaluation of the nine semipublicized cases. In doing so I am keenly aware of the fact that the available accounts are quite sketchy and incomplete; that evaluation must be deemed tentative.

Regarding Case 1, there was not enough evidence to prove the charge against the three British soldiers. No court of justice could have ruled any differently. Case 2, the decision of which was appealed to the Supreme Court at Shanghai, was never again reported. One may, therefore, assume that the outcome of the appeal satisfied the Japanese public. One may also make the same assumption concerning Case 3, for no complaint or criticism was ever reported against the British jury's verdict of not guilty against the defendant, the *Japan Weekly Mail*. It would seem that the adjudication of Case 4 was unfair. Immediate payment by the defendant probably accounts for absence of excoriation or even criticism of the trial outcome. It is virtually impossible to make any evaluation of Case 5 because the account explains neither the plaintiff's stance nor the Court's decision. But since the *Chōya shimbun* editorial inveighed against the decision, one may assume that at least the newspaper considered the decision unfair. This negative assessment is, of course, highly tentative. One may recall that the two *Hartley* cases were deemed not unfairly adjudicated, although their adjudication made the Japanese public irate. Case 6, like Case 4, seems to have been adjudicated fairly, for one reads nothing further about the process or outcome of the trial. As to Case 7, although the impending trial was reported, nothing further was printed about the outcome. This suggests that the Japanese public accepted the adjudication as fair and just. There is no room to doubt that Case 8 resulted in a fair trial. The Western defendant who failed to make an appearance at the consular court was sentenced to one month's imprisonment, and nothing more was heard of the case. Likewise, Case 9 appears to have been adjudicated with impartiality. No criticism was leveled against the decision that acquitted the American who had presumably been charged with an attempted homicide. Thus, of the nine cases, only two, Cases 4 and 5, may have been unfairly adjudicated.

Reading the two sets of newspapers has uncovered two additional cases, both of which may have been adjudicated unfairly. One wonders, if one could read all of the Japanese newspapers ever published in Japan during the Age of Extraterritoriality, how many more mixed cases might one find that were adjudicated unfairly?

One source of information for estimating this number is the major newspapers of Meiji Japan. Their number fluctuated between five and seven during the 1870s and the 1880s. As of the 1880s, the seven were the *Chōya shimbun*, the *Jiji shimpō*, the *Jiyū shimbun*, the *Mainichi shimbun*, the *Meiji shimbun*, the *Tokyo nichi nichi shimbun*, and the *Yūbin hōchi shimbun*.[17] Reading the first two newspapers has revealed two semipublicized cases that may have been adjudicated unfairly. One might be inclined to conjecture that reading all seven might uncover many more cases of this sort.

But this conjecture is probably incorrect; one might find just a few more, for two reasons. First, as already noted, fewer mixed cases were adjudicated during the 1890s than during the 1870s or the 1880s. (The case load of the U.S. consular court at Nagasaki was a notable exception to this trend, for the court adjudicated a greater number of cases during the 1890s than during any of the previous three decades.)[18]

Second, although throughout the Age of Extraterritoriality the number of newspapers covering current affairs was on the increase and although the newspapers began to print more pages, there was no corresponding increase in the reporting of mixed cases. Rather, there was an apparent absence during the last phase of the Age. This change probably reflected the Japanese newspapers' loss of interest in the subject of extraterritoriality consequent upon the signing, beginning in 1894, of a new Anglo-Japanese and other treaties promising the abolition of extraterritoriality in Japan.

In early Meiji Japan, numerous newspapers came into existence and lasted for varying periods of time. But not all of them, even those that continued to be printed throughout much of the period, reported the kind of news that had appeal to the minority in Japan who were interested in public affairs. In fact, newspapers of early Meiji Japan fell into two categories: *dai shimbun* (large newspapers) and *shō shimbun* (small newspapers). The two can be called major and minor newspapers, respectively. Twice as large in physical size as the minor newspapers, the major newspapers of the 1870s catered to intellectuals, while the minor newspapers appealed largely to nonintellectuals, females, and children. Therefore, the major newspapers provided that precious little coverage available on the mixed cases evaluated here. With the passage of time, however, the distinction in reader appeal tended to be blurred. For example, beginning in the early 1880s, even minor newspapers, like major ones, carried editorials. By the outbreak of the Sino-Japanese War of 1894–1895, the distinction ceased to be significant: all newspapers, major or minor, were both news-oriented and entertaining.[19]

The above developments might lead to the assumption that over the years an increased number of newspapers covered mixed cases, one aspect of current affairs. But this was not so. The *Chōya shimbun* reported Cases 2 and 3 in 1878, Case 4 in 1880, Case 5 in 1882, and Case 6 in 1884, but reported none from 1885 through 1893. (One may recall that I had no access to issues of this newspaper published after 1893.) Similarly, the *Jiji shimpō* reported Case 7 in 1888 and Case 8 in 1893, but none between 1894 and 1899. This absence is all the more remarkable, since from the mid-1880s no other major newspapers rivaled the *Jiji shimpō* in the extent of its news coverage, both domestic and overseas, in the thoroughness with which news was analyzed, and in the speed with which news was gathered and reported.[20] Not only did the newspapers multiply in number, but they also became thicker. In 1876, for example, the *Tokyo nichi nichi shimbun* was four pages long but was twice as long in 1885;[21] in mid-1891, the *Jiji shimpō* was lengthened from four pages to six.[22]

Nevertheless, these changes in no way boosted the newspapers' coverage of mixed cases. Instead, there seems to have been virtually no reporting during the last several years of the Age of Extraterritoriality. Two factors may explain this. First, as already pointed out, many consular courts in Japan adjudicated fewer mixed cases during the 1890s than during the 1880s, the U.S. consular court at Nagasaki being a notable exception. Second, after 1894, probably few mixed cases, if any, were considered worth being reported by Japanese newspapers largely because, with the signing of the Anglo-Japanese Treaty of that year in which Britain agreed to relinquish in due course its extraterritorial privileges in Japan, the Japanese knew that the Age of Extraterritoriality was about to fade into oblivion.

It should be evident, then, that even if one read all the Japanese newspapers ever published in Japan during the period, one might uncover only a handful of cases.

It is abundantly clear that adjudication of virtually all the estimated 3,500 cases went unchallenged by the Japanese. Those cases that outraged the people were the publicized ones, and there were only 5 of these. Of the 5, only the earliest, the *King* case, can truly be said to have been unfairly adjudicated. Of semipublicized cases, only a few *may* have been unfairly adjudicated. One may, therefore, assert that only a handful of the 3,500 cases, or far less than 1 percent, may have been adjudicated unfairly.

7

Conclusion

The functioning of the human mind requires simplicity in diversity, the universal in the particular. But it is also responsible in part for the bane of valid generalization: overcategorization. Psychologist Gordon Allport has observed: "Overcategorization is perhaps the commonest trick of the human mind. Given a thimbleful of facts we rush to make generalization as large as a tub."[1]

So it was with the Japanese view that the Western extraterritorial courts in Japan as a rule did not render equitable justice. F. C. Jones once wrote:

The various cases cited above to illustrate the defects of the consular courts attract notice because they are exceptional; doubtless in the great majority of cases reasonable justice was executed by the consuls and no more was heard of the affair. The evil that the consuls did lived after in appeal cases or diplomatic exchanges of notes, the good was usually interred in the archives of the court and lay forgotten.[2]

The present study has shown how few these exceptional cases were and how large "the great majority of cases" was. A conservative estimate of mixed cases adjudicated by the courts is 3,500. Of these, only a handful—or certainly less than 1 percent, even after making generous allowance for possible estimating errors—may have been adjudicated unfairly. The good that the consuls did in adjudicating virtually all the mixed cases satisfactorily to the Japanese litigants has lain forgotten. There is, therefore, no factual basis whatever to support the prevalent Japanese interpretation that, as a rule, no Japanese could expect justice in the Western consular courts.

Although the abolition of extraterritoriality was unquestionably the top national priority for both the Japanese government and all public affairs-conscious Japanese, extraterritoriality affected the lives of an infinitesimal fraction of the Japanese people. Proceedings of the Western consular courts were of no particular concern to most Japanese. Incontrovertible evidence of this disinterest is the fact that a reading of the two sets of daily newspapers covering the Age of Extraterritoriality reveals the reporting of only fourteen out of the estimated 3,500 mixed cases. In his draft communication to Foreign Secretary Granville dated November 20, 1882, British Minister to Japan Parkes observed that sweeping Japanese statements insinuating that "all sorts of extraordinary and lawless acts are being constantly committed by foreigners who shelter themselves under the extra territorial provisions are easy to make but very few instances indeed can be alleged of the Japanese government or any Japanese individual having suffered any appreciable harm through the operation of extra territoriality."[3] Why, then, has the Japanese view been accepted so tenaciously and so long?

Several factors that have been intimated throughout this study may be suggested as together constituting a plausible explanation: the lack of sufficient knowledge of law on the part of the consuls, the inadequate provisions and staff for the operation of consular courts, the Japanese difficulty in understanding Western legal principles, especially the differing substantive and procedural laws of the numerous treaty powers, and the like.

Much can be said of each of these factors. But probably none is more important than the determined and persistent Japanese drive to abolish the extraterritorial regime in Japan. Hatoyama Kazuo, a prominent Columbia- and Yale University-trained jurist, educator, and politician of Meiji Japan, precisely identified the primary causative factor when he wrote: "Practically, as the number of European and American residents was very small, I do not think it ["a peculiar system termed 'extraterritoriality' "] worked any serious harm, but, as a matter of principle, it was strongly objectionable to the highly sensitive Japanese."[4] In the nineteenth-century world, the militarily strong and technologically advanced Western powers forced the weaker and less technologically developed countries of the Orient to grant them extraterritoriality. Therefore, to the Japanese extraterritoriality was a badge of weakness and inferiority. It was an infringement upon the sovereign rights of Japan, a stigma to the self-esteem and pride of the highly sensitive Japanese. Therefore, once they realized this in the early 1870s,[5] they asserted, as Soejima Taneomi, the ex-foreign minister, put it, "that a great national wrong had been done her [Japan] by the Powers, whereby she had been robbed of her birth right, namely, Judicial . . . Autonomy. She alledged that it was prejudicial to the dignity of an independent and civilized State to have foreign law-courts sitting within its dominion."[6] Moreover, the Japanese bitterly resented the racial inferiority that they thought the extraterritorial system imputed to them.[7] The fact that Japan objected not only to specific abuses of extraterritoriality but also to extraterritoriality itself as a matter of principle made its abolition more than just an official diplomatic objective: it made it a compelling universal national obsession. The net result was that the Japanese became true believers in the indignity and unfairness of the extraterritorial system.

True believers need no truth; they already have it. All they need is proof, evidence, or mere signs. So it may have been with the Japanese historians and popular writers who have criticized or castigated the Western consular courts. They believed that extraterritoriality was basically unfair and unjust. They have, therefore, looked for any evidence they can find of this basic unfairness. Stated another way, already believing a generalization, they have searched for facts to substantiate that generalization. After having found what they believed to be the facts they sought in the five publicized cases, they subsequently highlighted them in their writings. For the writers, these cases have served as part of a larger body of collected evidence. In all probability, therefore, they have never stopped to think whether the five cases can fully support the sweeping generalization that this study has evaluated. As a result, the untenable interpretation has gone un-challenged and has remained erroneously accepted as historical fact.

Appendix ————————————

A Quantitative Process to Establish an Estimate of the Number of Mixed Cases Adjudicated by the British and the U.S. Consular Courts in Japan, 1859 to 1899

As pointed out in Chapter 6, an estimated 2,798 mixed cases were adjudicated by the British and the U.S. consular courts in Japan during the Age of Extraterritoriality. This figure is extrapolated from the 668 cases recorded in returns of the cases discovered during research of this study.

The process of extrapolation from hard data was predominantly quantitative and, therefore, not of sufficient interest to be included in the text. However, relegation of details of the extrapolation process to the Appendix should not be construed as meaning that the details are unimportant. On the contrary, they provide vital substantiation for the validity of the study's central thesis.

Before describing the process of extrapolation, I should explain why two figures—79 in each instance—in Appendix Table 1 that pertain to the U.S. consular court at Ōsaka and Hyōgo are identical. Inasmuch as the returns of cases adjudicated by the court for the entire period of its operation, thirty-one and a half years, were available for scrutiny, there was no need for extrapolation, a fact that explains why the "estimate" of mixed cases adjudicated by the court is the same as the number from which the "estimate" was derived. Furthermore, Chapter 6 discusses why the sum of estimated cases is less than the 100 percent count; that discussion is not repeated here.

Nagasaki

Fortunately, the records of a majority of mixed cases adjudicated by the British and the U.S. consular courts at Nagasaki were found. Therefore, estimating the respective numbers of the cases heard there was most reassuring.

Next to those of the U.S. court at Hyōgo and Ōsaka, the records of the U.S. court at Nagasaki represent the best preserved and most complete of all the consular court records located and examined. Although records of the U.S. court at Kanagawa have been equally faithfully recorded and kept, many of the unbound records there cannot be used for research because at a touch they crumble like old, fallen leaves. Missing from the records of the U.S. court at Nagasaki are the quarterly returns of lawsuits for

Appendix Table 1

Estimates of the Number of Mixed Cases Adjudicated at British and U.S Consular Courts in Japan, 1859-1899

	Consulate	Year Established	Number of Years of Operation Prior to July 1899(a)	A Number of Years for Which Mixed Cases Are Found	Number of Cases for A	B Number of Years for Which Estimate of Cases is Made	Estimate of Cases for B
BRITISH	Edo (Tokyo)(b)	1859(c)	40 1/2	11	44	40 1/2	118
	Hakodate	1859	40 1/2	15	30	30 1/2	74
	Hōyogo and Ōsaka(d)	1868	31 1/2	6(e)	97	31 1/2	538
	Kanagawa (Yokohama)(f)	1860	39 1/2	4	36	39 1/2	1,197
	Nagasaki	1859	40 1/2	31	174	40 1/2	212
	Niigata	1868(g)	15 (closed in 1882)	--(h)	--	--	--
	Subtotal		207 1/2	67	381	182 1/2	2,139
UNITED STATES	Edo	May 1869	2 3/4 (closed in March 1872)	--	--	--	--
	Hakodate	January 1865(i)	12 (closed in Oct. 1876)	0(j)	0	0	0
	Kanagawa	December 1861	37 1/2	11 3/4	149	37 1/2	507
	Nagasaki	May 1859	40 1/4	37 1/4	59	40 1/4	73
	Ōsaka-Hyōgo	January 1868	31 1/2	31 1/2	79	31 1/2	79
	Subtotal		124	80 1/2	287	109 1/4	659
	Total		331 1/2	147 1/2	668	291 3/4	2,798

SOURCES: BRITISH. Edo, FO 656/40, 656/49, 798/14, Hakodate, FO 656/41, Kanagawa, FO 656/14, 656/29, Nagasaki, FO 656/34, 656/34, 656/35, 656/49, Hyōgo and Ōsaka, FO 656/35, 656/34, 656/36, 656/42, 796/6, 796/10, Public Record Office, Kew, England; Great Britain, Foreign Office, Consular Establishments (London, 1870), p. 43; Great Britain, Foreign Office, Foreign Office List. UNITED STATES. Despatches from United States Consuls in Hakodate, 1856-1878 (T 113), Kanagawa, 1861-1897, and Yedo, 1869-1872 (Microcopy 135), 1897-1906 (Microcopy 136), Nagasaki, 1860-1906 (Microcopy 136), and List of United States Consular Officers, 1789-1939 (Microcopy 587), Appointment Records, General Records of the Department of State (Record Group 59); Records of the American Consulates at Kōbe, at Nagasaki, and at Yokohama, Records of the Foreign Service Posts of the Department of State (Record Group 84), National Archives, Washington, D.C.

(a) Extraterritoriality was abolished in Japan on July 17, 1899, except that France and Austria-Hungary continued it until August 4, 1899.

(b) The Foreign Office List for 1882 was the first one to refer to the British legation and the British consulate general at Tokyo as Tokyo rather than "Yedo." Letter from M. J. Callow, Library and Records Department, Foreign and Commonwealth Office, London, March 17, 1980.

(c) The exact months in which all of the British consulates were established cannot be ascertained from the sources. It is, therefore, assumed that each consulate was created at the beginning of the year during which the consulate is known to have been open.

(d) Hyōgo and Ōsaka were officially redesignated Kōbe and Hyōgo in 1898. Again, they were singly redesignated Kōbe in 1904. Foreign Office List, 1889,1904.

(e) The extant dockets of the Ōsaka sittings cover only three years from 1872 through 1874. FO 656/41. None of the cases recorded in the dockets are counted, since it is unknown how long the Ōsaka vice-consulate maintained dockets separate from those of the Hyōgo consulate.

(f) Kanagawa was officially redesignated Yokohama in 1885. Foreign Office List, 1885.

(g) Niigata reexisted as part of the Consular District of Hakodate–Niigata from 1885 to 1897. Ibid., 1885-1897.

(h) The dash (--) stands for "not found" or "not applicable."

(i) Elisha E. Rice was appointed commercial agent on June 26, 1856, and assumed charge at Hakodate on May 1, 1857. The post became a consulate with Rice's confirmation as consul on January 18, 1865. As a consulate, the post was officially closed on October 4, 1876, when it became a consular agency and remained so until August 20, 1878. "Introduction" to Microcopy 452. No U.S. consular agent was invested with judicial authority. John Bassett Moore, A Digest of International Law, 2.614.

(j) Examination of the records of the Hakodate consulate reveals that none of the consuls ever filed a return of cases, although they filed other kinds of returns. One may assume, therefore, that none of the consuls at Hakodate formed a consular court.

the years 1889, 1890, and 1891. For the ten-and-a-half year period from 1889 to July 1899, therefore, there are quarterly returns of the court for seven and a half years only. These returns record a total of 147 cases, of which 36 are mixed. Hence, the estimate of mixed cases at Nagasaki for the years from 1889 to mid–1899 was calculated as follows:

$$
\begin{array}{cc}
\textit{Years} & \textit{Cases} \\
7.5 & 36 \\
10.5 & X
\end{array}
$$

$$X = \frac{36 \times 10.5}{7.5}$$

$$X = 50$$

The Nagasaki estimate was not made on the basis of the total number of recorded cases for the longer period of thirty-seven and a quarter years because to do so would have produced a diminished estimate. The court adjudicated a greater number of cases during the period of ten and a half years than during any of the preceding decades of its operation, as may be seen in Appendix Table 2. During that period the court adjudicated 19.6 cases a year on the average, whereas during the immediate preceding decade (1879–1888), for example, it adjudicated only 1.4 cases a year. For the three preceding decades, the court adjudicated twelve, four, and seven *mixed* cases, respectively—twenty-three in all. The sum of this count and the estimated fifty for the last decade, a total of seventy-three, is the estimate for the entire four decades, as can be noted in Appendix Table 1.

Turning to the British court at Nagasaki, one finds that the extant records of the court lack information about the number of mixed cases for the first decade of its operation,

Appendix Table 2
Decennial Breakdown of the Number of Cases Adjudicated by the U.S. Consular Court at Nagasaki, 1859-1899

Years	A Number of Years for Which Mixed Cases Are Found	B Number of All (Mixed and Nonmixed) Cases for A	Mean of Cases per Year B/A
1859-1868	9 3/4	70	7.2
1869-1878	10	17	1.7
1879-1888	10	14	1.4
1889-1899	7 1/2	147	19.6

SOURCE: Records of the American Consulate at Nagasaki, Records of the Foreign Service Posts of the Department of State (Record Group 84), National Archives, Washington, D.C.

Appendix Table 3
Decennial Breakdown of the Number of Cases Adjudicated by the British Consular Court at Nagasaki, 1859-1899

Years	Mixed Cases	All Cases
1859-1868	X	299
1869-1878	57 ⎫	379 ⎫
1879-1888	58 ⎬ 172	246 ⎬ 898
1889-1899	57 ⎭	273 ⎭

SOURCES: FO 656/34, 656/36, 656/42, 756/6, 796/10, Public Record Office, Kew, England; Great Britain, Foreign Office, <u>Consular Establishments</u> (London, 1870), p. 43.

1859–1868. The number of cases for each of the other decades is presented in Appendix Table 3. The simplest way to arrive at an estimate of mixed cases for the first decade, X, would be to compute as follows:

	Mixed	All
1859–1868	X	299
1869–1899	172	898

$$X = \frac{172 \times 299}{898}$$

$$X = 57$$

The difficulty with this estimate, 57, is that it is probably too large, since the estimate represents 19 percent of the total 299 cases for the first decade. The basis for this conclusion is the well-known fact that there was, on the whole, little contact between Japanese and Westerners in nineteenth-century Japan. In 1883 the *Japan Weekly Mail*, a Yokohama English newspaper which was exceptionally friendly to the Japanese when compared with other foreign-language newspapers published in Japan, stated: "A dense cloud of mutual ignorance separates foreigners and Japanese. It would be difficult to determine which side knows less of the other's ways. Of social intercourse, there is very little, and what there is must be described as essentially superficial."[1] If there was "little of social intercourse" during the 1880s, there had been virtually none during the 1860s, a decade of xenophobia characterized by the slogan "Expel the Barbarian" (*jōi*). During this decade, many swashbuckling samurai were thirsty for and successful in lopping off the heads of Westerners with their long, curved swords.

An experimental attempt to establish an estimate smaller than 57, or 19 percent, required computation of an all British mixed/all cases ratio, as shown in Appendix Table 4. The ratio is .132. By multiplying this number to 299, the number of all cases adjudicated by the British court at Nagasaki, one arrives at an estimate of 39 mixed cases. To be sure, the data used in arriving at the ratio is incomplete. Therefore, one cannot

Appendix Table 4
Ratio of Mixed Cases to All Cases
Adjudicated by British Consular Courts, 1859–1899

	A	B	C	D	E	
Court	Years for Which Most Half-year Returns Are Found	Number of Half-year Returns(a) Presumably Filed for A	Number of Half-year Returns Actually Found	Number of Mixed Cases Recorded in C	Number of All Cases (Mixed and Nonmixed) Recorded	Percentage D/E
Edo	1871–1878	16	15	43	199	21.67%
	1885–1891	14(b)	7(b)	1(b)	4	
Hakodate	1866–1878	26	23	30	125	24.00
Hyōgo and Ōsaka	1869–1875	14	12	97(c)	649	14.95
Kanagawa	1865–1870	12	8	36	918	3.92
Nagasaki	1868–1899	64	38	174	1,070	17.40
Total		146	103	381	2,965	Mean 13.16

SOURCES: Same as the British sources cited in Appendix Table 1.
(a) Whereas all the U.S. consular courts filed quarterly returns of their lawsuits with the Department of State, all the British consular courts filed "half-year" returns with the British Foreign Office.
(b) During the seven-year period 1885 to 1891, the Edo court appears actually to have filed only twelve half-year returns, since only a single return was filed for each of the years 1886 and 1891. I was able to locate only seven of these twelve. Of the seven, six indicate that there were no cases adjudicated. The remaining return, the one for the latter half of 1889, shows that during that half-year the court adjudicated a mixed case and three nonmixed cases—four in all.
(c) Excluded from the 97 figure are six mixed cases recorded in the six half-year returns of the Osaka sittings. The reason for exclusion is that no one knows how long a separate docket was maintained; there is no basis for determining the number of years for which the six cases can be used for extrapolation. Hence, all data relating to the Hyogo-Osaka court pertain to the Hyogo sittings only; they represent an underevaluation of the entire caseload of that court.

Appendix Table 5
Mixed Versus All Cases
Adjudicated by the U.S.
and British Consular Courts
at Nagasaki, 1859-1899

Decade	U.S. at Nagasaki			British at Nagasaki		
	Mixed	All	M/A	Mixed	All	M/A
1859-1868	12	70	17.1%	39(a)	299	13.2%
1869-1878	4	17	23.4	57	379	15.0
1879-1888	7	14	50.0	58	246	23.6
1889-1899	50	205	24.5	57	273	20.8

SOURCES: Computed from Despatches from United States
          Consuls in Nagasaki, 1860-1906 (Microcopy 131), and
          Records of the American Consulate at Nagasaki, Records
          of the Foreign Service Posts of the Department of State
          (Record Group 84), National Archives, Washington, D.C.,
          and from FO 656/34, 656/36, 656/42, 796/6, 796/10,
          Public Record Office, Kew, England.
          (a)An estimate rather than a count.

assert with certainty that the number of mixed cases was 39, although one can state with assurance that 39 is closer than 57 to the indeterminable truth.

Appendix Table 5 provides critical data with which to corroborate the reasonableness of the estimate thus obtained. The table shows that the ratio of mixed/all cases adjudicated by the British court at Nagasaki for each of the other three decades is greater than that for the first decade, 13.2 percent. The same pattern applies to the U.S. court at Nagasaki where the ratio of mixed/all cases adjudicated by that court was smaller for the first decade than for any of the other three decades.

By substituting 39 for X in Appendix Table 3, one may obtain a total of 211 mixed cases as follows:

1859-1868	39
1869-1878	57
1879-1888	58
1889-1899	57

211

Kanagawa

Estimating the number of mixed cases adjudicated by the British court at Kanagawa (the Yokohama Court) was a rather difficult task. Unlike estimating the number of mixed cases of the British court at Nagasaki, the number at Kanagawa had to be calcuiated on the strength of only the small number of recorded cases actually found, which required extrapolation on a much greater scale than did estimating the like number for the Nagasaki court. Appendix Table 6 presents all of the meager data available to use in arriv-

Appendix Table 6
Number of Recorded Cases Adjudicated by the Yokohma (Kanagawa) Court

Years for Which Most Half-year Returns Are Found	A Number of Years for Which Cases Are Found	B Number of Mixed Cases for A	C Number of Non-mixed Cases for A	Number of All Cases, B + C
1865–1870	4	36	882	918

SOURCE: FO 656/34, 656/36, 656/42, 796/6, 796/10, Public Record Office, Kew, England.

ing at an estimate of the number of mixed cases adjudicated by the Yokohama Court during the entire period of its existence, thirty-nine and a half years. (See Appendix Table 1.)

The simplest and most obvious way of calculating the estimate, X, would lie in extrapolating as follows from the number of recorded cases found—36 (Appendix Table 6).

$$
\begin{array}{cc}
Years & Cases \\
4 & 36 \\
39.5 & X
\end{array}
$$

$$X = \frac{39.5 \times 36}{4}$$

$$X = 355.5$$

In all probability this estimate, 356, is too small. One may recall that the proportion of mixed cases to all cases adjudicated during the first decade was smaller than that of any of the other three decades (Appendix Table 5). Consequently, any extrapolation from such a four-year figure as 36 during the first decade to the other four decades is bound to yield an underestimate.

In an effort to arrive at another estimate that was not so depressed as the 356, the number of all cases was used as the basis for extrapolation. As seen in Appendix Table 6, the number of all cases for the four-year period is 918. On the basis of this count, the number of all cases for the thirty-nine and a half years, X, was estimated as follows:

$$
\begin{array}{cc}
Years & Cases \\
4 & 918 \\
39.5 & X
\end{array}
$$

$$X = \frac{918 \times 39.5}{4}$$

$$X = 9,065$$

To derive an estimate of *mixed* cases from the sum of *all* cases thus estimated, 9,065, one needs a percentage of mixed to all cases. Two percentages of this sort were computed, and the results, along with the all British mixed/all cases ratio presented in Appendix Table 4, are shown in Appendix Table 7. The figure used in obtaining the per-

Appendix Table 7
Mixed to All Cases Ratios

Consular Court	Number of Mixed Cases	Number of All Cases	Percentage
U.S. at Nagasaki	73	306	23.9%
British at Nagasaki	211	1,197	17.6
All British	381	2,965	13.2

SOURCE: Appendix Tables 4 and 5.

Appendix Table 8
Mixed and All Cases Recorded at the
U.S. Consular Court at Kanagawa, 1862–1899

Years	Number of Quarterly Returns Pre- sumably Filed	Number of Quarterly Returns Found	Number of Mixed Cases Recorded	Number of All Cases Recorded, Mixed and Nonmixed
1862–1968	28	--	--	--
1869–1878	40	2	24	47
1879–1888	40	29	123	265
1889–1899	42	16	12	76
Total	150	47	159	388

SOURCES: Despatches from United States Consuls in Kanagawa, 1861–1897, and
Yedo, 1869–1872 (Microcopy 135), Yokohama, 1897–1906 (Microcopy 136);
Records of the American Consulate at Kanagawa, Records of the Foreign
Service Posts of the Department of State (Record Group 84), National
Archives, Washington, D.C.

centage of mixed cases to all cases is the all British mixed/all cases ratio. Two reasons
account for this choice. The first is that this percentage is derived from a large number
of cases, 2,965; it has a relatively small sampling variability. The second reason is that,
since the percentage is the smallest of the three percentages, its choice is in harmony
with my consistent tendency toward conservative estimates. The multiplication of 9,065
by the ratio .132 yields 1,197, my estimate of mixed cases adjudicated by the Yokohama
Court.

The U.S. consular court at Kanagawa, created in December 1861, exercised extraterritorial jurisdiction for 150 quarters until July 1899. As indicated in Appendix Table
8, I was able to locate the Court's returns of lawsuits for 47 of these 150 quarters.

Assuming that there were no great variations in the court's incidence of adjudication
during the three decades from 1869 through mid-1899, one may extrapolate as follows
from the incomplete data presented in Appendix Table 8 an estimate of the number of
mixed cases adjudicated by the Kanagawa Court. X represents the estimated number for
the three decades, while X_1, X_2, and X_3 represent estimates of the numbers for the 1870s,
the 1880s, and the 1890s, respectively:

1869–1878	Quarters	Cases	
	2	24	$X_1 = \dfrac{40 \times 24}{2}$
	40	X_1	$X_1 = 480$
1879–1888	Quarters	Cases	
	29	123	$X_2 = \dfrac{40 \times 123}{29}$
	40	X_2	$X_2 = 170$
1889–1899	Quarters	Cases	
	16	12	$X_3 = \dfrac{42 \times 12}{16}$
	42	X_3	$X_3 = 32$

$$X = X_1 + X_2 + X_3 = 682$$

Although the years 1862 to 1868 are excluded from the estimated number, X, this estimate, 682, is too large because the estimate of *all* cases—1,506—which was arrived at in precisely the same way as 682 is too large. X, the 1,506, was extrapolated from data presented in Appendix Table 8 as follows:

1869–1878	Quarters	Cases	
	40	X_1	$X_1 = \dfrac{40 \times 47}{2}$
	2	47	$X_1 = 940$
1879–1888	Quarters	Cases	
	40	X_2	$X_2 = \dfrac{40 \times 265}{29}$
	29	265	$X_2 = 366$
1889–1899	Quarters	Cases	
	42	X_3	$X_3 = \dfrac{42 \times 76}{16}$
	16	76	$X_3 = 200$

$$X = X_1 + X_2 + X_3 = 1,506$$

This estimate, 1,506, is probably an overestimate because the estimate of all cases adjudicated by the court for the fourteen and a half years from 1871 through mid-1885 may be obtained with accuracy and confidence. Consul General Thomas B. Van Buren appears to have assumed charge at Kanagawa early in 1871 until he left the post as of June 30, 1885. The court's quarterly return of lawsuits for the second quarter of 1885 shows the following case numbers:[2]

Kind of Case	Case Number	Date of First Sitting
Civil	141	March 27, 1885
Criminal	158	April 4, 1885
Police	333	June 17, 1885

One may assume, therefore, that during his tenure Van Buren handled approximately 150 civil cases, 160 criminal cases, and 340 police cases—a total of 650 cases. On the basis of this figure, it is safe to assume that had he occupied the post for twenty years through 1890—the years roughly identical with the second and third decades of the court's existence—he could have adjudicated 897 cases or thereabouts. The estimated number of all cases adjudicated by the court for the second and third quarters, $X_1 + X_2$, is 1,306. Since 1,306 is incomparably larger than 897, it may be concluded that 1,506 is an overestimate.

To obtain a more accurate estimate of the mixed cases adjudicated during the 150 quarters, the per quarter mean of mixed cases adjudicated during the three decades from 1868 to mid-1899 was used as the basis for computing the estimate. From Appendix Table 8 one may readily calculate this mean, the quotient of 159 and 47, or 3.38. If this mean were found to be a conservative estimate, one could arrive at a conservative estimate of the mixed cases by multiplying the mean by 150.

One way to test whether or not the mean, 3.38, is a conservative figure lies in testing whether the per quarter mean of all cases found, 388, is a conservative one (Appendix

Table 8). A similar test on 388 can be conducted by comparing it with the per quarter mean of all cases estimated, 1,506, an overestimate. Should the per quarter mean of 388 be much smaller than that of 1,506, one would be justified in concluding that the 388 figure is a relatively conservative estimate. From Appendix Table 8 one may calculate the two means: 8.26 (388/47) and 12.34 (1,506/122). Since 8.26 is much smaller than 12.34, one may conclude that the 8.26 figure is a relatively conservative estimate of the per quarter mean of all cases. Hence, one may likewise conclude that the mean, 3.38, is also a conservative one. By multiplying the mean by 150, one obtains 507, an estimate of the mixed cases which is closer to the true, but unascertainable, figure than the estimate extrapolated from the known figures for the 122 quarters—682 cases. Appendix Table 1 shows 507 as the estimate of the mixed cases adjudicated by the U.S. consular court at Kanagawa.

So much for explaining the method of estimating the mixed cases adjudicated by the Kanagawa and Nagasaki consular courts. How the estimates of mixed cases adjudicated by the other British and the U.S. consular courts were arrived at is not explained here, for two reasons. First, the Nagasaki and Kanagawa courts adjudicated an estimated total of 1,989 cases, or approximately 71 percent of all the mixed cases estimated; the foregoing has already covered a large majority and, therefore, provides the reader with a good idea of how all the estimates shown in Appendix Table 1 were obtained. Second, one might find a lengthy explanation of how all the estimates were obtained exceedingly redundant, boring, and tedious. At his request, however, I would be glad to inform any interested reader of how the other estimates of mixed cases not explained in the Appendix were obtained.

Notes

Preface

1. Tatui Baba, *The Treaty Between Japan and England* (London, 1876), p. 7.
2. Trans. in the *Japan Weekly Mail*, July 15, 1894.
3. Moriya Hidesuke, Jōyaku kaisei," *Iwanami kōza Niohon rekishi*, 8 (Tokyo, 1934), 14f.; Yamamoto Shigeru, *Jōyaku kaiseishi* (Tokyo, 1943), pp. 213f.; Inoue Kiyoshi, *Jōyaku kaisei* (Tokyo: Iwanami shinsho, 1955), p. 34; and Kikujiro Ishii, *Diplomatic Commentaries*, trans. and ed. William R. Langdon (Baltimore, 1937), p. 17.

Chapter 1. The Western Consular Courts in Nineteenth-Century Japan: An Overview

1. See W. E. Hall, *A Treatise on the Foreign Powers and Jurisdiction of the British Crown* (Oxford, 1894); F. T. Piggott, *Extraterritoriality: The Law Relating to Consular Jurisdiction and to Residence in Oriental Countries*, 2d ed. (Hong Kong, 1907); and Shih Shun Liu, *Extraterritoriality: Its Rise and Its Decline* (New York, 1925).
2. F. C. Jones, *Extraterritoriality in Japan and the Diplomatic Relations Resulting in Its Abolition, 1853–1899* (New Haven, Conn., 1931), pp. 35–44. This monograph, the only English-language study on the important subject of the revision of the unequal treaties in Japan, has served generations of scholars and students well. But the author's analysis of the working of the British and the U.S. consular courts contains serious inaccuracies. For example, he states: "Further, whenever he [the litigant] was . . . prevented [from appealing to the higher courts], the concurrent jurisdiction of the Supreme Court at Shanghai and, after 1878, of the Court for Japan at Kanagawa, with the provincial courts, enabled the verdicts of the latter to be reviewed and, if necessary, amended without the parties concerned having to appear in the higher courts themselves." Ibid., p. 42. This statement contains three errors. First, the Supreme Court had power to review not only verdicts but also sentences. Second, the Court for Japan had no appellate jurisdiction. Finally, the Supreme Court reviewed cases by virtue of its appellate jurisdiction and not of its concurrent jurisdiction. See China and Japan Order in Council, 1865, Arts. 119–123; and China and Japan Order in Council, 1878, Art. 8.

3. FO 46/313/167.

4. Richard B. Hubbard, *The United States in the Far East; or, Modern Japan and the Orient* (Richmond, Va., 1899), pp. 366f.

5. FO 46/313/167.

6. Clive Parry, "United Kingdom," *Legal Advisers and Foreign Affairs*, ed. H.C.L. Merillat (New York, 1964), p. 150.

7. See FO 46/260.

8. FO 46/314/164; Hiezuka Ryū ["On Japan's Foreign Trade"], *Shidankai sokki-roku*, ed. Shidankai, 196 (Tokyo, 1909), 54, reprint ed., 28 (Tokyo, 1973), 554—here-after cited as Hiezuka ["On Japan's Foreign Trade"]; and Jones, *Extraterritoriality in Japan*, pp. 34f.

9. China and Japan Order in Council, 1865, Arts. 65, 63, 70.

10. Ibid., Art. 71.

11. Ibid., Art. 33; and Jones, *Extraterritoriality in Japan*, p. 38.

12. China and Japan Order in Council, 1868, Art. 77.

13. Ibid., Arts. 9–12.

14. Ibid., Arts. 30, 32.

15. Ibid., Art. 62.

16. Ibid., Art. 119.

17. Ibid., Arts. 121, 120.

18. Ibid., Art. 131.

19. Letter from J. K. Dixon, Chief Clerk of the Privy Council, London, February 17, 1977.

20. China and Japan Order in Council, 1878, Arts. 5, 6, 3, 9.

21. FO 46/234/191.

22. China and Japan Order in Council, 1878, Arts. 1, 9.

23. Jones, *Extraterritoriality in Japan*, p. 42.

24. Ibid.

25. FO 46/313/167.

26. Consul General C. R. Greenhouse to Assistant Secretary of State James D. Porter, January 19, 1887, Despatches from United States Consuls in Kanagawa, 1861–1897, and Yedo, 1869–1872 (Microcopy 135/16), General Records of the Department of State (Record Group 59), National Archives, Washington, D.C.

27. John Bassett Moore, *A Digest of International Law*, 2 (Washington, D.C., 1906), 613.

28. Revised Statutes of the United States, 20 *Statutes at Large* 131, Secs. 4089, 4105.

29. Ibid., Sec. 4106.

30. Ibid., Secs. 4090, 4102.

31. Ibid., Sec. 4107.

32. Ibid., Sec. 4095.

33. Ibid., Sec. 4107.

34. Ibid., Secs. 4092, 4093.

35. Ibid., Sec. 4094.

36. Ibid., Secs. 4086, 4118, 4119.

37. Frank E. Hinckley, *American Consular Jurisdiction in the Orient* (Washington, D.C., 1906), p. 62.

38. Herbert H.D. Pierce, *Report to the Honorable John Hay, Secretary of State,*

upon a Tour of Consular Inspection in Asia (Washington, D.C., 1904), p. 9. Since judgments in civil cases had been appealable to the Circuit Court in California only when the matter in dispute exceeded $2,500, for sums under $2,500 appeal still lay to the U.S. minister at Tokyo. Ibid.

39. Quoted in Hinckley, *American Consular Jurisdiction in the Orient*, p. 74.

40. Ibid., p. ix.

41. DeB. Randolph Keim, *A Report to the Hon. George S. Boutwell, Secretary of the Treasury, upon the Condition of the Consular Service of the United States of America* (Washington, D.C., 1872), p. 183.

42. Pierce, *Report*, p. 15.

43. For Dennett's long-lasting influence on the current historiography of American-East Asian relations, see Ernest R. May, ed., *American-East Asian Relations: A Survey* (Cambridge, Mass., 1972).

44. Tyler Dennett, *Americans in Eastern Asia* (New York, 1922, reprint ed., 1941), pp. 669, 670, 672.

45. Keim, *A Report*, pp. 3–11. An American historian of Japanese history who as a boy grew up in Shanghai under extraterritorial law wrote me: "Given the low calibre of American consuls, I am . . . doubtful as to the quality of justice in the American consular courts [in nineteenth-century Japan]." The conclusion that the justice of the American courts was of doubtful quality flows quite logically from the premise that the calibre of the consuls was low. But this logical conclusion is contrary to the facts as it applies to Japanese litigants at the American courts.

46. Dennett, *Americans in Eastern Asia*, p. 672.

47. *Jiji shimpō*, January 1, 1885.

48. Letters from Dr. Anna Coreth, Direktor des Hous-, Hof- und Staatsarchiv, Vienna, August 24, 1976, February 2, 1977.

49. Letters from P. H. Desneux, Archiviste, Ministère des Affaires étrangères et du Commerce Extérieur, Bruxelles, August 27, 1976.

50. Ibid.

51. Letters from Frank Jørgensen, Archivist, Second Department, Rigsarkivet, København, October 11, 1976, February 10, 1977; FO 46/313/167.

52. Letters from Directeur des Archives et de la Documentation, Ministère des Affaires Étrangères, Paris, April 18, 1975, October 24, 1975, July 5, 1979. Inquiries about the possible existence of documents or studies on the organization, jurisdiction, and distribution of the consular courts set up in Japan by France were directed to the Press and Information Division of the French Embassy in Washington, D.C.; the editor of the *French Colonial Studies*; and Archives du Ministère de la Justice, Archives Nationales, and the Bureau for Asian and South Pacific Affairs at the French Foreign Ministry, all in Paris. The French Embassy suggested that I get in touch with the Bureau for Asian and South Pacific Affairs, but the other parties did not respond.

53. FO 46/313/167.

54. Letter from Dr. W. Meyrat, Archivist, Swiss Federal Archives, Bern, July 27, 1976.

55. Tsurutaro Senga, *Gestaltung und Kritik der heutigen Konsulargerichtsbarkeit in Japan* (Berlin, 1897), pp. 63, 66, 67.

56. Letter from Dr. Maria Keipert, Auswärtiges Amt, Bonn, June 10, 1975; letters from Zentrales Staatsarchiv, Potsdam, August 28, 1975, December 12, 1975.

57. Ralph S. Kukendall, *The Hawaiian Kingdom*, 2 (Honolulu, 1953), 233f.

58. Liu, *Extraterritoriality*, p. 208.

59. Miss Agnes C. Conrad, State Archivist, Public Archives, Department of Accounting and General Services, the State of Hawaii, responded to my inquiry as follows: "Hawaii did not claim extra-territorial rights and consequential [*sic*] had no courts." Two subsequent pleas for search for the possible existence of a consular file elicited no response.

60. Letter from il Capo del Servizio Storico e Documentazione, Ministero degli Affari Esteri, Roma, April 18, 1977.

61. Ishii Takashi, *Meiji shoki no kokusai kankei* (Tokyo, 1977), pp. 334, 99, 98–109. Hereafter cited as Ishii, *Meiji shoki*.

62. See n. 60.

63. Letters from E. Van Laar, Keeper of the Second Section, General State Archives, The Hague, May 13, 1975, August 18, 1976, February 4, 1977.

64. FO 46/313/167.

65. My own counting. There are no records of mixed cases adjudicated by the Portuguese consular courts in Japan that have been preserved in Peru. Letter from Director del Archivo General de la Nacion, Lima, February 9, 1977. An inquiry into the possible existence of such records in Japan and a few questions concerning the Portuguese consulates were directed to the Portuguese Embassy in Tokyo, but no response came.

66. George Alexander Lensen, *Russian Diplomatic and Consular Officials in East Asia* (Tokyo, 1968), pp. 156–193.

67. Records of the Russian consulates in Japan were not published, nor are there any quantitative data on mixed cases tried at those consulates among materials in the Russian Foreign Ministry's possession. Letter from V. Mazaev, Chief of the Historical Diplomatic Division, Ministry of Foreign Affairs, USSR, December 21, 1976.

68. Inquiries were made to the Spanish Embassy in Tokyo and to the Ministerio de Asuntos Exteriores and the Archivo Historico Nacional, both in Madrid.

69. FO 46/313/167.

70. Letters from E. van Laar, General State Archives, The Hague, August 18, 1976, and Folke Ludwigs, Riksarkivet, Stockholm, July 29, 1976.

71. Letters from W. Meyrat, Archivist, July 27, 1976, and O. Gauye, Director, August 11, 1976, of Swiss Federal Archives, Bern.

72. Hiezuka ["On Japan's Foreign Trade"], 28.550.

73. Ishii, *Meiji shoki*, p. 342.

74. FO 46/251/101.

75. FO 46/360/189; and Japan, Gaimushō, *Nihon gaikō bunsho* (NGB), 47 vols. (Tokyo, 1936–1963), 12.431.

76. Hiezuka ["On Japan's Foreign Trade"], 28.550; D. W. Smith, *European Settlements in the Far East* (New York, 1900), p. 31.

77. FO 46/313/167; Smith, *European Settlements*, p. 35; and Basil Hall Chamberlain, *Japanese Things* (Rutland, Vt., 1971), p. 389.

78. FO 46/313/167f.

79. Townsend Harris, *The Complete Journal of Townsend Harris*, rev. ed. (Rutland, Vt., 1959), p. 516.

80. Ishii Takashi, *Nihon kaikokushi* (Tokyo, 1972), pp. 265–268, 272, 252.

81. Ibid., pp. 251f.

82. All treaty provisions documented and quoted in this study are from Japan, Gai-

mushō Jōyakukyoku, ed., *Kyū jōyaku isan*, 4 vols. (Tokyo, 1930–1934). Therefore, specific references will not be cited.

83. Ōyama Azusa, *Kyū jōyaku moto ni okeru kaishi kaikō no kenkyū* (Tokyo, 1967), pp. 2–7. Hereafter cited as Ōyama, *Kaishi kaikō*.

84. Ishii, *Nihon kaikokushi*, pp. 269f.

85. Ōyama, *Kaishi kaikō*, p. 17; Jones, *Extraterritoriality in Japan*, pp. 22f.; and John Peter Stern, *The Japanese Interpretation of the "Law of Nations," 1854–1874* (Princeton, N.J., 1979), pp. 41–43.

86. Harold S. Williams, *Tales of the Foreign Settlements in Japan* (Rutland, Vt., 1958), p. 35.

87. Ōyama, *Kaishi kaikō*, pp. 321–324; and letter from Professor Ōyama Azusa, October 2, 1979.

88. Letter from M. J. Callow, Library and Records Department, Foreign and Commonwealth Office, London, March 17, 1899.

Chapter 2. The Honor of a Japanese Girl: The *King* Case (1875)

1. Baba, *The Treaty Between Japan and England*, p. 7.

2. Taguchi Ukichi, *Jōyaku kaiseiron*, in *Meiji bunka zenshū*, ed. Meiji Bunka Kenkyūkai, 3d ed., 31 vols. (Tokyo, 1967–1969), 11.358f. Hereafter cited as Taguchi, *Jōyaku*.

3. Yamamoto, *Jōyaku kaiseishi*, p. 214.

4. Inoue, *Jōyaku kaisei*, p. 38.

5. Richard T. Chang, "A British Trial in Japan: *Regina* v. *Archibald King*," *Journal of Asian History* 10 (1976): 134–150.

6. Vice-Consul Martin Dohmen to Sir Edmund Hornby, Judge of the Supreme Court, June 19, 1875, Embassy and Consular Archives: Yedo Correspondence, FO 656/40, Public Record Office, Kew.

7. Ibid.

8. Ibid.

9. Ibid.

10. *Japan Weekly Mail*, June 19, 1875.

11. China and Japan Order in Council, 1865, Art. 77.

12. *Keihō*, 1880, Arts. 348 and 22.

13. In passing sentence, the Japanese judge was bound by the provisions of the Penal Code. He could not vary the maximum and minimum sentences stipulated by those provisions. To make it doubly certain that this was in fact so, the *Daishin'in hanketsuroku* volumes in the Library of Congress, which cover the years 1892–1906, were examined by Dr. Sung Yoon Cho, Acting Chief, Far Eastern Law Division, Law Library, Library of Congress. His time-consuming examination reveals that twelve rape cases are reported in those volumes and that of these cases only four indicate the sentences imposed by the lower courts (his letter of March 25, 1975). My evaluation of the four sentences shows that they were all in conformity with the appropriate provisions of the Penal Code in force and that none of the prison terms was shorter than two years.

14. *Kaitei ritsurei*, 1873, Art. 260. The text of this code may be found in Hōmu Sōgō Kenkyūjo, comp., *Keiji kankei kyū hōreishū (Keihōhen)* (Tokyo, 1969), pp. 96–139.

15. See n. 12.

16. *Keihō*, 1907, Arts. 117 and 12.

17. *Halsbury's Laws of England*, 3d ed., 43 vols. (London, 1952–1964), 10.431. General verdicts "in criminal matters are findings of guilty or not guilty." Special verdicts, on the other hand, are "findings of specific facts, upon which it is the duty of the court . . . in criminal cases to direct the jury to return the general verdict warranted by their special findings." Ibid., 24.34f.

18. China and Japan Order in Council, 1865, Arts. 33 and 34.

19. Jones, *Extraterritoriality in Japan*, p. 38.

20. China and Japan Order in Council, 1865, Arts. 68, 70, 72.

21. *The Japan Gazette*, June 22, 1875.

22. (24 & 25 Vict. ch. 100), Sec. 48.

23. The British law reports normally record only the verdict pronounced and not the sentence imposed on a case. Therefore, I would like to thank Miss Eve Johansson of the British Library in London for calling my attention to *Judicial Statistics*.

24. All but one were males. The annual mean for the seven years (1,010/7) was 144.4. The like figure for the years 1861 through 1870 (1,419/10) was 141.9. It would seem, therefore, that in the third quarter of the nineteenth century there was a high degree of consistency in the number of rape offenders committed for trial.

25. W. R. Cornish, et al., *Crime and Law in Nineteenth Century Britain* (Dublin, 1978), pp. 21f.

26. *Oxford English Dictionary*, 7.632.

27. See n. 25.

28. Edward Jenks, *A Short History of English Law*, 5th ed. (London, 1938), pp. 349f.; R. M. Jackson, *The Machinery of Justice in England*, 2d ed. (Cambridge, 1953), pp. 184f.

29. Cornish et al., *Crime and Law*, p. 46.

30. For details, see Chang, "A British Trial in Japan," pp. 144–146.

31. China and Japan Order in Council, 1865, Arts. 71 and 72.

Chapter 3. Extraterritoriality on Trial: The *Hartley* Cases (1878)

1. Hanabusa Nagamichi, *Meiji gaikōshi* (Tokyo, 1966), p. 65.

2. Inoue, *Jōyaku kaisei*, p. 41; and Kawashima Shintarō, *Jōyaku kaisei keika gaiyō* in *Jōyaku kaisei kankei Nihon gaikō bunsho*, ed. Nihon Gakujutsu Shinkōkai, 6 (Tokyo, 1950), 169. Hereafter cited as Kawashima, *Jōyaku kaisei*.

3. Yamamoto, *Jōyaku kaiseishi*, pp. 205f.; and Roy Hidemichi Akagi, *Japan's Foreign Relations, 1542–1936* (Tokyo, 1936), pp. 93–95.

4. Quoted in Liu, *Extraterritoriality*, pp. 28, 65, 77.

5. Henry Wheaton, *Elements of International Law*, Dana's ed. (Boston, 1866), p. 302, quoted in Liu, *Extraterritoriality*, p. 18.

6. Liu, *Extraterritoriality*, pp. 31, 47, 96.

7. Not all the treaties stipulated *actor sequitor forum rei* concerning civil disputes. A notable exception was the Anglo-Japanese Treaty of 1858, Article 6 of which provided:

A British subject having reason to complain of a Japanese, must proceed to the Consulate and state his grievance. The Consul will . . . do his utmost to arrange it amicably. In like manner, if a Japanese have reason to complain of a British subject, the Consul shall no less listen to his complaint, and endeavour to settle it in a friendly manner. If disputes take place of such a nature that the Consul cannot arrange them amicably, then he shall request the assistance of the Japanese authorities, that they may together . . . decide it amicably.

But the British never implemented this provision. *Law Reports, Appeal Cases, 1895*, p. 653. Instead they followed, in practice, Article 5 of the Austro-Hungarian Japanese Treaty of 1869 which embodied *actor sequitor forum rei*: "If an Austro-Hungaryan citizen has a complaint or grievance against a Japanese subject, the case shall be decided by the Japanese authorities. If on the contrary a Japanese has a complaint or grievance against a citizen of the said Monarchy, the case shall be decided by the Imperial Royal Authorities." The Austrian treaty was largely the work of Sir Harry Parkes, the British minister to Japan, and consequently reflected his view of the optimum arrangement.

8. U.S. Department of State, *Papers Relating to the Foreign Relations of the United States, 1874*, Washington, D.C., 1875, pp. 658f.

9. Substantive law creates or defines rights; procedural law "prescribes [the] method of enforcing the rights or obtaining redress for their invasion." Relating to crimes, procedural law provides or regulates the steps whereby one who commits a criminal offense is punished. *Black's Law Dictionary*, rev. 4th ed. (1968), pp. 1598, 1367.

10. G. H. Scidmore, A *Digest of Leading Cases Relating to Consular Court Jurisdiction in Japan* (Yokohama, 1882), p. 19; "Judgment Book," pp. 39–43, Records of the American Consulate at Nagasaki, Records of the Foreign Service Posts of the Department of State (Record Group 84), National Archives, Washington, D.C.

11. Eli T. Sheppard, *Extra-Territoriality in Japan* (Tokyo, 1879), pp. 49, 46. In 1877, Sheppard, U.S. consul general at Tientsin, assumed the post, a vacancy created by the expiration of E. P. Smith's term late in 1876. J. Payson Treat, *Diplomatic Relations Between the United States and Japan, 1853–1895*, 2 vols. (Stanford, 1932), 2.42.

12. Sheppard, *Extra-Territoriality in Japan*, pp. 26f.

13. FO 46/362/231.

14. FO 46/360/201; and FO 46/362/231.

15. Jerome H. Jaffe, "Narcotic Analgesics," *Pharmacological Basis of Therapeutics*, eds. Louis S. Goodman and Alford Gilman, 4th ed. (New York, 1970), p. 237.

16. I. D. Macht, "The History of Opium and Some of Its Preparations and Alkaloids," *Journal of the American Medical Association* 64 (1915): 481.

17. Jaffe, "Narcotic Analgesics," p. 253.

18. FO 46/360/196, 83, 189.

19. FO 46/362/233. In the nineteenth century, not all varieties of opium were used for medicinal purposes. Opium was classified into medicinal, smoking, and eating opium, but in East Asia only the first two varieties seem to have mattered. This dichotomous distinction was one of both form and substance. Medicinal opium was a dessicated gum or powder; smoking opium had the consistency of molasses. Medicinal opium contained a higher proportion of morphine than smoking opium. Apothecary North testified that, although the British Pharmacopoeia did not insist on a standard of morphine, it was generally agreed that the morphine content of smoking opium was approximately one-fifth that of medicinal opium. Indian opium—more specifically, the Bengal brands, the best known of all smoking opium brands—contained 2 or 3 percent of morphine. Japanese opium, the use of which the Japanese government once suggested to the British during the opium controversy, contained only 4 percent of morphine; the British considered it unfit for medicinal use. The term "Turkish opium," as used in this study, is synonymous with medicinal opium. Strictly speaking, however,

not all brands of Turkish opium contained a higher percentage of morphine than did Indian opium. About three-quarters of the opium prepared in Turkey was produced in Anatolia and exported by way of Smyrna. The remainder was produced in the hilly districts of provinces near the southern coast of the Black Sea and found its way into Constantinople. According to North, the Smyrna varieties contained 9 to 11 percent of morphine, and Smyrna morphine was the only medicinal opium recognized by the British Pharmacopoeia. FO 46/360/86, 189; and *Encyclopaedia Britannica*, 11th ed. (1910–1911), 20.131–134.

20. FO 46/360/106, 197–200.

21. Maruyama Kanji, *Soejima Taneomi haku* (Tokyo, 1936), p. 224; Fujii Jintarō, et al., *Sōgō Nihonshi taikei*, 12 (Tokyo, 1934), 642–646; Zaidan Hōnin Kaikoku Hyakunen Kinen Bunka Jigyōkai, ed., *Nichibei bunka kōshōshi*, 1 (Tokyo, 1956), 318; and Imai Shōji, *Oyatoi gaikokujin: gaikō* (Tokyo, 1975), pp. 49–60. In his *Soejima Taneomi haku*, p. 199, Maruyama states that the *Japan Advertiser* once reported that Sir Edmund Hornby, who died in Japan in 1896, aided the Japanese government in its disposition of the *Maria Luz* incident. Maruyama then adds that since there is no corroborating evidence, one cannot know how true this report is. At the time of the incident, Sir Edmund was in charge of the Supreme Court for China and Japan at Shanghai. It would not have been possible for him to render any assistance to Tokyo across the Yellow Sea; moreover, it would have been highly unethical of him to act as adviser to Tokyo while serving as the "chief" judge of Her Majesty's Supreme Court, a post from which he retired in 1876. FO 796/1/187. One has to conclude that the *Japan Advertiser* report quoted by Maruyama was unfounded.

22. FO 46/360/191–194, 382–384; and NGB, 11.504, 12.413, 419. Here was the earliest instance of Japan asserting that the treaty powers could not enjoy any right not specifically conceded by Japan. According to Shimomura Fujio, *Meiji Ishin no gaikō* (Tokyo, 1948), pp. 248–250, it was only in 1876 that the Japanese government concluded that Japan's treaties with the Western powers in no way limited its executive power (*gyōseiken*) and that Japan retained the right to impose executive punishments (*gyōsei shobun*) on Westerners resident in Japan. In view of Acting Foreign Minister Ueno's action, however, that date should be pushed back to 1873.

23. FO 46/360/194–196.

24. FO 46/360/197–205.

25. FO 46/360/225–374.

26. FO 46/360/232, 370; and FO 46/361/33f, 37, 47.

27. See n. 95.

28. FO 46/360/179f, 235, 241.

29. FO 46/360/218–220; and FO 46/362/76. Early Meiji legislation left much to be desired. It was "full of ambiguities and even of internal contradictions." Letter from Robert M. Spaulding, Jr., the author of *Imperial Japan's Higher Civil Service Examination* (Princeton, N.J., 1967), who has read a great deal of that legislation, January 31, 1980.

30. FO 46/360/196; and FO 46/361/52.

31. FO 46/360/407f.

32. Unpublished content analysis of (a) leading articles on Japan in *The Times* and (b) editorials on Japan in the *New York Times* for the years 1868–1899.

33. Sheppard, *Extra-Territoriality in Japan*, p. 48.

34. NGB, 13.578–590.

35. FO 46/362/72.

36. Dennett, *Americans in Eastern Asia*, p. 515.

37. Ujita Naoyoshi, *Shidehara Kijūrō* (Tokyo, 1958), p. 40.

38. S. Lane-Poole and F. V. Dickins, *The Life of Sir Harry Parkes*, 2 vols. (London, 1894), 2.258. For E. P. Smith's involvement in drafting diplomatic notes and policy statements in *English*, see Inō Tentarō, *Nihon gaikō shisōshi ronkō*, 2 vols. (Tokyo, 1966–1967), 1.117–119, 2.6, 8, 19, 23, 33f. Hereafter cited as Inō, *Nihon gaikō*.

39. This incredulity may have been current among the Japanese public. An editorial of the *Chōya shimbun*, dated September 28, 1880, which criticized the decisions on the *Hartley* cases to be discussed shortly, read: "Opium is medicinal if it is said to be put to medicinal use; it is smoking if it is said to be used for smoking purposes."

40. FO 46/360/213, 379–384; and NGB, 11.442–444, 507.

41. FO 46/360/70–104.

42. FO 46/360/61–63, 104–109.

43. NGB, 13.588.

44. The words "judgment" and "decision" are sometimes used interchangeably. *Black's Law Dictionary*, rev. 4th ed., p. 977. But in my own writing, not quotations, the word "judgment" has a wider meaning than the word "decision": "judgment" includes not only the official decision of a court of justice, but also the reason that the court gives for its decision.

45. *Encyclopaedia Britannica*, 11th ed., 20.136.

46. FO 46/360/4–9; and NGB, 11.487f. Cf. *Japan Weekly Mail*, April 14, 1878.

47. FO 46/360/110f.

48. FO 46/360/25–36; and NGB, 11.476f, 491–495.

49. FO 46/360/73–75; and NGB, 11.504.

50. FO 46/360/7, 44–46; and NGB, 11.504.

51. Parry, "United Kingdom," p. 110; FO 46/360/123; *Chōya shimbun*, February 9, 1979; and NGB, 12.427.

52. FO 46/361/347, 352–354, 387f.

53. See FO 46/362.

54. FO 46/361/315–318.

55. In consular court documents examined for this study, the senior judge of the Supreme Court at Shanghai was referred to as "Chief Judge." But the correct title, under the 1865 China and Japan Order in Council, was simply "the Judge."

56. FO 46/361/319–341, 415–418.

57. FO 834/12/X–K 4860.

58. H.W.R. Wade, *Administrative Law*, 3d ed. (Oxford, 1971), pp. 53f.

59. Ibid., p. 104; and Amnon Rubinstein, *Jurisdiction and Illegality: A Study in Public Law* (Oxford, 1965), pp. 3–6.

60. Rubinstein, *Jurisdiction and Illegality*, pp. 194, 229.

61. Ibid., p. 48. The earliest instance cited by Rubinstein is an 1848 case. Ibid.

62. NGB, 11.502; FO 656/238/188f; and FO 46/360/131–135.

63. China and Japan Order in Council, 1878, Arts. 3, 11, 6.

64. FO 46/360/58–60, 121.

65. FO 46/360/65f; FO 46/361/31; and letters from J. K. Dixon, Chief Clerk of the Privy Council Office, London, February 17, May 2, 1977. At the end of 1880, Foreign Minister Inoue instructed the Japanese chargé d'affaires in London to inform the Foreign Office that Japan had decided not to apply for leave to appeal in the *Hartley* cases. FO/46/362/52.

66. FO 46/361/314f.

67. FO 46/360/167.

68. *NGB*, 12.398, 414; and FO 46/362/232–241.

69. *NGB*, 12.427.

70. The Egyptian government, for example, had an attitude similar to that of the Japanese government. See Lord McNair, *International Law Opinions*, 3 vols. (Cambridge, 1956), 1.100.

71. These opinions were rendered by the same distinguished lawyers: John Holker, attorney–general (1875–1880) and later lord justice of appeal (1881–1882); Hardinge S. Gifford, solicitor-general (1875–1880) and afterwards Lord Halsbury, who became lord chancellor thrice (1885–1886, 1886–1892, 1895–1905); and J. Parker Deane, legal adviser to the Foreign Office (1872–1886) who filled the void created by the death in 1872 of Sir Travers Twiss, the last queen's advocate-general. With the elimination of the post of the queen's advocate-general, the two law officers, attorney-general and solicitor-general, required some specialist help on points of international law. Therefore, Dr. Deane, though not a law officer, worked with them and signed all opinions rendered to the Foreign Office between 1872 and 1886. Lord McNair, *International Law Opinions*, 3.426; and J.L.J. Edwards, *The Law Officers of the Crown* (London, 1964), pp. 3, 83, 134–140, 312, 314.

72. Lord McNair, *International Law Opinions*, 1.xvii; and Sir Arnold D. McNair, *The Law of Treaties* (Oxford, 1938), p. viii.

73. Lord McNair, *International Law Opinions*, 1.xix; and Edwards, *The Law Officers of the Crown*, pp. 256–262.

74. This office was subsequently redesignated that of the legal adviser. Previously, Pauncefote had occupied a like post at the Colonial Office from 1867 to 1876. Parry, "United Kingdom," p. 138.

75. This society, composed largely of clergymen and members of Parliament, took the view that the two *Hartley* decisions opened a door to uncontrolled and unlimited introduction of opium into Japan in direct contravention of "the letter and spirit" of the prohibition in the Anglo-Japanese Treaty of 1858 and in the Tariff Convention of 1866. The society repeatedly petitioned Lord Salisbury to direct Parkes to have the British in Japan obey Japanese regulations on the importation and sale of opium. The society, however, never succeeded in having Salisbury receive its deputations. Although the pressure exerted on the Foreign Office by the society probably had no effect on the ultimate outcome of the opium controversy, it undoubtedly helped to sharpen the issue in the minds of key Foreign Office officials and served to comfort Japanese officials like Ueno and Terashima who were waging a series of forlorn, legal, and diplomatic battles with courage, determination, and persistence. See FO/46/360/1, 141–160; and *NGB*, 11.498.

76. FO 46/360/14, 21; and *NGB*, 11.479–483.

77. FO 46/360/23.

78. FO 46/360/137–140.

79. FO 46/360/149; and *NGB*, 12.413.

80. FO 46/361/29; and *NGB*, 11.511–514.

81. FO 46/361/55–60, 127, 182.

82. *NGB*, 12.424f; and FO 46/361/90f.

83. *NGB*, 12.423f.

84. FO 46/362/76–78; and FO 46/361/129–132. For Wilkinson's defense, see FO 46/361/31–40; and FO 46/360/448–459.

85. FO 46/361/148–151.

86. *NGB*, 12.428f, 431.

87. FO 46/362/231.

88. Ibid.; and *NGB*, 13.586f.

89. See, for example, *Jiji shimpō*, October 8, 1890; Yamamoto, *Jōyaku kaiseishi*, p. 181; Kawashima, *Jōyaku kaisei*, p. 153; Inoue, *Jōyaku kaisei*, p. 80; and Konishi Shirō, *Nihon zenshi* 8 (Tokyo, 1962), 305.

90. See, for example, Kawashima, *Jōyaku kaisei*, p. 168; Inoue, *Jōyaku kaisei*, p. 113; and Inō, *Nihon gaikō*, 1.113.

91. FO 46/361/58.

92. See n. 83; and FO 46/361/136.

93. The Librarian's Department, an inadequate and misleading appellation, was concerned with, among other things, the printing of the law officers' reports; the custody of manuscript correspondence, original treaties, etc.; the compilation of complete collections of treaties, conventions, etc.; and the preparation of memoranda on the interpretation of treaties and treaty questions. Sir J. Tilley and Sir S. Gaselee, *The Foreign Office* (London, 1933), pp. 299f.

94. FO 46/361/88–90. Article 4 of the 1854 Convention provided that "British ships in Japanese waters shall conform to the Laws of Japan." Parkes insisted that this convention had been superseded by the 1858 treaty. FO 46/362/82.

95. Tilley and Gaselee, *The Foreign Office*, pp. 126, 171, 159, 161f., 164.

96. FO 46/362/86f.

97. FO 46/362/231.

98. See n. 88.

99. *In re* Ross, 140 U.S. at 475 (1890).

100. J. L. Brierly, *The Law of Nations*, 6th ed., ed. Sir Humphrey Waldock (Oxford, 1963), p. 318.

101. Some might argue, therefore, that Japan's ignorance of the stigma its people would associate with extraterritoriality could in no way account for Japan conceding extraterritoriality. I find it impossible to accept this argument. It is exceedingly doubtful that the leaders of the Bakufu or the early Meiji government would have conceded extraterritoriality as readily as they did if they had had an appreciable knowledge of Western diplomacy and international law. I have come across plenty of evidence that they had no such knowledge prior to the early 1870s. Perhaps the best known piece of evidence is the consternation among members of the Iwakura Mission in Washington, D.C., in 1871 upon learning that the 1858 treaties contained such a thing as a unilateral most-favored-nation clause. But I have not yet found any evidence that the Bakufu leadership had enough knowledge of international law and diplomacy before conceding what extraterritoriality meant, objectively, in the context of the nineteenth-century world.

102. *Kaitei ritsurei*, Art. 126.

103. Harold J. Berman and William R. Greiner, *The Nature and Functions of Law*, 3d ed. (Mineola, N.Y., 1972), p. 32.

104. FO 410/19/10.

105. *McNabb* v. *United States*, 318 U.S. 332 (1943), quoted in Wade, *Administrative Law*, p. 17.

106. Wade, *Administrative Law*, p. 17.

107. FO 46/360/420.

108. See, for example, *Chōya shimbun*, June 24, 1875; September 2, 1876.

109. FO 46/360/34f.

Chapter 4. Captain Drake's Failure to Discharge His Trust: The *Drake* Case (1886)

1. See, for example, *Chōya shimbun*, September 20, 1890; and *Jiji shimpō*, September 20, 1890.

2. Inoue Karoru Kō Denki Hensankai, *Segai Inoue Kō den*, 5 vols. (Tokyo, 1933–1934), 3.736. Hereafter cited as *Segai Inoue*.

3. *Chōya shimbun*, November 18, 1886.

4. See "The Pilgrim-Ship Episode" in Joseph Conrad, *Lord Jim*, ed. Thomas C. Moser (New York: Norton Critical ed., 1968), pp. 309–336.

5. FO 46/349/83–87.

6. FO 46/349/86.

7. Ibid.

8. FO 46/349/84, 86.

9. Today's Japanese intellectuals accept this explanation. For example, a Japanese judge who recently has written on the *Drake* case has observed:

It had been only nineteen years since the Meiji Restoration, and only a little while since Japan's contact with the modern civilization of Western Europe. In the eyes of the English, who regarded Japan as a small, weak country in the Orient, the Japanese were nothing but a colored people like those of Southeast Asia and Africa. Had the *Normanton* been a vessel plying near the coast of Europe with Europeans on board, an incident of the sort that actually took place could not have occurred.

Kikuchi Hiroshi, "Norumantongō senchō no saiban," *Hōsō*, no. 234 (April 1970): 46. Hereafter cited as Kikuchi, "Saiban."

10. FO 46/348/262; and *Japan Weekly Mail*, November 27, 1886.

11. *Jiji shimpō*, November 6, 1886.

12. *Jiji shimpō*, November 13, 1886; and Ashida Tsukao, *Norumantongō chimbotsu jijō* (Tokyo, 1887), p. 80. See also the Appendix to Soga Kashi, ed., *Eikoku kisen Norumantongō saibanroku* (Tokyo, 1887). Hereafter cited as Soga, ed., *Saibanroku*.

13. *Jiji shimpō*, November 17, 1886.

14. Trans. in *Japan Weekly Mail*, November 13, 1886. See also *Jiji shimpō*, November 17, 1886.

15. The text of the finding may be found in Tanaka Tokihiko, "Norumantongō jiken," *Nihon seiji saiban shiroku*, ed. Wagatsuma Sakae, et al., 2 (Tokyo, 1969), 141f.

16. FO 46/349/8.

17. Kikuchi, "Saiban," p. 39; *Segai Inoue*, 3.736; and FO 46/349/9.

18. The British Minister Sir Francis R. Plunkett in Tokyo expressed to the Foreign Secretary, the Earl of Iddlesleight, the view that the Ministry of Foreign Affairs had whipped up public excitement about the *Normanton*. But the evidence does not support his statement. For example, Plunkett reported that it was not until November 15 that "any excitement in connection with it [the *Normanton* incident] commenced." This is not true. The excitement began as early as November 7. Plunkett took as proof the Ministry's encouragement of Cambridge-trained Nabeshima's letter of November 13, part of which has already been quoted (see n. 10). In no way did the letter foster the press's agitation. Rather, it commended the Tokyo newspapers' drive for subscription for support of the surviving families of the perished passengers, a drive that had already been in progress. See FO 46/348/253–257, 260–262; FO 46/349/1–7, 209–213. It would seem

that the public indignation over the *Normanton* affair was far more geniune, intense, and widespread than Plunkett depicted it in his report.

19. Kikuchi, "Saiban," pp. 39f.

20. FO 46/349/87–89.

21. In his "Saiban," p. 42, Judge Kikuchi speculates at length as to why five, not twelve, men made up the jury. Part of this speculation is quite illuminating. There is, however, no room for speculation if one examines the terms of the China and Japan Order in Council, 1865. See the text of Chapter 1 documented by n. 15.

22. FO 46/349/89.

23. Okata Akio, et al., *Nihon no rekishi*, 11 (Tokyo, 1959), 55.

24. Taguchi, *Jōyaku*, p. 359.

25. Shimomura Fujio, *Nihon zenshi* 9 (Tokyo, 1968), 162.

26. Inoue, *Jōyaku kaisei*, p. 39.

27. Glanville Williams, *Textbook of Criminal Law* (London, 1978), pp. 25–27.

28. Kikuchi, "Saiban," p. 45; and Tanaka, "Norumantongō jiken," p. 140. According to English law, however, "the number of persons affected by a single act of negligence does not affect the degree of negligence." *Halsbury's Laws of England*, 3d ed., 10.716.

29. *Chōya shimbun*, November 17, 1886.

30. Soga, ed., *Saibanroku*, pp. 4–6.

31. 26 Fed. Cas. 360 (1840). Frederick C. Hicks, *Human Jettison: A Sea Tale from the Law* (St. Paul, Minn., 1927), provides a full account and comprehensive analysis of the case.

32. Ibid.

33. Hicks, *Human Jettison*, pp. 295, 386.

34. Ibid., pp. 35f.

35. Ibid., pp. 121f, 285.

36. J.W. Cecil Turner, *Kenny's Outlines of Criminal Law*, 16th ed. (Cambridge, 1952), p. 142.

37. Justin Miller, *Handbook of Criminal Law* (St. Paul, Minn., 1934), pp. 279, 285.

38. Ibid., pp. 262, 263.

39. Hicks, *Human Jettison*, p. 287.

40. Ibid., p. 31.

41. Ibid., pp. 28, 329, 332.

42. George E. Dix and M. Michael Sharlot, *Criminal Law: Cases and Materials* (St. Paul, Minn., 1973), p. 1042.

43. Two such translations are cited in n. 12.

44. (24 & 25 Vict. ch. 100), Sec. 5.

45. Cornish, et al., *Crime and Law in Nineteenth Century Britain*, p. 46.

Chapter 5. In the Name of the Emperor: The *Chishima* Case (1893–1895)

1. *Shimbun shūsei Meiji hennenshi*, 15 vols. (Tokyo, 1936–1941), 8.328, 330. Hereafter cited as *Shimbun*.

2. Ibid., 9.48; and *Dai Nippon Teikoku gikaishi*, 18 vols. (Tokyo, 1926–1930), 449f. Hereafter cited as *Gikaishi*.

3. *Japan Weekly Mail,* December 31, 1892; and *Gikaishi,* 2.474, 3.162.

4. Trans. in *Japan Weekly Mail,* January 28, 1893. For the Japanese text, see *Shimbun,* 8.363.

5. FO 46/480/31, 5f.

6. *Gikaishi,* 3.1644, 1753; *Japan Weekly Mail,* December 31, 1892; *Shimbun,* 8.328, 9.298; *Meiji bunka zenshū,* 11.541; and *NGB,* 28.1.301.

7. *Japan Weekly Mail,* June 24, 1893.

8. The following table lists the sitting and judgment days of the British courts involved and the sources for the trial records utilized in this study.

Court	Sitting or Judgment Day	Japan Weekly Mail Issue in Which Trial Records May Be Found
Yokohoma	May 25, 1893	May 27, 1893
	May 31, 1893	June 10, 1893
	June 5, 1893	" " "
	June 12, 1893	June 24, 1893
	June 13, 1893	" " "
	June 29, 1893	July 1, 1893
Shanghai	Oct. 10, 1893	Oct. 21, 1893
	Oct. 11, 1893	" " "
	Oct. 13, 1893	" " "
	Oct. 14, 1893	" " "
	Oct. 25, 1893	" " "
London	May 21, 1895	The only record available proved to be the summary in Law Reports, Appeal Cases, 1895, pp. 644-660.
	May 22, 1895	
	May 24, 1895	
	May 28, 1895	
	July 3, 1895	

As a rule, no legal arguments presented in the text are documented, for the following reason. Virtually all of them were repeated in all of the three British courts and on almost every one of the sitting days, except the first court's first sitting day. Therefore, it would amount to an intolerable exercise in footnoting to document these arguments. However, all verbatim quotations from the trial records are documented.

The Japanese translation of the excerpts of the Yokohama and Shanghai courts' judgments are available in *Meiji bunka zenshū,* 10.524–540; and *NGB,* 26.241–257. Also, the judgment of the Privy Council in Japanese translation may be found in *NGB,* 28.1.307–313. Any account based on these and other Japanese sources only is likely to be incomplete, misleading, and lopsided. See, for example, Inoue, *Jōyaku kaisei,* pp. 36–38.

The *Chishima* case dealt with several important legal issues, such as the conflict between treaty and municipal law, claim and counterclaim, jurisdiction, territorial waters, and sovereign immunity. The legal mind may find the examination of these issues in itself quite exciting. In this study, however, they will be touched upon only so far as they impinge upon the line of inquiry set forth.

9. FO 46/480/45; NGB, 26.260; and *Japan Weekly Mail*, June 10, 1893.

10. Once a master was held liable for every act of his servant while in his employment, whether within or without the scope of his employment. Today a master is liable only if such acts are committed within the scope of his servant's employment. The scope-of-employment rule became established about 1800. K. Krishina Menon, *Outlines of Jurisprudence*, 4th ed. (Bombay, 1961), pp. 197f.

11. George W. Patton and David P. Derham, A *Textbook of Jurisprudence*, 4th ed. (Oxford, 1972), pp. 338, 352. Today sovereign immunity is no longer absolute. The British government, like the United States government (The Fed. Tort Claims Act, 1946), is liable in tort (Crown Proceedings Act, 1947). Consequently, an intriguing question has been raised: "If the Crown may make itself liable in civil cases, why not in criminal cases?" Ibid., 352f.

12. T. J. Lawrence, *The Principle of International Law*, 7th ed. rev. by Percy H. Winfield (London, 1925), pp. 233f.

13. See, for example, *Law Reports, Appeal Cases*, 1895, pp. 652–654.

14. FO 46/480/72–75.

15. *Black's Law Dictionary*, revised 4th ed. (St. Paul, 1968), p. 125. The terms "general appearance" and "special," expressions explicitly recognized by the Civil Procedure of the U.S. Federal Court, were not actually used in the *Chishima* trials. There the issue was couched in terms of whether submission was *general* or not.

16. Ibid., p. 520.

17. *Japan Weekly Mail*, October 21, 1893.

18. Ibid., June 24, 1893.

19. Ibid., November 4, 1893.

20. *Shimbun*, 8.485, 487, 494, 9.48; Hōchisha, *Chishimakan jiken* (Tokyo, 1893), in *Meiji bunka zenshū*, ed. Meiji Bunka Kenkyūkai, 3d ed., 31 vols. (Tokyo, 1967–1969), 11.521–561; and *Gikaishi*, 2.1108.

21. NGB, 26.257–259.

22. Ōkubo Toshiaki, ed., *Taikei Nihonshi sōsho 3, Seijishi 3* (Tokyo, 1967), 275–277; Hōchisha, *Chishimakan jiken*, 540–551; and Osatake Takeshi, "Chishimakan jiken kaidai," *Maiji bunka zenshū*, ed. Meiji Bunka Kenkyūkai, 3d ed., 31 vols. (Tokyo, 1967–1969), 11.38–40 (*kaidai*). Hereafter cited as Osatake, "Kaidai."

23. Osatake, "Kaidai," p. 39. Concise and comprehensive, the "Kaidai" has been widely utilized by Japanese historians. This may very well continue. Therefore, two small, additional errors should be pointed out. First, the "Kaidai" indicates that the P & O paid Tokyo court costs of ¥ 12,076. This amount is probably a printing error; the sum was ¥ 12,176. *Gikaishi*, 3.1753. Second, Osatake states that the *Chishima* case was the first action ever brought to a foreign court by the Japanese government. This statement is incorrect. In 1879, the government sued certain Englishmen in a British court in Japan and had to appear in the Supreme Court at Shanghai as the respondent. Kudō Takeshige, *Teikoku Gikai shikō*, rev. ed. (Tokyo, 1927), pp. 248f. Moreover, prior to 1893 many prefectural governors had brought actions to consular courts on behalf of the central government. My own examination of the law reports of the *Japan Weekly Mail*.

24. Hanabusa, *Meiji gaikōshi*, p. 89.

25. See n. 22.

26. A–694, "Gunkan Chishima soshō jiken shinsa hōkoku," Goin Bunko (Inoue Kowashi papers), Kokugakuin University, Tokyo. The other five committee members were Tanabe Kaoru, *sanjikan*, Shihōshō; Yokota Kuniomi, chief of the Civil and Criminal Bureau, Shihōshō; Kurino Shin'ichirō, chief of the Political Affairs Bureau, Gaimushō; Kaneko Kentarō, secretary-general, Kizokuin; and Itō Senkichi, vice-minister of the Navy.

27. A–694, A–705, A–706, Goin Bunko, Kokugakuin University.

28. *Shimbun*, 9.18; and *NGB*, 26.260.

29. For details, see FO 46/480/183, 195–204; *NGB*, September 5, 1895; and Mutsu Munemitsu Monjo, 68.7, National Diet Library (NDL). Hereafter cited as Mutsu Monjo, 68.7, NDL.

30. *Gikaishi*, 3.1619f.

31. *NGB*, 28.1.303.

32. (57 & 58 Vict. ch. 60). The £8-per-ton provision is in Sec. 502 (1).

33. *Halsbury's Laws of England*, 36.423–428.

34. The only case which approximated the type of case mentioned in the pre-1972 period was *Bank of Athens* v. *Royal Exchange Assurance* (1938), 1 K.B. 771, which decided that a court could award interest on damages under a statute passed after the proceedings had begun. In other words, the court held that the measure of interest on damages was a matter of procedure.

35. *Wilson* v. *Dagnall* (1972) 1 Q.B. 509 (C.A.); and A.K.R. Kiralfy, *The English Legal System*, 5th ed. (London, 1973), p. 105.

36. *The Ironsides* (1862), Lush, 458. See also *Halsbury's Laws of England*, 36.427f.

37. Louis Franck, "Collisions at Sea in Relation to International Maritime Law," *Law Quarterly Review* 12 (1896): 260f.; and Alfred Huger, "The Proportional Damage Rule in Collision at Sea," *Cornell Law Quarterly* 13 (1927): 532, 540.

38. Some astute readers may wonder why the *Chishima* would have had to pay the *Ravenna* one-half of its damage, $50,000, despite the fact that the Privy council decided that no counterclaim could be entertained. In its judgment, the Privy Council noted that in an 1848 case, where the fact that a plaintiff was a foreigner made it impossible for the British defendant to prosecute a cross-action against him, the Admiralty Court of England had withheld the payment of one-half of the damage sustained by the plaintiff's ship until he agreed to pay one-half of the damage sustained by the other ship. In other words, if this precedent were to be followed, the *Chishima* would not be allowed to recover $425,000 until the plaintiff agreed to let the *Ravenna* recover $50,000. One may construe this *obiter dictim* as meaning that while the highest court was ruling that no counterclaim could be filed, it was simultaneously hinting that the defendant should be able to recover his counterclaim all the same in the event that both were found to be at fault. From this point of view, one should not jump to the conclusion that the Privy Council had rendered an underhanded judgment. Hearing a claim and a counterclaim together is taken for granted today, and this practice had been well established when the *Chishima* case was instituted. Moreover, as it has been shown in the early part of this study, the defendant strongly argued the sentiment that complete justice demanded that both claims be heard together. The assistant judge of the Shanghai Supreme Court persuasively expressed this feeling when he stated: "The question is, has the Emperor of Japan any right, as he contends, to ask that his claim be determined wholly without reference to the damage sustained by defendants [the P & O] and that he be at liberty to recover his damages even in the event of both vessels being found to

blame, leaving the defendants to the chances of an action in the Japanese Courts against the wrong-doer?" *Japan Weekly Mail*, November 14, 1893. One may assume, therefore, that the Privy Council intended that the *obiter dictum* would balance the likelihood of injustice which could result from faithful observance of the limits of the treaty. This was an instance of what a lawyer calls *equity*.

39. *Halsbury's Laws of England*, 35.774f.

40. See n. 32.

41. Thanks are due to Professor Tanigawa Hisahshi, a noted Japanese authority on maritime law, of Seikei University, Tokyo, for the kind aid I received in constructing this table in April 1974.

42. NGB 28.1.303. For still another piece of the evidence mentioned, see Mutsu Monjo, 68.7, NDL. At this time, all telegram instructions and dispatches were still sent in English.

43. See no. 29.

44. *NGB*, 28.1.305. A copy of this letter was transmitted by London to Tokyo. Ibid., 304–306.

45. The conversion rates used in this study for the yen, the dollar, and the pound are the average rates for 1895, as given in *Nihon Teikoku dai jūgo tōkei nenkan*, p. 674, as follows: £1 = $4.73; $1 = ¥2.01. The only exception is the yen equivalent to the £10,000 compromise, which comes from the *Jiji shimpō*, September 21, 1895. *Shimbun*, 9.298.

46. See n. 6.

47. *Gikaishi*, 3.1753; and *Shimbun*, 9.298.

48. *NGB*, 28.1.304, 310f; and Mutsu Monjo, 68.7, NDL.

49. Etō Jun, "Umi wa yomigaeru—Yamamoto Gonnohyōe to kaigun," *Bungei shunjū* 52 (October 1974): 379f.

50. For examples, see Osatake, "Kaidai," p. 40; and Inoue, *Jōyaku kaisei*, pp. 37f.

51. (7 George II ch. 15), Sec. 1. See also Sir William Holdsworth, *A History of English Law*, 7th ed., 16 vols. (London, 1956–1966), 11.448.

52. George C. Sprague, "Divided Damage," *New York University Law Review* 6 (1929): 21; and Huger, "The Proportional Damage Rule," p. 532.

Chapter 6. How Many Unfair Cases?

1. Robert William Fogel, "The Limits of Quantitative Methods in History," *American Historical Review* 80 (April 1975): 337.

2. FO 656/68–70.

3. See the "Introduction" to any of the microfilm rolls of Despatches from United States Consuls, General Records of the Department of State (Record Group 59), National Archives, Washington, D.C.

4. Delmar Karlen, *Anglo-American Criminal Justice* (New York and Oxford, 1967), p. 210.

5. FO 410/21/59–88 (1883), 152–167; FO 796/6/14f (1884); and FO 796/10/187, 190f (1890).

6. FO 410/21/85f, 160–162.

7. Letter from Professor Yamamoto Sōji of Tōhoku University, Sendai, February 15, 1977.

8. Julian D.M. Lew, "The Extra-Territorial Criminal Jurisdiction of English Courts," *International and Comparative Law Quarterly* 27 (January 1978): 198.

9. Brierly, *The Law of Nations*, pp. 223–225.

10. Edwards, *The Law Officers of the Crown*, p. 3.

11. Lord McNair, *International Law Opinions*, 1.76. See also ibid., 2.160f.

12. Ibid., 2.169.

13. FO 46/314/3, 36.

14. FO 46/341/38.

15. *Yūbin hōchi shimbun*, July 3, 1877.

16. In analyzing quantitatively the content of newspapers, researchers often have used measures of space expressed in the term "column inches" to describe the relative emphasis accorded a given report. These measures were not used here because the purpose of this examination did not call for them. The purpose was merely to ascertain whether there existed publicized cases other than the five and then to obtain a simple measure of frequency with which the five were reported or condemned. I was not concerned with such attributes as focus of attention, intensity, length, value, and importance. My assumption was that newspaper coverage making value judgment was seldom favorable to any of the publicized cases. This assumption was proved correct by a reading of the two sets of newspapers. Therefore, I simply counted reports and editorials that referred to any of the five cases and, as already noted, indicated those dates on which the reports or editorials were carried.

17. Ono Hideo, *Nihon shimbun hattatsushi* (Ōsaka, 1922), p. 158.

18. See Appendix Table 2.

19. Ono, *Nihon shimbun*, pp. 99f., 108–110, 158–160, 242.

20. Ibid., pp. 247f.

21. Ibid., p. 186.

22. My own counting.

Chapter 7. Conclusion

1. Gordon W. Allport, *The Nature of Prejudice*, (Garden City, N.Y.: Anchor Books ed., 1958), p. 9.

2. Jones, *Extraterritoriality in Japan*, p. 69.

3. Memorandum No. 10, Memoranda and Miscellaneous MS., Sir Harry Parkes Papers, Cambridge University Library, Cambridge.

4. Kazuo Hatoyama, "The Civil Code of Japan Compared with the French Civil Code," *Yale Law Journal* 11 (April 1902): 298.

5. See Chapter 3, n. 101.

6. Taneomi Soyeshima, *"Japan's Foreign Relations,"* Fifty Years of Japan, ed. Shigenobu Okuma, 2d ed., 1 (London, 1910), 103.

7. Though resentful, many Meiji intellectuals believed the Japanese to be truly inferior to Westerners. See Oka Yoshitake, "Jōyaku kaisei ron'gi ni arawareta tōji no taigai ishiki (1)," *Kokka Gakkai zasshi*, 67 (August 1953): 1–24.

Appendix

1. *Japan Weekly Mail*, August 4, 1884.

2. Vice-Consul General G. E. Rice to the Department of State, June 30, 1885 (Enclosure 6 in Dispatch no. 904), Despatches from United States Consuls in Kanagawa, 1861–1897, and Yedo, 1869–1872, Microcopy 135/15, General Records of the Department of State (Record Group 59), National Archives, Washington, D.C.

Bibliography

Unpublished Materials

Cambridge, England. Cambridge University Library, Sir Harry Parkes Papers.
Kew, England. Public Record Office, Records of the Foreign Office.
   Confidential Print: Japan, FO 410
   Embassy and Consular Archives: Japan, FO 656, 796
   Embassy and Consular Archives: China, FO 656, 798
   General Correspondence: Japan, FO 46
Tokyo, Japan. Kokugakuin University, Goin Bunko (Inoue Kowashi Papers).
Tokyo, Japan. National Diet Library, Mutsu Munemitsu Monjo.
Washington, D.C. National Archives, Records of the Department of State.
   General Records, Record Group 59: Despatches from United States Consuls in
   Hakodate (T 113), Kanagawa and Yedo (Microcopy 136),
      Yokohama (Microcopy 136), Nagasaki (Microcopy 136), and
      List of United States Consular Officers (Microcopy 587)
   Records of the Foreign Service Posts, Record Group 84: Records of the American
   Consulates at Kōbe, Nagasaki, and Yokohama.

Published Materials

Books, Series, Chapters, and Articles

Akagi, Roy Hidemichi. *Japan's Foreign Relations, 1542–1936*. Tokyo, 1936.
Allport, Gordon W. *The Nature of Prejudice*. Garden City, N.Y.: Anchor Books ed.,
   1958.
Ashida Tsukao. *Norumantongō chimbotsu jijō*. Tokyo, 1887.
Baba, Tatui. *The Treaty Between Japan and England*. London, 1876.
Berman, Harold J., and William R. Greiner. *The Nature and Functions of Law*. 3d ed.
   Mineola, N.Y., 1972.
Black's Law Dictionary. Rev. 4th ed., 1968.

Brierly, J. L. *The Law of Nations*. Ed. Sir Humphrey Waldock. 6th ed. Oxford, 1963.

Chamberlain, Basil Hall. *Japanese Things*. Rutland, Vt., 1971.

Chang, Richard T. "A British Trial in Japan: *Regina* v. *Archibald King*." *Journal of Asian History* 10 (1976): 134–150.

Conrad, Joseph. *Lord Jim*. Ed. Thoms C. Moser. New York: Norton Critical ed., 1968.

Cornish, W. R., et al. *Crime and Law in Nineteenth Century Britain*. Dublin, 1978.

Dai Nippon Teikoku Gikaishi. 18 vols. Tokyo, 1926–1930.

Dennett, Tyler. *Americans in Eastern Asia*. New York, 1922. Reprint ed. 1941.

Dix, George E., and M. Michael Sharlot. *Criminal Law: Cases and Materials*. St. Paul, Minn., 1973.

Edwards, J.L.J. *The Law Officers of the Crown*. London, 1964.

Encyclopaedia Britannica. 11th ed. (1910–1911). Vol. 20.

Etō Jun. "Umi wa yomigaeru—Yamamoto Gonnohyōe to kaigun." *Bungei shunjū* 52 (October 1974): 378–390.

Fogel, Robert William. "The Limits of Quantitative Methods in History." *American Historical Review* 80 (April 1975): 329–365.

Franck, Louis. "Collisions at Sea in Relation to International Maritime Law." *Law Quarterly Review* 12 (1896): 260–273.

Fujii Jintarō, et al. *Sōgō Nihonshi taikei*. Vol. 12. Tokyo, 1934.

Great Britain. Foreign Office. *Foreign Office List*. Annual.

———. Parliament. *Parliamentary Papers (Commons)*. 1870, 63, Cmnd. 195; 1871, 64, Cmnd. 442; 1872, 65, Cmnd. 600; 1873, 70, Cmnd. 871; 1874, 71, Cmnd. 1055; 1875, 81, Cmnd 1315; 1876, 79, Cmnd. 1595; 1881, 95, Cmnd. 3088; 1882, 75, Cmnd. 3333; 1883, 77, Cmnd. 3763; 1884, 86, Cmnd. 4170; 1884–1885, 86, Cmnd. 4518; 1886, 72, Cmnd. 4808; 1887, 90, Cmnd. 5155.

Hall, W. E. *A Treatise on the Foreign Powers and Jurisdiction of the British Crown*. Oxford, 1894.

Halsbury's Laws of England. 3d ed. 43 vols. London, 1952–1964. Reference made to Vols. 10, 24, 35, and 36.

Hanabusa Nagamichi. *Meiji gaikōshi*. Tokyo, 1966.

Harris, Townsend. *The Complete Journal of Townsend Harris*. Rev. ed. Rutland, Vt., 1959.

Hatoyama, Kazuo. "The Civil Code of Japan Compared with the French Civil Code." *Yale Law Journal* 11 (April, May, June 1902): 296–303, 354–370, 403–419.

Hicks, Frederick C. *Human Jettison: A Sea Tale from the Law*. St. Paul, Minn., 1927.

Hiezuka Ryū. ["On Japan's Foreign Trade"]. *Shidankai sokkiroku*. Ed. Shidankai, 196 (Tokyo, 1909), 29–56. Reprint ed., 28 (Tokyo, 1973), 529–550.

Hinckley, Frank E. *American Consular Jurisdiction in the Orient*. Washington, D.C., 1906.

Hōchisha. *Chishimakan jiken*. Tokyo, 1893. In *Meiji bunka zenshū*. Ed. Meiji Bunka Kenkyūkai. 3d ed. 31 vols. Tokyo, 1967–1969, 11.521–561.

Holdsworth, Sir William. *A History of English Law*. 7th ed. 16 vols. London, 1956–1966.

Hubbard, Richard B. *The United States in the Far East; or, Modern Japan and the Orient*. Richmond, Va., 1899.

Huger, Alfred. "The Proportional Damage Rule in Collision at Sea." *Cornell Law Quarterly* 13 (1927): 531–558.

Imai Shōji. *Oyatoi gaikokujin: gaikō*. Tokyo, 1975.

Inō Tentarō. *Nihon gaikō shishōshi ronkō*. 2 vols. Tokyo, 1966–1967.

Inoue Kaoru Kō Denki Hensankai. *Segai Inoue Kō den*. 5 vols. Tokyo, 1933–1934.

Inoue Kiyoshi. *Jōyaku kaisei*. Tokyo: Iwanami shinsho, 1950.

Ishii, Kikujiro. *Diplomatic Commentaries*. Trans. and ed. William R. Langdon. Baltimore, 1937.

Ishii Takashi. *Meiji shoki no kokusai kankei*. Tokyo, 1977.

————. *Nihon kaikokushi*. Tokyo, 1972.

Jackson, R. M. *The Machinery of Justice in England*. 2d ed. Cambridge, 1953.

Jaffe, Jerome H. "Narcotic Analgesics." *Pharmacological Basis of Therapeutics*. Eds. Louis S. Goodman and Alford Gilman. 4th ed. New York, 1970, pp. 237–275.

Japan. Gaimushō. *Nihon gaikō bunsho*. 47 vols. Tokyo, 1936–1963. Reference made to Vols. 11, 12, 26, 28.

————. Gaimushō Jōyakukyoku. Ed. *Kyū jōyaku isen*. 4 vols. Tokyo, 1930, 1934.

Jenks, Edward. *A Short History of English Law*. 5th ed. London, 1938.

Jones, F. C. *Extraterritoriality in Japan and the Diplomatic Relations Resulting in Its Abolition, 1853–1899*. New Haven, Conn., 1931.

Karlen, Delmar. *Anglo-American Criminal Justice*. New York and Oxford, 1967.

Kawashima Shintarō. *Jōyaku kaisei keika gaiyō*. In *Jōyaku kaisei kankei Nihon gaikō bunsho*. Ed. Nihon Gakujutsu Shinkōkai, 6. Tokyo, 1950.

Keim, DeB. Randolph. *A Report to the Hon. George S. Boutwell, Secretary of the Treasury, upon the Condition of the Consular Service of the United States of America*. Washington, D.C., 1872.

Kikuchi Hiroshi. "Norumantongō senchō no saiban." *Hōsō*, no. 234 (April 1970): 38–46.

Kiralfy, A.K.R. *The English Legal System*. 5th ed. London, 1973.

Konishi Shirō. *Nihon zenshi 8*. Tokyo, 1962.

Kudō Takashige. *Teikoku Gikai shikō*. Rev. ed. Tokyo, 1927.

Kukendall, Ralph S. *The Hawaiian Kingdom, 2*. Honolulu, 1953.

Lane-Poole, S., and F. V. Dickins. *The Life of Sir Harry Parkes*. 2 vols. London, 1894.

Law Reports, Appeal Cases, 1895.

Lawrence, T. J. *The Principle of International Law*. 7th ed. revised by Percy H. Winfield. London, 1925.

Lensen, George Alexander. *Russian Diplomatic and Consular Officials in East Asia*. Tokyo, 1968.

Lew, Julian D.M. "The Extra-Territorial Criminal Jurisdiction of English Courts." *International and Comparative Law Quarterly* 27 (January 1978): 168–214.

Liu, Shih Shun. *Extraterritoriality: Its Rise and Its Decline*. New York, 1925.

Lord McNair. *International Law Opinions*. 3 vols. Cambridge, 1956.

Macht, I. D. "The History of Opium and Some of Its Preparations and Alkaloids." *Journal of the American Medical Association* 64 (1915): 477–481.

McNair, Sir Arnold D. *The Law of Treaties*. Oxford, 1938.

Maruyama Kanji. *Soejima Taneomi haku*. Tokyo, 1936.

Meiji Bunka Kenkyūkai, ed. *Bakumatsu Meiji shimbun zenshū*. Reprint ed. 8 vols. 1961–1962.

————. *Meiji bunka zenshū*. 3d ed. 31 vols. Tokyo, 1967–1969. Vols. 4, 10.

Menon, Krishna. *Outlines of Jurisprudence*. 3d ed. Bombay, 1961.

Miller, Justin. *Handbook of Criminal Law*. St. Paul, Minn., 1934.

Moore, John Bassett. *A Digest of International Law, 2*. Washington, D.C., 1906.

Moriya Hidesuke. "Jōyaku kaisei." *Iwanami kōza Nihon rekishi*, 8. Tokyo, 1934, pp. 1–62.

Nihon Teikoku . . . tōkei nenkan, annually, 1882–1940. Reference made to volumes for 1885, 1891, 1894, and 1895.

Oka Yoshitake. "Jōyaku kaisei ron'gi ni arawareta tōji no taigai ishiki (1)." *Kokka Gakkai zasshi* 67 (August 1953): 1–24.

Okata Akio, et al. *Nihon no rekishi*, 11. Tokyo, 1959.

Ōkubo Toshiaki, ed. *Taikei Nihonshi sōsho 3, Seijishi 3*. Tokyo, 1967.

Ono Hideo. *Nihon shimbun hattatsushi*. Ōsaka, 1922.

Osatake Takeshi. "Chishimakan jiken kaidai." In *Meiji bunka zenshū*. Ed. Meiji Bunka Kenkyūkai. 3d ed. 31 vols. Tokyo, 1967–1969, 11.38–40.

Ōyama Azusa. *Kyū jōyaku moto ni okeru kaishi kaikō no kenkyū*. Tokyo, 1967.

Oxford English Dictionary. Vol. 7.

Parry, Clive. "United Kingdon." In *Legal Advisers and Foreign Affairs*. Ed. H.C.L. Merillat. New York, 1964, pp. 101–152.

Patton, George W., and David P. Derham. *A Textbook of Jurisprudence*. 4th ed. Oxford, 1972.

Pierce, Herbert H.D. *Report to the Honorable John Hay, Secretary of State, upon a Tour of Consular Inspection in Asia*. Washington, D.C., 1904.

Piggott, F. T. *Extraterritoriality: The Law Relating to Consular Jurisdiction and to Residence in Oriental Countries*. 2d ed. Hong Kong, 1907.

Rubinstein, Amnon. *Jurisdiction and Illegality: A Study in Public Law*. Oxford, 1965.

Scidmore, G. H. *A Digest of Leading Cases Relating to Consular Court Jurisdiction in Japan*. Yokohama, 1882.

Senga, Tsurutaro. *Gestaltung und Kritik der heutigen Konsulgerichtsbarkeit in Japan*. Berlin, 1897.

Sheppard, Eli T. *Extra-Territoriality in Japan*. Tokyo, 1879.

Shimbun shūsei Meiji hennenshi. 15 vols. Tokyo, 1936–1941.

Shimomura Fujio. *Meiji Ishin no gaikō*. Tokyo, 1948.

———. *Nihon zenshi 9*. Tokyo, 1968.

Smith, D. W. *European Settlements in the Far East*. London, 1900.

Soga Kashi, ed. *Eikoku kisen Norumantongō saibanroku*. Tokyo, 1887.

Soyeshima, Taneomi. "Japan's Foreign Relations." *Fifty Years of Japan*. Ed. Shigenobu Okuma. 2d ed. 1 (London, 1910), 93–121.

Sprague, George C. "Divided Damage." *New York University Law Review* 6 (1929): 15–31.

The Statesman's Year-Book, Annual. Reference made to volumes for 1890, 1895, and 1896.

Stern, John Peter. *The Japanese Interpretation of the "Law of Nations," 1854–1874*. Princeton, N.J., 1979.

Taguchi Ukichi. *Jōyaku kaiseiron*. In *Meiji bunka zenshū*. Ed. Meiji Bunka Kenkyūkai. 3d ed. 31 vols. Tokyo, 1967–1969, 11.351–363.

Tanaka Tokihiko. "Norumantongō jiken," *Nihon seiji saiban shiroku*. Ed. Wagatsuma Sakae, et al., 2. Tokyo, 1969, pp. 125–142.

Tilley, Sir J., and Sir S. Gaselee. *The Foreign Office*. London, 1933.

Treat, J. Payson. *Diplomatic Relations Between the United States and Japan, 1853–1895*. 2 vols. Stanford, 1932.

Turner, J.W. Cecil. *Kenny's Outlines of Criminal Law*. 16th ed. Cambridge, 1952.

Ujita Nāoyoshi. *Shidehara Kijūrō*. Tokyo, 1958.
U.S. Department of State. *Papers Relating to the Foreign Relations of the United States, 1874*. Washington, D.C., 1875.
Wade, H.W.R. *Administrative Law*. 3d ed. Oxford, 1971.
Williams, Glanville. *Textbook of Criminal Law*. London, 1978.
Williams, Harold S. *Tales of the Foreign Settlements in Japan*. Rutland, Vt., 1958.
Yamamoto Shigeru. *Jōyaku kaiseishi*. Tokyo, 1943.
Zaidan Hōnin Kaikoku Hyakunen Kinen Bunka Jigyōkai, ed. *Nichibei bunka kōshōshi*, 1. Tokyo, 1956.

Statutes

China and Japan Order in Council, 1865.
China and Japan Order in Council, 1878.
Kaitei ritsurei, 1873. In *Keiji kankei kyū hōreishū (Keihōhen)*. Comp. Hōmu Sōgō Kenkyūjo. Tokyo, 1969, pp. 96–138.
Keihō, 1907. In *Kyū hōreishū*. Eds. Wagatsuma Sakae, et al. Tokyo, 1968, pp. 448–450. Revised provisions of *Keihō*, 1880.
Merchant Shipping Act, 1894, 57 & 58 Vict. ch. 60.
Offences against the Person Act, 1861, 24 & 25, Vict. ch. 100.
Revised Statutes of the United States, Secs. 4083–4130, Act of June 14, 1878, 20 *Statutes at Large* 131. Note: Since the British statutes and orders cited above have been published in a variety of sources—for example, law reports, *The London Gazette*, and single bound volumes—no specific sources are cited here.

Newspapers

Chōya shimbun. Daily, 1874–1893.
The Far East. Weekly, 1870–1874.
Japan Weekly Mail. Weekly, 1875, 1876, 1884, 1886, 1893, 1895, 1896.
Jiji shimpō. Daily, 1882–1899.
Nihon. Daily, 1895–1899.
Niroku shimpō. Daily, 1893–1895.
Yūbin hōchi shimbun. Daily, 1872–1882.

Index

About the Author

RICHARD T. CHANG is Professor of History at the University of Florida. His earlier books include *From Prejudice to Tolerance: A Study of the Japanese Image of the West, 1826–1864*, *Historians and Meiji Statesmen*, and *Historians and Taishō Statesmen*. His articles have appeared in the *Journal of Asian Studies*, *Monumenta Nipponica*, and the *Journal of Asian History*.